MW00844922

Extending Microsoft Power Apps with Power Apps Component Framework

A complete guide to creating, deploying, and improving your code components

Danish Naglekar

BIRMINGHAM—MUMBAI

Extending Microsoft Power Apps with Power Apps Component Framework

Publishing Product Manager: Denim Pinto

Senior Editor: Nitee Shetty

Content Development Editor: Vaishali Ramkumar

Technical Editor: Gaurav Gala

Copy Editor: Safis Editing

Project Coordinator: Deeksha Thakkar

Proofreader: Safis Editing

Indexer: Rekha Nair

Production Designer: Prashant Ghare

First published: February 2021

Production reference: 1250221

Published by Packt Publishing Ltd.

Livery Place

35 Livery Street

Birmingham

B3 2PB, UK.

ISBN 978-1-80056-491-6

www.packt.com

I would like to express my very great appreciation to Scott Durow for his meticulous review and guidance throughout the process.

I would like to offer my special thanks to Julian Sharp for providing helpful reviews.

I wish to acknowledge the help provided by Diana Birkelbach and Ivan Ficko.

My special thanks are extended to the following people at Packt: Denim Pinto, who believed that we could make this book happen; Nitee Shetty, who provided important structural design and writing guidelines; Prajakta Naik, who made sure everyone kept the book on schedule; and editors Tiksha Lad and Vaishali Ramkumar, who provided useful suggestions to improve my drafts.

Last but not least, I beg forgiveness of all those who have been with me through the course of the book and whose names I have failed to mention.

Readers can reach me on Twitter: @DanzMaverick.

Contributors

About the author

Danish Naglekar, also known as *Power Maverick*, is a full-stack software engineer, consultant, and architect with a wide technical breadth and deep understanding of Power Platform. He is a Microsoft MVP in Business Applications. He has created a tool called the PCF Builder that makes the development and deployment of code components easier. He likes to help the technical community by writing blogs on his personal website and enjoys making technical videos on his YouTube channel. He has provided training on getting started with the Power Apps Component Framework. He also runs a weekly newsletter focused on Power Platform for professional developers. Danish earned a master's degree in computer applications from Mumbai University in 2011. Originally from a small town named Ratnagiri in Maharashtra, India, Danish currently resides in Fort Mill, South Carolina, USA with his wife.

When I started writing this book, I did not know it would have so much content. Even though I have written many blogs, writing a book was definitely a different experience. None of this would have been possible without my wife, Minal. She has been so patient with me, pushing me to keep me on track, reading early drafts, providing feedback, and supporting me throughout the book.

I am particularly grateful for the assistance given by Hemant Gaur, who is a driving force in the PCF community and is always available to answer any questions or provide assistance as much as possible.

Foreword

The Power Apps component framework is by far the most successful and high impact project I've had the privilege to work on in my time spanning over 13 years at Microsoft. It started as a small effort to create specialized controls tailored for mobile apps but soon morphed into the foundation for brand new Unified Interface for Dynamics 365 powering web, embedded, and mobile applications. With Power Platform bringing model-driven and canvas apps together, this framework was a natural fit for canvas apps. All the new experiences, including AI builder, Mixed reality, and Microsoft Dataverse for Teams, were built using this framework. The ability to code just the missing piece and integrate it seamlessly with a rapid application development platform is what makes this framework unique. You can use your existing web development skills, code, along with external libraries and services to create packaged reusable components, which then can be used by all citizen developers.

Danish Naglekar was one of the early insider program participants and has been part of this journey for few years now. He has created and shared multiple controls and built amazing tools to accelerate the control development. From the introduction and fundamentals in the initial chapters to deeper technical topics, this book has good coverage with relevant examples, development tips, community resources, and best practices. Danish is a natural teacher, which is quite evident from his community participation, newsletters, and mentorship sessions. These combined with his first-hand framework experience makes this book a great read for anyone using and working on Power Platform/Dynamics 365.

Hemant Gaur

Principal Program Manager, Power Apps

Microsoft

To my parents, for always being there, encouraging me, and believing in me. To my wife, for her endless love, support, and strength. And to the Power Platform community, who have given so much love and encouragement.

"Learn new things, share your knowledge, and grow together as a community!"

– Danish Naglekar

About the reviewer

Scott Durow has been a Microsoft Business Applications MVP since 2013, specializing in Dynamics 365 and the Power Platform. He is a passionate software architect, technologist, blogger, and speaker, as well as the author of multiple tools including the Ribbon Workbench. His software career spans more than 20 years and he has moved from assembly language device driver programming, to industrial control software, and then into enterprise business applications. Scott has recently moved from the UK to beautiful British Columbia in Canada, with his wife and three children. Find him on Twitter as @ ScottDurow .

Julian Sharp is a Dynamics 365 and Power Platform solutions architect and Microsoft Certified Trainer. He holds many certifications in configuring, customizing, and developing for several Microsoft products. Julian is a Microsoft MVP who has been building solutions on the Microsoft stack for 20 years. He uses a combination of Microsoft Dynamics 365, Power Platform, and Azure to create solutions to meet complex business needs. Julian is the author of *Microsoft Power Platform Functional Consultant: PL-200 Exam Guide*. Extending Power Platform both on the server side and the client side to enhance the user experience has recently led Julian into utilizing code components in his solutions.

Table of Contents

Preface

Section 1:
Fundamentals of the Power Apps Component Framework

1
Introduction to the Power Apps Component Framework

Learning some terminology	4	Node.js or npm	9
Overview of the Power Apps component framework	4	TypeScript	10
		.NET Framework	10
What is the Power Apps component framework?	5	Visual Studio Code	11
		Power Apps CLI	12
Who is it focused on?	6		
How are code components different from HTML web resources?	7	Downloading the example library and using the practice questions	12
Getting to know the licensing requirements	8	Summary	13
Exploring the advantages of PCF	8	Test your knowledge	13
		Further reading	14
Preparing your development machine	9		

2
Power Apps CLI

Technical requirements	15	What is Power Apps CLI?	16

What is npm?	17	project using Power Apps CLI	20
Initializing a Power Apps component framework project	19	Summary	22
		Test your knowledge	22
Exercise – creating a PCF		Further reading	23

3

Community Tools and Resources

Technical requirements	26	Integrating PCF Generator in PCF Builder	46
PCF Builder	26	Exercise – Creating a PCF project using PCF Generator	47
Graphical user interface version	26		
Guided experience version	32	PCF Gallery	55
PCF Generator	41	Using a code component from PCF Gallery	56
Installing PCF Generator	42		
Initializing a PCF project using PCF Generator	42	Submitting your own code component on PCF Gallery	57
Using command-line arguments	45	Summary	58
Benefits of using PCF Generator over Power Apps CLI for PCF	45	Test your knowledge	58
		Further reading	58

4

Project Overview and the Component Life Cycle

Technical requirements	60	Dataverse solution projects using Power Apps CLI	66
The types of project	60		
The component makeup	60	Understanding the ControlManifest file	67
The manifest file	61		
The component implementation	62	Manifest file for field type code component	70
The resource files	62		
		Manifest file for dataset type code components	74
Getting to know the files and the folder structure	63	The supported data types	75
PCF projects using Power Apps CLI	63	Supported features	76
The author's recommended folder structure	65	Exploring the index.ts file	78
PCF projects using a PCF Generator	66	The init function	78

The updateView method   79
The getOutputs method   79
The destroy method   79

**Understanding the component
life cycle   80**
Page load   80

Data changes by the user   80
Data changes by the app   80

Summary   84
Test your knowledge   85
Further reading   86

Section 2:
Building and Managing Code Components

5

Code, Test, and Repeat

Technical requirements   90
**Building the code component
for a field   90**
Initializing a new PCF project for a field   90
Updating the control manifest file for a
field   91
Adding logic to the field code component 94
Testing the field code component   97
Fixing the issues observed in the field
code component   99
Adding styling to a field code
component   101
Enriching the field code component by
using a preview image   103

Building a code component for

a view or
sub-grid   105
Initializing a new PCF project for a
dataset   105
Updating the control manifest file for a
dataset   106
Adding logic to a dataset code
component   106
Adding styling to a dataset code
component   114
Testing the dataset code component   115

Summary   117
Testing your knowledge   117
Further reading   118

6

Debugging Code Components

Technical requirements   120
Overview of the test harness   120
Debugging using the test

harness   121
Inspecting elements in a code
component   122
Inspecting console logs to evaluate

scripts   123
Debugging using breakpoints   125

Debugging in model-driven apps   127
Installing and configuring Fiddler Classic 127
Debugging using AutoResponder   129

Debugging in canvas apps   132
Debugging using DevTools   132
Debugging using AutoResponder   134

Summary   135
Test your knowledge   136
Further reading   136

7

Authentication Profiles

Technical requirements   138
Understanding authentication profiles   138
Creating authentication profiles 138
Creating profiles using Power Apps CLI   138
Creating profiles using PCF Builder   139

Managing authentication profiles   141
Changing profiles using Power Apps CLI   141
Deleting profiles using Power Apps CLI   142
Retrieving the details of a selected

profile using Power Apps CLI   143
Managing profiles using PCF Builder   144

Deploying using authentication profiles   147
Deploying using Power Apps CLI   148
Deploying code components using PCF Builder   150

Summary   151
Test your knowledge   152
Further reading   152

8

Introduction to the Dataverse Project

Technical requirements   154
Overview of the Dataverse solution project   154
Initializing the solution project and adding a code component   155
Building a Dataverse project and obtaining the output   161
Understanding the default build process   162
Generating different types of solution

packages   162
Creating a production version   163

Adding multiple code components to a single Dataverse solution   166
Deploying new code components to an existing solution   168
Using the solution clone command of the Power Apps CLI   168

Using PCF Builder to add new
components to an existing solution   170

Exporting the solution's ZIP
file using the Power Apps CLI
commands   172

Understanding the complete
development cycle   174
Summary   175
Test your knowledge   176
Further reading   176

9

Configuring Code Components in Power Apps

Technical requirements   178
Adding a field type code
component to
a model-driven app   178
Configuring a dataset code
component in
a model-driven app   181
Adding a code component to a specific
view of a table   181
Adding a code component to a table   184
Adding a code component to a sub-grid   186
Configuring a code component on a
dashboard   189

Adding a code component to a
canvas app   192
Configuring a field type code
component on a screen   194
Configuring a dataset type code
component on
a screen   197
Adding a code component to a gallery
component   199

Summary   201
Test your knowledge   202
Further reading   202

Section 3:
Enhancing Code Components and Your
Development Experience

10

Diving Deep into the Features Provided by PCF

Technical requirements   206
Understanding the context   206
Exploring the updateView
method   208
Understanding the importance
of the getOutputs method   214

Setting a null value on the field   217
Setting values on the field based on a
condition   218
Omitting updates to a field   220

Inspecting the caching
mechanism   222

Working with external devices   227
Exploring the Web API   231
Summary   236
Test your knowledge   236
Further reading   237

11
Creating Advanced Dataset Code Components

Technical requirements   240
Recap of what was built   240
Sorting the data in a dataset   241
Implementing pagination on a
dataset   244
Integrating code components
with out-of-the-box options   249
Understanding the technique to
open a record from a dataset   253
Defining properties on a
dataset   256
Summary   259
Test your knowledge   259
Further reading   260

12
Enriching Your Dev Experience

Technical requirements   262
Using Lint and Prettier   262
Understanding the process of linting
your code   262
Integrating Prettier with a linter 264
Working with ESLint and Prettier   266
Setting up a testing framework 269
Using React and Fluent UI to
build code components   272
Summary   277
Test your knowledge   277
Further reading   278

Answers to Knowledge Tests

Chapter 1   279
Chapter 2   280
Chapter 3   280
Chapter 4   281
Chapter 5   281
Chapter 6   282
Chapter 7   283
Chapter 8   283
Chapter 9   284
Chapter 10   285
Chapter 11   285
Chapter 12   286
Why subscribe?   287

Other Books You May Enjoy

Index

Preface

Power Apps component framework, also known as PCF, is used to create code components for Microsoft Power Apps. This provides a new way of enhancing the user interface by providing enriched controls in model-driven and canvas apps.

This book will provide a practical guide that will cover the basics of creating, updating, and deploying a code component. It will also provide useful insights into the life cycle of the code component. With a hands-on approach to implementation and associated methodologies, this book will have you up and running and productive in no time. Complete with step-by-step explanations of essential concepts, practical examples, and self-assessment questions, you will begin to explore your knowledge of Power Apps component framework.

You will learn the basics of Power Apps component framework and about the usage of the different tools available, along with their benefits while building or deploying code components. You will also learn how to create, test, debug, and deploy your code components and take a deep dive into essential components of Power Apps component framework. Finally, you will learn advanced modern web development techniques to improve your development experience. By the end of this book, you will be able to build, test, debug, and deploy your own code component using Power Apps component framework, addressing key pain points encountered in the component life cycle.

Who this book is for

This book is aimed at developers who are working with the Power Platform and Microsoft Dataverse. It is also aimed at developers aspiring to work on the Power Platform and Microsoft Dataverse. To benefit from this book, it is helpful to have some basic knowledge of TypeScript.

What this book covers

Chapter 1, Introduction to the Power Apps Component Framework, teaches the basics of Power Apps component framework, who it is aimed toward, why it should be used, and how it is different from HTML web resources. It also details some of the advantages of using this framework and mentions the prerequisites for getting started with building code components using this framework.

Chapter 2, Power Apps CLI, defines what Power Apps CLI is and provides you with a basic understanding of the npm package. It also describes how to get started with Power Apps CLI.

Chapter 3, Community Tools and Resources, covers community tools that simplify building and managing code components. It also covers the community repository of all publicly available code components.

Chapter 4, Project Overview and the Component Life Cycle, explains the types of projects provided by Power Apps CLI. It also explains the makeup of code components along with file and folder structures. It showcases the structure of the Control Manifest and `index.ts` files in detail. At the end of the chapter, it covers the component life cycle and how events interact with each other and their host.

Chapter 5, Code, Test, and Repeat, explains the process of initializing a PCF project, editing the manifest file, and writing code to create components. It also showcases methods to add styling and preview images. It provides a step-by-step guide to create code components for a field and view.

Chapter 6, Debugging Code Components, provides an overview of the test harness included with the framework and guides you through different debugging processes. It also provides information on how to debug a code component when it is already deployed to model-driven or canvas apps using Fiddler AutoResponder.

Chapter 7, Authentication Profiles, provides an overview of authentication profiles and how to create them. It also describes the ways to manage them, from changing the default profile to deleting a profile. It shows the process to quickly deploy your code components to a preferred Microsoft Dataverse environment.

Chapter 8, Introduction to the Dataverse Project, provides an introduction to the Microsoft Dataverse Project and how to initialize, add, and build your code components in that project. It also covers the process of building and deploying multiple code components in a single solution to the Microsoft Dataverse environment.

Chapter 9, Configuring Code Components in Power Apps, showcases how to configure field and datatype code components on both model-driven and canvas apps. It also details differences in the rendering of code components on model-driven and canvas apps.

Chapter 10, Diving Deep into the Features Provided by PCF, explains in depth about events, important features, and methods provided by the framework and how to use them in each scenario with examples.

Chapter 11, Creating Advanced Dataset Code Components, explains advanced features, such as sorting, paging, opening a selected record, and integrating out-of-the-box options available on views and sub-grids that can be added to a dataset code component to enhance the user experience.

Chapter 12, Enriching Your Dev Experience, provides guidance on the process of using modern web techniques to make your code look pretty and set up a pattern to analyze the code for potential errors. It will show you the process of setting up a testing framework. It will also teach you how to use React and Fluent UI by providing a step-by-step guide to create your own code component.

To get the most out of this book

You will need access to a Microsoft Dataverse environment and administrator permissions to create and customize model-driven and canvas apps. If you do not have access to a Microsoft Dataverse environment, then you can start a 30-day trial using the following link: `https://bit.ly/PowerAppsSignUpTrial`.

Example data in this book was curated using *Visual Studio Code*, and *Power Apps CLI version 1.4.4*.

The installation prerequisites to get started with Power Apps component framework are explained as a step-by-step guide in *Chapter 1, Introduction to the Power Apps Component Framework*.

If you are using the digital version of this book, we advise you to type the code yourself or access the code via the GitHub repository (link available in the next section). Doing so will help you avoid any potential errors related to the copying and pasting of code.

Danish is active on various channels where he posts interesting content, code snippets, video tutorials, and information about PCF and the Power Platform mainly aimed at professional developers. You may benefit from following him on:

- YouTube: `https://youtube.com/PowerMaverick`
- GitHub: `https://github.com/PowerMaverick`
- Twitter: `https://twitter.com/DanzMaverick`
- Blogs: `https://powermaverick.dev`
- Weekly newsletter: `https://www.powerplatformdevelopersweekly.com`

Download the example code files

You can download the example code files for this book from GitHub at `https://github.com/PacktPublishing/Extending-Microsoft-Power-Apps-with-Power-Apps-Component-Framework`. In case there's an update to the code, it will be updated on the existing GitHub repository.

We also have other code bundles from our rich catalog of books and videos available at `https://github.com/PacktPublishing/`. Check them out!

Download the color images

We also provide a PDF file that has color images of the screenshots/diagrams used in this book. You can download it here: `https://static.packt-cdn.com/downloads/9781800564916_ColorImages.pdf`

Conventions used

There are a number of text conventions used throughout this book.

`Code in text`: Indicates code words in text, database table names, folder names, filenames, file extensions, pathnames, dummy URLs, user input, and Twitter handles. Here is an example: "The index of a profile needs to be provided based on the indexes shown when you executed the `pac auth list` command."

A block of code is set as follows:

```
public getOutputs(): IOutputs
{
    return {
        characterCounterDataInput: this.textbox.value
    };
}
```

When we wish to draw your attention to a particular part of a code block, the relevant lines or items are set in bold:

```
<resources>
        <code path="index.ts" order="1"/>
        <css path="css/MyCharacterCounter.css" order="1" />
</resources>
```

Any command-line input or output is written as follows:

```
pac auth delete --index <index of the profile>
```

Bold: Indicates a new term, an important word, or words that you see onscreen. For example, words in menus or dialog boxes appear in the text like this. Here is an example: "Click on **Authentication Profiles**. This will reveal two options: **Create Profile** and **List Profiles**."

Tips or important notes
Appear like this.

Get in touch

Feedback from our readers is always welcome.

General feedback: If you have questions about any aspect of this book, mention the book title in the subject of your message and email us at customercare@packtpub.com.

Errata: Although we have taken every care to ensure the accuracy of our content, mistakes do happen. If you have found a mistake in this book, we would be grateful if you would report this to us. Please visit www.packtpub.com/support/errata, selecting your book, clicking on the Errata Submission Form link, and entering the details.

Piracy: If you come across any illegal copies of our works in any form on the Internet, we would be grateful if you would provide us with the location address or website name. Please contact us at copyright@packt.com with a link to the material.

If you are interested in becoming an author: If there is a topic that you have expertise in and you are interested in either writing or contributing to a book, please visit authors.packtpub.com.

Reviews

Please leave a review. Once you have read and used this book, why not leave a review on the site that you purchased it from? Potential readers can then see and use your unbiased opinion to make purchase decisions, we at Packt can understand what you think about our products, and our authors can see your feedback on their book. Thank you!

For more information about Packt, please visit packt.com.

Section 1: Fundamentals of the Power Apps Component Framework

This first section focuses on the basics of the Power Apps component framework. First, we get an introduction to the Power Apps component framework, the advantages of using the framework, and the prerequisites needed to get started. Then, we look into details such as what Power Apps CLI is and its importance when building code components.

After that, we get introduced to some community tools that can help build and manage code components. Some of these tools also help in making the deployment of code components easy.

Then, we gain an understanding of the structure of the projects provided by Power Apps CLI and the makeup of the code components. We also look at the structure of the control manifest and index code files. Lastly, we cover the component life cycle and how each event interacts with itself and the host.

This section comprises the following chapters:

- *Chapter 1, Introduction to the Power Apps Component Framework*
- *Chapter 2, Power Apps CLI*
- *Chapter 3, Community Tools and Resources*
- *Chapter 4, Project Overview and the Component Life Cycle*

1

Introduction to the Power Apps Component Framework

One of the most sought-after new features for developers using Power Apps was the introduction of the Power Apps component framework, an extensibility framework for professional developers to create their own code components that can be natively added to model-driven or canvas apps. This chapter aims to introduce you to the framework and how it improves user interaction with an application. In a step-by-step manner, we will look at the various facets of the Power Apps component framework and end the chapter by preparing our machine for the upcoming chapters.

In this chapter, we are going to cover the following main topics:

- Overview of the Power Apps component framework
- Understanding the difference between the Power Apps component framework and HTML web resources

- Getting to know the licensing requirements
- Exploring the advantages of the Power Apps component framework
- Preparing your development machine

Learning some terminology

Before we begin, there is some terminology used throughout the book, and in this section, we are going to get familiar with it.

Dataverse is a platform that not only stores data in a logical manner but also provides security and audit capabilities around data. It provides a rich set of APIs and connectors. It also enables developers to extend the platform to accomplish their custom requirements. It was previously known as **Common Data Service (CDS)**.

Web resources are special files that help extend the Dataverse platform. There are different types of web resources. One such type is HTML, which extends the Dataverse platform by providing the ability to embed HTML components on forms, sitemaps, and dashboards.

Xrm context is an object provided by the Dataverse platform that helps developers to extend the platform by providing access to data, metadata, and some additional functions. Xrm context is crucial to extending the platform as it enables developers to integrate web resources with the platform to fulfill custom requirements.

Now that we understand some of the terminology, let's get an overview of the Power Apps component framework.

Overview of the Power Apps component framework

This section is all about gradually familiarizing ourselves with the framework. Let's first understand what exactly the Power Apps component framework is and why we need it. It is important to understand how the Power Apps component framework evolved before we move on to learning about the differences between the Power Apps component framework and HTML web resources, as well as the licensing requirements and the advantages of using this framework.

What is the Power Apps component framework?

The **Power Apps component framework**, otherwise known as **PCF**, is defined by Microsoft as a framework that empowers professional developers and app makers to create code components for *model-driven apps* and *canvas apps* to provide enhanced user experience for users to work with data on forms, views, and dashboards. But what does that mean? It means that now professional developers can create widgets that can be configured by the system customizer or an app maker easily, extending the capabilities of any application. Some examples include transforming a numeric field into a slider or transforming a list of appointments into an entirely different visual, such as a calendar.

Originally, it was named **Custom Control Framework (CCF)** and later renamed to *Power Apps Control Framework*, but that name did not stick for too long and it was finally renamed to the **Power Apps component framework (PCF)**. Before releasing this framework for public use, Microsoft was using it internally to create a lot of components on a unified interface, one such component being editable grids.

PCF allows professional developers to use a multitude of libraries and services of their choice and add these reusable components to any model-driven or canvas app. Other than providing usability, the framework also provides powerful capabilities for advanced interactions. To facilitate the development of code components, the **Microsoft Power Apps CLI** tool enables component creation, easy debugging, built-in validation, and testing using a code editor of your choice.

PCF resolves some of the drawbacks we had for a long time with HTML web resources, such as the lack of flexibility and portability, by providing the ability to package a component with parameters. This means your component is abstracted from an environment and made into a truly reusable component. For example, say you want to show a weather forecast depending on the zip code from an entity record. If we had to do this using an HTML web resource, we would have to keep the forecast API information either hardcoded or in a configuration entity. To do the latter would mean an extra line of code. Also, because we want to read the zip code from the entity record, we would have to fetch the Xrm context using the `window.parent` method. This is simplified using PCF by using the parameters on the control configuration form. With the same example, you can capture the forecast API information as a component property and access the zip code data using the framework's context object, which provides a neat out-of-the-box way to access an attribute's data. We will be looking into this framework's context object further in later chapters.

> **Note**
> At the time of writing this book, PCF does not work on on-premises instances.

Now that you understand what PCF is and its history, let's look at who exactly it caters to.

Who is it focused on?

When Microsoft introduced the *low-code-no-code* platform, there were two terms used within the realm of business applications: citizen developer and professional developer. Citizen developers are not developers in the regular sense, and they may not know a coding language, but they are still involved in the development process through using low-code tools, such as canvas apps, Power Automate, and so on. These tools may not necessarily be straightforward and there is a bit of learning needed to use them. Professional developers are the ones who are more heavily involved in the development process and extend their platforms using various programming languages. These developers may create reusable components that can be utilized by citizen developers.

PCF is targeted more at professional developers, as along with knowledge of the framework, you also need basic knowledge of TypeScript, npm, and the web development process. This framework enables you to create **code components** that can be used by citizen developers on model-driven or canvas apps. Hence, now more than ever, we need a collaborative effort between citizen developers and professional developers to create holistic and usable systems.

If you are a professional developer with basic knowledge of JavaScript and Dataverse but you do not possess working knowledge of TypeScript or npm, do not worry, as this book will provide ample support for you to understand the basics needed to build a code component.

> **Note**
> The code components built using PCF are sometimes also referred to as custom controls.

Next, we will learn the difference between HTML web resources and code components and understand the reasoning behind keeping both HTML web resources and code components.

How are code components different from HTML web resources?

Now, you may wonder, *do you need HTML web resources if you have code components?* The answer is *yes*, we still need HTML web resources, and as of today, both have their own distinct ways that offer you full flexibility in customizing your system. For instance, code components can only be tied to a field or a dataset; so, if you have a requirement to add a custom piece of functionality to a dashboard that cannot be accomplished using iFrames or charts, you will still have to resort to HTML web resources.

The following table shows us some of the notable differences between HTML web resources and code components:

HTML web resource	Code component
Xrm context is not easily accessible to code inside an HTML web resource.	PCF context is readily available for a control, which provides full framework capabilities.
Control loads after all out-of-the-box controls load.	Loads at the same time as any other out-of-the-box components.
May not provide a seamless experience for users; for example, controls cannot be rendered outside of a web resource boundary.	Provides a seamless experience for users; for example, the control intelligently uses only the space that is required and is responsive in design without any effort on your part.
Deployment can become complex as you are responsible for maintaining multiple files and dependencies.	Deployment is simplified with one single file.
Reusing on multiple projects or across different entities and forms can be a hassle, because an HTML web resource may be tightly coupled with a particular environment or entities.	Code components can be reused many times on multiple projects and across different entities and forms due to the abstraction from an environment, simply by providing parameters.
Cannot dynamically allocate height to a web resource on a model-driven form.	Ability to dynamically allocate the height of a control on a model-driven form.
Not supported on canvas apps.	Supports both canvas and model-driven apps.
Not a bound control. It can be added to a model-driven sitemap without binding it to a field or dataset.	Must be bound to a field or a dataset. Cannot be used on a dashboard or a direct link on a sitemap.

Table 1.1 – HTML web resources versus code components

As you can see from the preceding table, HTML web resources help where PCF lacks and vice versa, providing you with full flexibility in customizing your application. Let's now look at the licensing needs.

Getting to know the licensing requirements

How a code component interacts with an external service determines the licensing scheme for the app that consumes the code component. The two license classifications are as follows:

- When an app uses a code component that connects with an external service, it becomes premium, and end users need to have a Power Apps license.

- If code components do not consume an external service, then the usage of such components in an app requires users to at least have a license for Office 365.

> **Note**
> A code component cannot be used in Dataverse for Teams.

Now that we understand the licensing requirements, let's go through the advantages of using PCF.

Exploring the advantages of PCF

When developing code components using PCF, it is important for you to know some of the advantages of the framework. They are as follows:

- Access to a rich set of framework APIs that grant capabilities such as managing component life cycles and getting contextual data and metadata information.

- Seamless server access through a web API, utility, and data formatting methods.

- Access to device features, such as camera, location services, and microphone.

- Provides a quickstart template that uses npm packages and webpack.

- Optimized for performance.

- Unlike HTML web resources, which get rendered as an iFrame, code components are rendered as part of the DOM, which provides an enhanced and seamless user experience.

- Developers can utilize Power Apps capabilities to the fullest; for example, they can use the command bar on sub-grids.

- Based on how code components are created, PCF can support both model-driven and canvas apps. We will be looking at the cases when a code component cannot support canvas apps in later chapters.

These are just some of the advantages of PCF. Let's now look at how to prepare your machine, which will help us develop the code components.

Preparing your development machine

There are some prerequisites you need to install before you can start building the code components that we will be using in this book. In the following subsections, we will look at each of these prerequisites in detail and examine the processes required to get these tools installed.

Node.js or npm

The first prerequisite is Node.js or npm; you do not need both because if you install one, the other gets installed as part of it.

Node.js helps users to build scalable applications using an asynchronous event-driven runtime engine.

npm is an open source JavaScript and TypeScript package registry. It has a command-line interface that enables developers to interact with it.

For installation, browse to `https://nodejs.org` and choose the latest LTS version available for download. Once the file is downloaded, execute it to install it on your machine:

Node.js® is a JavaScript runtime built on Chrome's V8 JavaScript engine.

Download for Windows (x64)

Other Downloads | Changelog | API Docs   Other Downloads | Changelog | API Docs

Or have a look at the Long Term Support (LTS) schedule.

Figure. 1.1 – Node.js download

Once the installation is complete, you can check the status by opening a command prompt and running the `npm version` command, which should show you the npm version installed on the machine.

TypeScript

Once you have installed these prerequisites, you need to make sure you have TypeScript installed on the machine. To check whether TypeScript is already installed on your machine, open the command prompt and execute the following command:

```
tsc -v
```

If the response from the command shows a version number, then you already have TypeScript installed on your machine, but if the response states that the command is not recognized, then you need to install TypeScript on your machine.

TypeScript can be installed through npm using the following command:

```
npm install -g typescript
```

`-g` means it is installed on your system globally so that the TypeScript compiler can be used in any of your projects. Once the installation is complete, you can execute `tsc -v` to confirm it.

.NET Framework

Next, you need to make sure the .NET Framework 4.6.2 developer pack is installed on your machine. To check whether 4.6.2 version is already installed on your machine, do the following:

1. Open **Visual Studio Installer**. If you do not have Visual Studio Installer, then you can download the latest version of Visual Studio from `https://visualstudio.microsoft.com/downloads`.

2. From the **More** option for the latest version of Visual Studio, select **Modify**, which will bring up the **Installation details** window.

3. Make sure the **ASP.NET and web development** option is checked.

4. On the right-hand panel, under **ASP.Net and web development**, confirm that **.NET Framework 4.6.2 development tools** is checked. If it is not installed, then check the box and click on the **Install while downloading** button, as seen in the following screenshot:

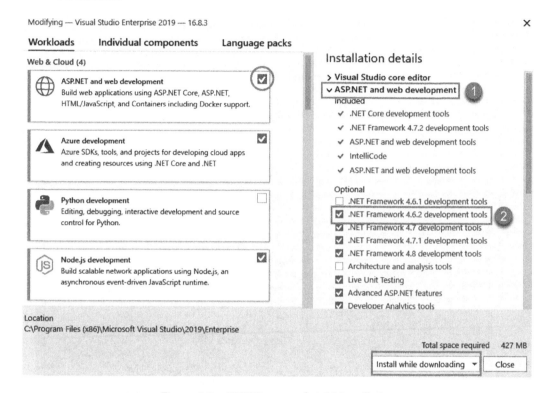

Figure. 1.2 – .NET Framework 4.6.2 installation

Visual Studio Code

While you can use any preferred integrated development environment, for the development in this book, we are going to use Visual Studio Code.

Visual Studio Code is a free source code editor made by Microsoft for Windows, Linux, and macOS. Its features include support for debugging, syntax highlighting, intelligent code completion, snippets, code refactoring, and embedded Git.

If you do not have Visual Studio Code installed on your machine, you can install it from `https://code.visualstudio.com/download`.

Power Apps CLI

The most important tool in enabling a developer to interact with PCF and empowering them to create, test, debug, and deploy code components is Power Apps CLI. To download it, browse to `https://aka.ms/PowerAppsCLI`. Once downloaded, install it on your machine.

> **Note**
>
> Currently, Power Apps CLI is only supported on Windows 10.

To confirm the installation, open the command prompt and run the `pac` command. It should show an output as follows:

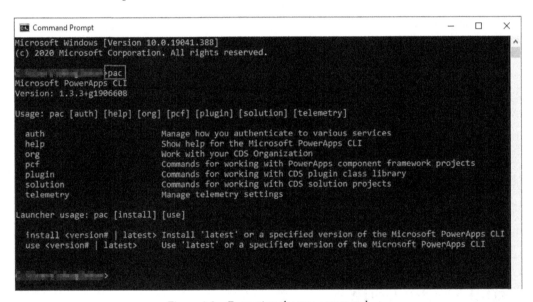

Figure 1.3 – Executing the pac command

Once your machine has been prepared with all the prerequisites, you need to download the example library.

Downloading the example library and using the practice questions

Throughout this book, you will be creating some sample controls, and to help you validate those controls, a library has been published on GitHub for you to download.

To download the library, navigate to `https://github.com/PacktPublishing/Extending-Microsoft-Power-Apps-with-Power-Apps-Component-Framework`.

In this book, at the end of each chapter, you will find questions to test the knowledge and skills you have acquired. Each question will show you the points you will earn if you answer it correctly. There are *5,000* points to be earned overall. The answers to those questions can be found at the end of the book.

At this point, you should have all the tools and content you need to build your own code components throughout the book.

Summary

Power Apps component framework is the next level of development framework, enabling developers to extend any type of Power Apps app. We introduced PCF, looked at the key differences between code components and HTML web resources, learned about the licensing requirements, and talked about PCF's advantages. We ended the chapter by learning about the installation processes for all the prerequisites of the book to set ourselves up for the upcoming chapters.

In the next chapter, we will look at the Power Apps CLI tool, which helps in the initialization of various projects.

Test your knowledge

1. Are HTML web resources still needed when we can just use code components built using PCF? (*100 points*)

    a. Yes

    b. No

2. When does an app that has implemented a code component built using PCF need a premium Power Apps license? (*100 points*)

    a. When a code component does not use an external service

    b. When a code component uses an external service

3. What is the one crucial application that you need to install in order to prepare your development machine for building code components? (*200 points*)

    a. Visual Studio Code

    b. Power Apps CLI

Further reading

- Additional information related to PCF can be found in the Microsoft documentation at `https://bit.ly/PCFOverview`.

- To learn the basics of TypeScript for JavaScript programmers, go to `https://www.typescriptlang.org/docs/handbook/typescript-in-5-minutes.html`.

- If you are new to TypeScript and JavaScript, then read this article: `https://www.typescriptlang.org/docs/handbook/typescript-from-scratch.html`.

2
Power Apps CLI

Now that we know a little about the history of the **Power Apps component framework** (**PCF**) and have our development environment set up, let's take our next steps into the world of Power Apps – getting to know Power Apps CLI. This chapter will focus on getting you introduced to the basics of the Power Apps command-line interface and provide an overview of npm. In a step-by-step manner, we will understand the process for initializing your first PCF project using Power Apps CLI. By the end of this chapter, you will be ready to create code components for the chapters that come next.

In this chapter, we are going to cover the following main topics:

- Overview of Power Apps CLI
- Understanding npm
- Initializing a PCF project using Power Apps CLI

Technical requirements

In order to work through this chapter, you need to install all the prerequisites and download the example library that will help you with the development process mentioned in *Chapter 1, Introduction to the Power Apps Component Framework*. Download the example library from `https://github.com/PacktPublishing/Extending-Microsoft-Power-Apps-with-Power-Apps-Component-Framework/tree/master/Chapter02`.

What is Power Apps CLI?

Power Apps CLI is a command-line interface that provides developers with a set of commands to work with PCF, Dataverse solutions, plugins, and much more. It is the first step toward a comprehensive **application lifecycle management** (**ALM**) story where the developers can create, build, and publish their projects quickly and effectively.

A set of commands provided by Power Apps CLI helps you to create a PCF project that will enable you to develop code components. It also provides you with a command to create a **Dataverse** solution project that will help you package your code components, which can be deployed to any Dataverse environment. The command related to a plugin project initializes a class library with a plugin base and example plugin classes. It also provides commands to authenticate and manage various Dataverse environments.

There are multiple community-built tools to begin your journey of building code components but beneath all those tools, the core to initializing your code component is Power Apps CLI. Other tools provide additional functionality where Power Apps CLI lacks.

Using Power Apps CLI currently can help you manage three types of projects, namely, a PCF project, a Dataverse solution project, and a plugin project. In this chapter, we will be looking at a PCF project.

A PCF project is used to create a code component, whereas a Dataverse solution project is used to reference the solution components and deploy them from a local machine to your preferred Dataverse environment.

If you already have Power Apps CLI installed on your machine, then you can easily update it to the latest version by executing the following command:

```
pac install latest
```

Power Apps CLI helps you to initialize projects but to develop and build code components, you need some basic understanding of modern web development. So, we need to first look at some of the basics of modern web development. This is covered in the next section.

What is npm?

npm, short for **Node Package Manager**, is an online repository for publishing open source projects built on Node.js. It also provides a command-line utility for interacting with an online repository that helps in package installation, version management, and dependency management. For more information on npm, you can visit `https://www.npmjs.com/`.

To help maintain project dependencies, scripts, and versioning, each Node.js project provides a `package.json` file. When you initialize your **PCF** project, you will get a `package.json` file as part of the project template. This file will contain a `script` section that will help you execute certain commands, such as `build` and `test`. It will also contain a list of dependencies that can be easily restored from the npm package registry to your local machine.

During the course of this book, we will be using the following npm commands:

- `npm install`: This command installs all dependencies from the npm package registry to the local `node_modules` folder, which are listed in the `package.json` file.

- `npm build`: This command executes the specified `build` script mentioned under the `scripts` section in the `package.json` file.

- `npm start`: This command is similar to `build`, in the sense that it executes the specified `start` script mentioned under the `scripts` section in the `package.json` file.

The PCF project provides a set of npm scripts that will help you during the development of your code component. If you are using VS Code, you can access npm scripts from the **EXPLORER** pane as shown in the following screenshot:

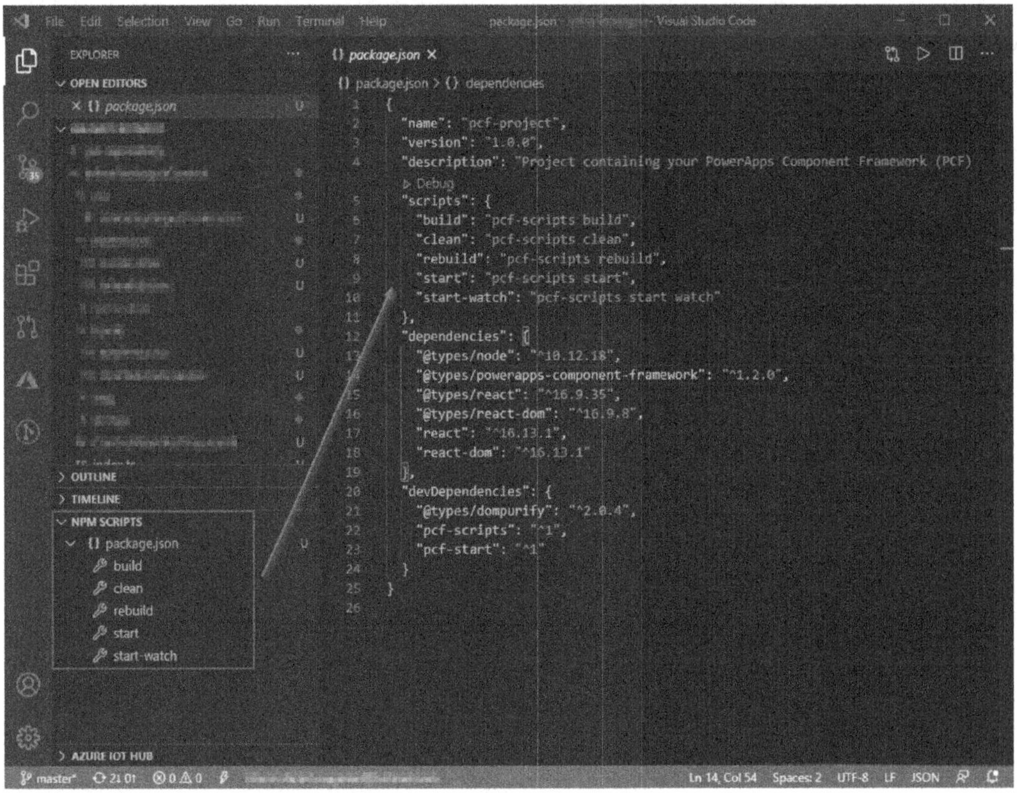

Figure 2.1 – Accessing npm scripts in VS Code

In the preceding screenshot, you can see that the dependencies are also listed in the package.json file. So, if you have downloaded code from a new source (let's say GitHub), then to make sure you have all the dependencies installed on your local machine, you need to execute the npm install command. This command will install all the dependencies listed in the package.json file.

Now, that you understand what Power Apps CLI and npm are, let's get started with the initialization of the code component.

Initializing a Power Apps component framework project

After you have installed all the prerequisites mentioned in *Chapter 1*, *Introduction to the Power Apps Component Framework*, let's begin with initializing the code component. In this section, we will execute the commands that will initialize a Power Apps component framework project that is used to create the code component.

> **Note**
> Visual Studio Code will be used as the development tool throughout this book.

To begin initializing your first PCF project, perform the following steps:

1. Create a folder that will serve as your workspace for building the code component.

2. Start VS Code and within VS Code, navigate to the folder that you just created.

3. Open an integrated terminal of VS Code; the default command to open a terminal in VS Code is *Ctrl + `*.

4. To initialize a PCF project, you will have to run the following Power Apps CLI command in the terminal:

    ```
    pac pcf init --namespace <your_namespace> --name
    <component_name> --template <field|dataset>
    ```

    When providing your namespace and component name, you cannot use spaces or any special characters except (.) dot; you also cannot name your control PCF. The `template` attribute takes in two values: `field` or `dataset`. We will investigate the details of each of those types in later chapters.

5. Once the PCF project is initialized, the next step is to install all its dependencies using this command:

    ```
    npm install
    ```

This should create several files and folders under your workspace and one of the files will have the .pcfproj extension. We will look into the details of each file and folder that gets created as part of the project in *Chapter 4, Project Overview and the Component Life Cycle.*

Now that you have seen the steps, let's try to replicate these steps to create our own project.

Exercise – creating a PCF project using Power Apps CLI

Let's initialize a new PCF project using Power Apps CLI by performing the following steps:

1. Create a folder named CustomTagsCLIProject.

2. Open this folder in VS Code.

3. Open an integrated terminal of VS Code.

4. Run the following command to initialize the project:

    ```
    pac pcf init --namespace PowerMeUp --name CustomTagsCLI
    --template field
    ```

5. Execute the installation command:

    ```
    npm install
    ```

If you have executed the steps just mentioned, you should be able to compare them with the following screenshot:

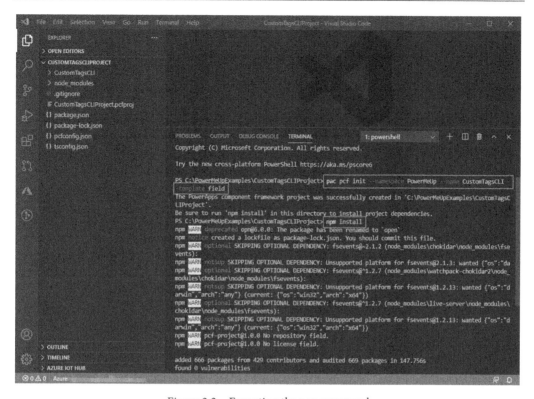

Figure 2.2 – Executing the pac command

Once you have successfully executed the commands, you should see several folders and files created under the CustomTagsCLI project and the folder structure should look something like the following screenshot:

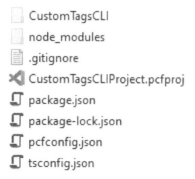

Figure 2.3 – Outcome after executing the pac command

See how easy it was to create our own PCF project? I encourage you to try and create your own projects and get familiar with the CLI tool.

Summary

In this chapter, we learned about the basics of Power Apps CLI and the npm package. We saw different types of projects that are supported by Power Apps CLI and the differences between some of them. We initialized a Power Apps component framework project using Power Apps CLI that will help us build a code component and we saw that Power Apps CLI plays an important role when it comes to initializing any of the project types mentioned.

In the next chapter, we will look at some of the community-built tools that enhance the development experience.

Test your knowledge

1. Which command allows you to upgrade the version of Power Apps CLI to the latest? (*100 points*)

    a. `pcf install latest`

    b. `pac install latest`

2. What is the extension of the PCF project file? (*100 points*)

    a. `.pcfproj`

    b. `.pcf`

3. Which of the following commands is correct? (*200 points*)

    a. `pac pcf init --namespace Power Me Up --name SuperControl --template field`

    b. `pac pcf init -ns PowerMeUp -n SuperControl -t field`

Further reading

- Additional information related to Power Apps CLI can be found in Microsoft's documentation at `https://bit.ly/PowerAppsCLI`.

- Information on the basics of the `package.json` file can be found at `https://nodejs.dev/learn/the-package-json-guide`.

- Additional information on `npm install` can be found at `https://nodejs.dev/learn/where-does-npm-install-the-packages`.

3
Community Tools and Resources

In the last chapter, we saw what Power Apps CLI is and how we can initialize a project for code components. Let's now take a look at what the Power Platform community has built to improve the development process: a rich set of tools and a collection of community-built code components. These tools overcome the drawbacks of Power Apps CLI by either providing a **graphical user interface (GUI)** or by allowing developers to execute commands quickly. These tools also provide you with different templates and features that minimize the time taken to build code components.

We will begin this journey by getting to know PCF Builder, followed by PCF Generator, and finally we will look at PCF Gallery. By the end of this chapter, you will be familiar with these tools and library, which will help you to build code components more quickly.

In this chapter, we are going to cover the following main topics:

- An overview of PCF Builder
- Using PCF Builder for XrmToolBox
- Using PCF Builder for Visual Studio Code
- An overview of PCF Generator
- Exploring the installation guide and initializing projects

- Understanding the benefits of using PCF Generator over Power Apps CLI

- Integration between PCF Builder and PCF Generator

- Exploring code components on PCF Gallery

Technical requirements

In order to work through this chapter, you need to install all the prerequisites and download the example library that will help you with the development process mentioned in *Chapter 1, Introduction to the Power Apps Component Framework*. Download the example library from `https://github.com/PacktPublishing/Extending-Microsoft-Power-Apps-with-Power-Apps-Component-Framework/tree/master/Chapter03`. You will also need to install **XrmToolBox** and **Visual Studio Code**. You can download the latest version of XrmToolBox from `https://www.xrmtoolbox.com/`.

PCF Builder

PCF Builder enables you to build code components with ease where you do not need to write the CLI commands but still use Power Apps CLI under the hood. Most of the commands are consolidated, making it easier to build controls. It has two versions of itself; one provides a GUI as opposed to a command-line interface provided by Power Apps CLI, and the other version provides a guided experience for users. Both these versions are community built, with their source code available on **GitHub**, while links to the source code are provided in *Further reading* section of this chapter. PCF Builder also has a community chat room, where you can discuss new features or open issues. To join the chat room, you can use the following link: `https://bit.ly/PCFBuilderChat`.

Graphical user interface version

The version that provides a graphical user interface is a tool created for **XrmToolBox**, which is a Windows application that enables developers or admins to connect to the **Dataverse** environment, providing an array of tools to facilitate customization, configuration, and operation. PCF Builder for XrmToolBox provides an easy-to-use GUI that helps users to create, build, test, and deploy code components without writing a single command. This enhances the developer's experience by allowing them to focus on the core logic of the code components by eliminating the need for them to remember commands to execute. The tool allows you to view the output from Power Apps CLI in an embedded console view. It also provides access to Microsoft documentation, forums, ideas, and sample code.

The following screenshot gives us a preview of PCF Builder for XrmToolBox:

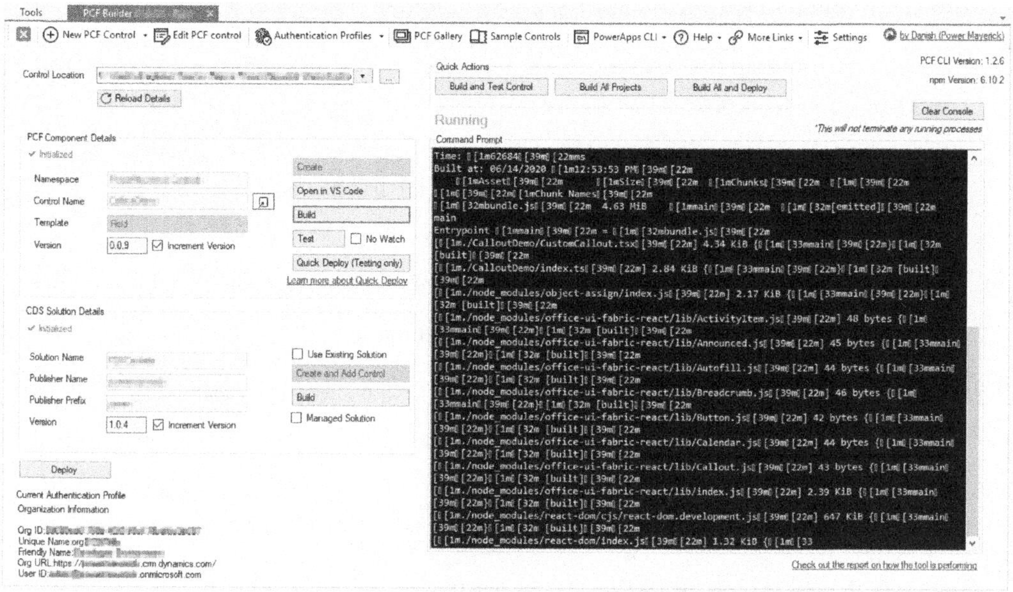

Figure 3.1 – PCF Builder for XrmToolBox version 2.2020.06.011

Advantages of PCF Builder for XrmToolBox

Let's now explore the advantages of PCF Builder for XrmToolBox when developing code components using the Power Apps component framework. They are as follows:

- It provides a graphical user interface so that you do not need to remember the Power Apps CLI commands.

- It consolidates multiple commands with a single click of a button, thereby reducing the complexity of using Power Apps CLI.

- It gives easy access to Microsoft documentation, forums, and sample codes.

- It shows statuses, such as running, failed, and succeeded.

- It auto-increments versions of projects.

As you can see, PCF Builder enhances the development of code components by reducing the developer's efforts and adding tons of cool features.

Installing PCF Builder from the XrmToolBox tool library

To install PCF Builder from XrmToolBox, perform the following steps:

1. Open XrmToolBox. If you do not have it installed on your machine, install it from `https://www.xrmtoolbox.com/`.

2. From the menu bar, navigate to **Configuration** and then click on **Tool Library**. This will show you a list of all the available tools on XrmToolBox.

3. Search for `PCF Builder` in the search textbox.

4. Click on the checkbox provided next to the **PCF Builder** record.

5. Finally, click on the **Install** button on the menu bar.

The following screenshot highlights the installation steps we just learned:

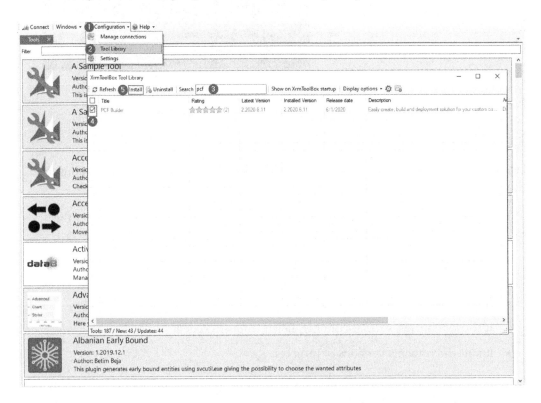

Figure 3.2 – Installation page in XrmToolBox

Initializing a PCF project using PCF Builder for XrmToolBox

Once you have installed PCF Builder in XrmToolBox, let's now learn how to initialize a PCF project using this tool:

1. Start by creating a new folder or by selecting an existing empty folder.

2. Populate the complete path in the textbox provided with the **Control Location** label.

3. Provide your preferred `namespace` and `name` for the control and select your `template type` from the dropdown.

4. Now, click the **Create** button in the **PCF Component Details** section. This will initialize the PCF project and install the project dependencies.

5. The tool will show the status as running and, once it finishes processing, the status will be hidden, indicating that the initialization process is complete. You can check the output in the embedded console view.

6. Once the project is initialized, all the fields related to the PCF project will be read-only. You can open the project in VS Code by clicking on the **Open in VS Code** button.

7. You also have a choice to open the folder location by clicking the button next to the textbox provided to enter the **Control Name** field.

By the end of these steps, you should have initialized a PCF project just by clicking a few buttons.

Rating the tool in XrmToolBox

As PCF Builder is a community tool, it is always recommended to provide your feedback and support the tool. It helps developers to implement new features, which can improve the efficiency of the tool and benefits the entire community. To provide a rating, perform the following steps:

1. From the **XrmToolBox** menu bar, navigate to **Configuration** and click on **Tool Library**, showing a list of all the available tools.

2. Search for `PCF Builder` and then select it from the list.

3. This will bring up the details for PCF Builder, and in the top-right corner of that panel will be a link called **Rate this tool**.

4. Clicking this link will take you to the XrmToolBox portal where, after you log in (may need to create an account), you can enter your rating and feedback comments relating to the tool.

5. You can also rate the tool directly on the XrmToolBox portal by going to this link: `https://bit.ly/PBXrmToolBox`.

Exercise – Creating a PCF project using PCF Builder for XrmToolBox

Let's now initialize a PCF project using PCF Builder for XrmToolBox. Perform the following steps:

1. Create a folder named `CustomTagsPBXProject`.

2. Open XrmToolBox and invoke `PCF Builder` for the list of tools.

3. You can skip the prompt for connecting to the Dataverse environment.

4. Copy the full path of the folder created in *Step 1* and paste it into the textbox named **Control Location**.

5. Populate the namespace with `PowerMeUp`.

6. Type `CustomTagsPBX` in the **Control Name** field.

7. Select the **Field** option from the dropdown.

8. Click on the **Create** button within the **PCF Component Details** section.

Once you have executed these steps, you should be able to compare them with the following screenshot:

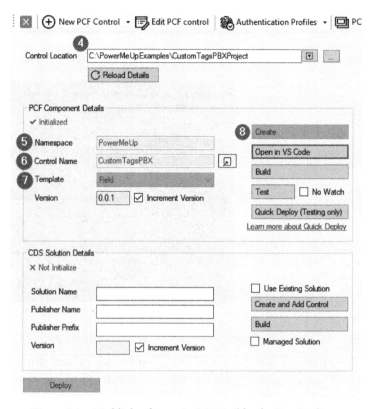

Figure 3.3 – Highlighted steps in PCF Builder for XrmToolBox

Following successful execution of all the aforementioned steps, the output of the tool should look as follows:

Figure 3.4 – Outcome of PCF Builder for XrmToolBox

Now that we have undergone the process of initializing a PCF project using PCF Builder for XrmToolBox, let's take a look at what the experience would be if we were just using VS Code and didn't have to leave that interface.

Guided experience version

The version that provides guided experience is created as an extension for VS Code. PCF Builder for VS Code enables users to initialize, build, test, and deploy code components from within the coding interface, making it easy for developers to build code components without switching between multiple tools. As with the GUI version, it enhances the developer's experience by allowing them to focus on the core logic of the code components by eliminating the need for them to remember the commands to execute.

The following screenshot shows us a preview of a few commands that are available on PCF Builder:

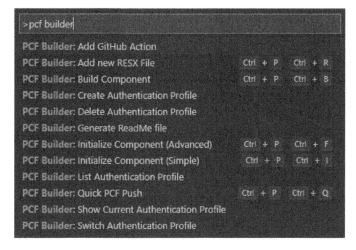

Figure 3.5 – All commands from PCF Builder for VS Code

Advantages of PCF Builder for VS Code

Let's take a look at the advantages of PCF Builder for VS Code:

- There is no need to switch between different tools.

- It consolidates multiple commands in a single command, thereby reducing the complexity of using Power Apps CLI.

- It provides Intellisense on the manifest file.

- It has the ability to add additional resource files and a reference is automatically added to the manifest file.

As you can see, the advantages of PCF Builder for VS Code are different to those of PCF Builder for XrmToolBox.

Installing PCF Builder from VS Code

To install PCF Builder from VS Code, perform the following steps:

1. Open VS Code. If you do not have it installed on your machine, install it from `code.visualstudio.com/download`.

2. From the menu, navigate to **View** and then click on **Extensions** to reveal the extensions sidebar. Search for `PCF Builder` in the search box and select it from the list.

3.   This will open the extension information page, with the **Install** button in the top section. Click on the **Install** button to add it to your extensions.

4.   Alternatively, you can also install PCF Builder from this link: `https://bit.ly/ PBVSCode`.

Initializing a PCF project using PCF Builder from VS Code

To initialize a PCF project using PCF Builder from VS Code, perform the following steps:

1.   Identify an empty folder that will serve as your workspace for creating your code component. If no such folder exists, create a new folder.

2.   Within VS Code, open the folder that you have deemed to be your workspace.

3.   Invoke the command palette by either navigating to **View** from the menu bar and selecting the **Command Palette** option, or by using keyboard shortcut *Ctrl + Shift + P*.

4.   Type `PCF Builder` to reveal the list of commands. Select **PCF Builder: Initialize Component (Simple)** from the list.

5.   The application will then show prompts to enter additional values. First, enter your preferred namespace, followed by the control name, and select your template type.

6.   Then you will be shown an option to select additional packages to install, such as React and/or Fluent UI. You can either press the *Esc* key or select **None** if you do not want any additional packages.

7.   The extension will start executing the Power Apps CLI commands to initialize the project. The output will be visible in the integrated terminal window.

8.   Once the project is initialized, you will see some files and folders created in the explorer pane of VS Code.

By the end of these steps, you should have initialized a PCF project just by answering a few questions.

Rating the tool on Visual Studio Marketplace

This extension is free, hence, it is always recommended to provide your feedback and support in relation to the tool. To provide a rating, perform the following steps:

1.   Browse to `marketplace.visualstudio.com/vscode` and search for `PCF Builder`.

2.   Open the **PCF Builder** extension from the list.

3. Navigate to the **Rating & Review** tab and click on **Write a Review**.

4. This will prompt you to log in to your Visual Studio account. If you do not have one, you can create an account for free.

5. Provide your rating and, optionally, you can submit your comments.

6. Alternatively, you can provide your ratings and comments using this link: `https://marketplace.visualstudio.com/ items?itemName=danish-naglekar.pcf-builder#review-details`.

Exercise – Creating a PCF project using PCF Builder for VS Code

Let's initialize a PCF project using the PCF Builder extension for VS Code. Perform the following steps:

1. Create a folder named `CustomTagsPBVSProject`.

2. Start VS Code and open the folder created in *Step 1*:

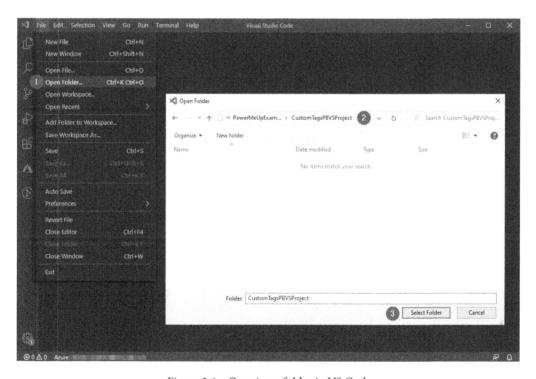

Figure 3.6 – Opening a folder in VS Code

3. From the menu, select **View | Command Palette…**:

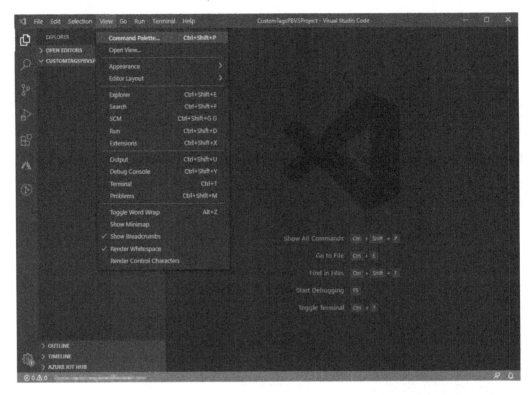

Figure 3.7 – Command Palette

4. Type `PCF Builder` and select **PCF Builder: Initialize Component (Simple)** from the list of commands:

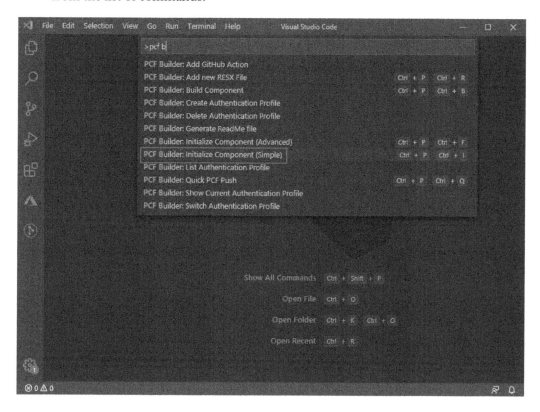

Figure 3.8 – PCF Builder Initialize command

5. Populate the namespace with `PowerMeUp` and hit *Enter*:

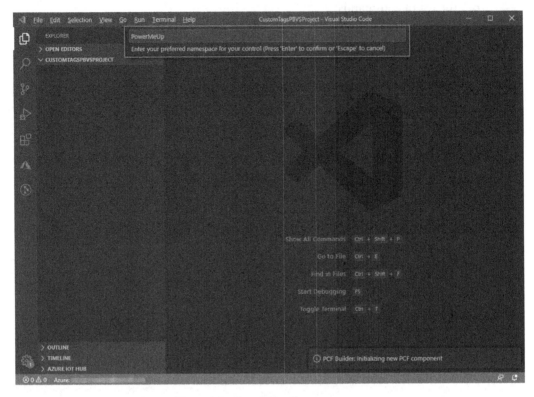

Figure 3.9 – Populating the namespace

6.   Populate the name as `CustomTagsPBVS`:

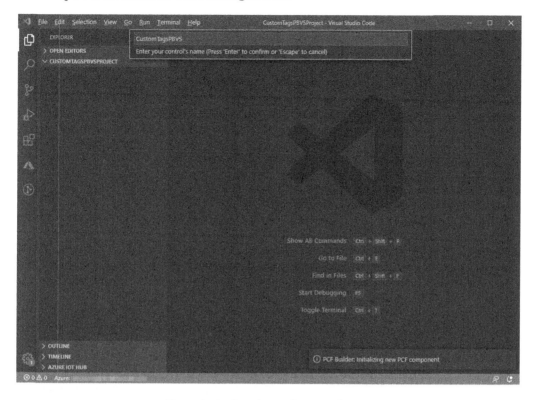

Figure 3.10 – Populating the control name

7. Choose **field** from the options provided for the template type:

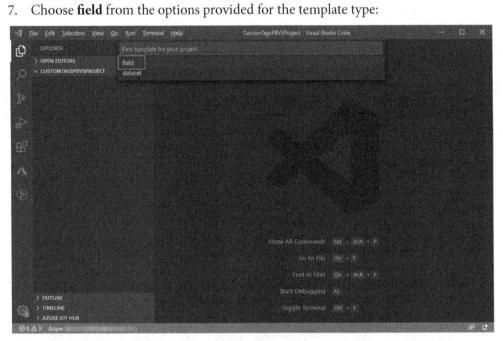

Figure 3.11 – Selecting the field type of control

8. Select **None** from the options provided for npm packages:

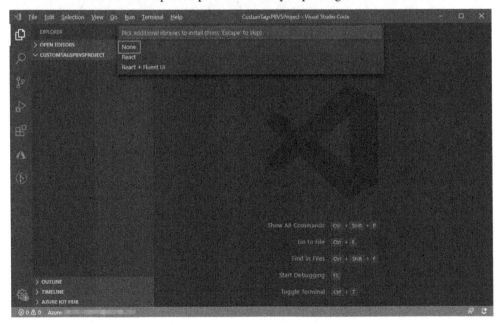

Figure 3.12 – No additional library selected to install

Finally, once execution of all the steps is complete, you should see the following output:

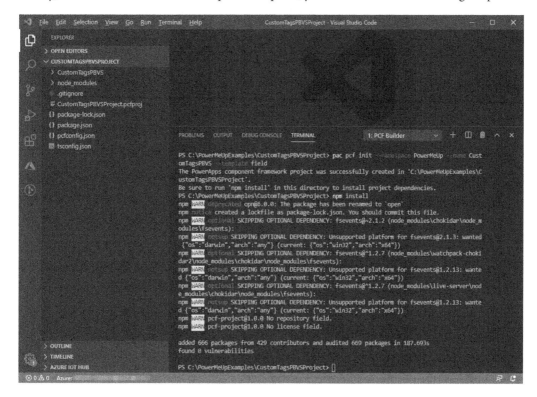

Figure 3.13 – Outcome of PCF Builder for VS Code

You can choose to close the terminal, but there is no need to delete it. Now that you have initialized a couple of PCF projects and understood the process, let's look at one more tool that provides easy-to-use templates.

PCF Generator

PCF Generator is another CLI package sourced from the npm library that helps you create boilerplate code using a scaffolding tool called **Yeoman**. The package not only creates necessary files and folders, but also initializes the Dataverse solution while correctly configuring references in the manifest file. It follows the recommended programming guidelines for creating folder structures and files. The source code for PCF Generator is available on **GitHub** and links to the source code are provided in the *Further reading* section of this chapter.

Installing PCF Generator

Perform the following steps to install PCF Generator:

1. Before you begin using PCF Generator, you need to install **Yeoman** by running the following command:

```
npm install -g yo
```

2. You also need to install the PCF Generator package from npm with the following command:

```
npm install -g generator-pcf
```

For the installation of Yeoman and PCF Generator, we have used the -g attribute. Hence, these packages will be installed globally for the logged-in user, which means you need to run these commands only once.

Initializing a PCF project using PCF Generator

There are a few ways in which you can use this package. You can use the Windows Command Prompt, or you can even run the commands from within VS Code by using its integrated terminal, or you can supply a few arguments that will skip the guided process. However you choose to run the package, you still need an empty folder to start with, and if you do not have any empty folder, create one. Let's take a look at the different ways to use this package.

Using Command Prompt for initialization

After deciding on the folder, navigate to that folder from Command Prompt using the cd <full folder path> command. Now, run the following command:

```
yo pcf -force
```

This will guide you through the selection process. Once you have answered all the questions, it will initialize a PCF and Dataverse solution project for you.

Using VS Code for initialization

Before we run the initialization command for PCF Generator, we will want to register the path of the MSBUILD file in the environment variable. Usually, the MSBUILD executable file is found under your latest Visual Studio folder. If you are unsure of where to find the MSBUILD executable file, then start PCF Builder for XrmToolBox and open the **Settings** window. You will be able to see **MS Build Path** on the settings window; copy this path. Now, by executing the following steps, register the copied MSBUILD path in the environment variable:

1. Press your *Windows* key and search for environment variable. Clicking on it will open **System Properties**.

2. Click on the **Environment Variable** button. This will open the **Environment Variable** window.

3. Under the **User variable** section, select **Path** and then click on the **Edit** button. This will bring up the **Edit** window.

4. Click the **New** button and paste the copied path.

5. Click the **OK** buttons on all the open windows.

This should set the MSBUILD path. Let's now understand how to use PCF Generator to initialize the project.

> **Note**
>
> Setting the MSBUILD path in the environment variable is useful for running any msbuild command.

Open VS Code. If you do not have it installed on your machine, install it from code . visualstudio.com/download. Open the folder that you have deemed to be your workspace and invoke the integrated terminal by either navigating to **View** from the menu bar and selecting the **Terminal** option, or by using the keyboard shortcut *Ctrl + `*. Within the terminal, run the following command:

```
yo pcf -force
```

Once you have invoked PCF Generator, answer the questions asked by the package to initialize your PCF and Dataverse solution projects.

> **Tip**
>
> Using the `-force` attribute avoids getting too many confirmation questions.

How to answer the questions?

When you run the initialization command, you will be asked a few questions before the project is initialized. The following list explains each of the questions and how to answer them:

- **Control namespace**: This is your preferred namespace for the control. It cannot contain spaces.

- **Control name**: This is an internal control name. It cannot contain spaces.

- **Choose control template**: Use your keyboard's up and down arrow keys to make your preferred selection.

- **Additional NPM packages**: Three options are provided here. Again, use your keyboard's up and down arrow keys to make your preferred selection.

- **Publisher prefix**: This is the **Dataverse** solution package prefix. It must be less than or equal to five character in length.

- **Publisher name**: This is the **Dataverse** solution publisher name and cannot contain spaces.

- **Type of solution to build**: There are three options provided; `Both`, `Unmanaged`, and `Managed`. Based on your preferences, using your keyboard's up and down arrow keys, select a value.

Once you have answered all the necessary questions, PCF Generator will initialize a PCF project, install all the needed dependencies, structure the project with community standardization, initialize the Dataverse solution project, add the code component reference to the Dataverse solution project, and initiate the build process.

Next, we will be looking at how to avoid answering those questions by supplying the values as arguments to the command.

Using command-line arguments

The package also takes in command-line arguments, which, when supplied, skips the questions for which the value was provided. The following table shows what the different options are and their requirements:

Full Name	Short Name	Type	Description
controlNamespace	ns	string	Your preferred namespace for the control.
controlName	n	string	An internal name for your control.
controlTemplate	t	string	Valid values: field or dataset.
npmPackage	pkg	int	Valid values: 0 – None. 1 – React. 2 – React + Fluent UI.
publisherPrefix	pp	string	Prefix for your Dataverse solution.
publisherName	pn	string	Dataverse solution publisher name.
solutionPackageType	spt	string	Dataverse solution type to be created after the project is built. Valid values: Both, Unmanaged, Managed.
skip-solution	ss	bool	If true, then it does not create a Dataverse solution project.
skip-msbuild	sb	bool	If true, then it does not build a Dataverse solution project.

Table 3.1 – Details regarding each command-line argument

Benefits of using PCF Generator over Power Apps CLI for PCF

Power Apps CLI for PCF and the solution offer only a basic project creation. However, PCF Generator, on the other hand, creates both the projects in a single command with all the recommended folder structure and boilerplate code, which simplifies the development process.

Some of the advantages of using PCF Generator are as follows:

- It creates a complete solution with boilerplate code.

- It has the ability to add new resource files just by selection and a reference is maintained in the manifest file.

- It automatically generates a README file by analyzing the manifest file.

Next, we would look at how PCF Generator is integrated with PCF Builder to allow an enhanced development experience.

Integrating PCF Generator in PCF Builder

Even though you can use PCF Generator by itself, it is nicely integrated into PCF Builder for VS Code. The command in PCF Builder to look for is called **PCF Builder: Initialize Component (Advanced)**, and the shortcut key in VS Code for this is *Ctrl + P* followed by *Ctrl + F*. With this, you must answer a series of questions and it will initiate the boilerplate PCF and Dataverse solution project for you, as shown in the following screenshot:

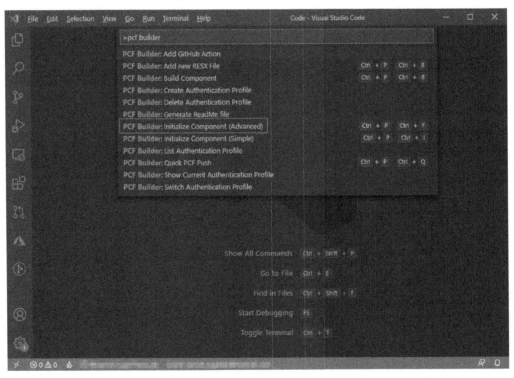

Figure 3.14 – PCF Generator inside PCF Builder

Exercise – Creating a PCF project using PCF Generator

Before we start with our exercise, we need to make sure that we install the prerequisites. This is a one-time activity. To install the prerequisites, open Command Prompt and execute the following two commands:

```
npm install -g yo
npm install -g generator-pcf
```

The -g attribute denotes that these packages are installed globally on your system so that they can be used by any project.

Let's now initialize a PCF project using PCF Generator. Perform the following steps:

1. Create a folder named CustomTagsPGVSProject.

2. Start VS Code and open the folder created in *Step 1*.

3. From the **View** menu, select **Terminal**:

Figure 3.15 – Opening the terminal in VS Code

4. Bypass the PowerShell execution policy by using the following command:

```
Set-ExecutionPolicy -Scope Process -ExecutionPolicy
Bypass
```

5. Type yo pcf -force and hit *Enter*:

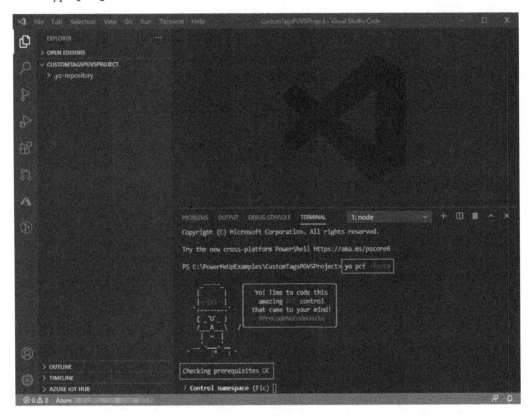

Figure 3.16 – Executing the yo pcf command

6. Populate the namespace with `PowerMeUp`. Hit *Enter* and wait for the repository to get created.

7. Populate the name as `CustomTagsPCVS`:

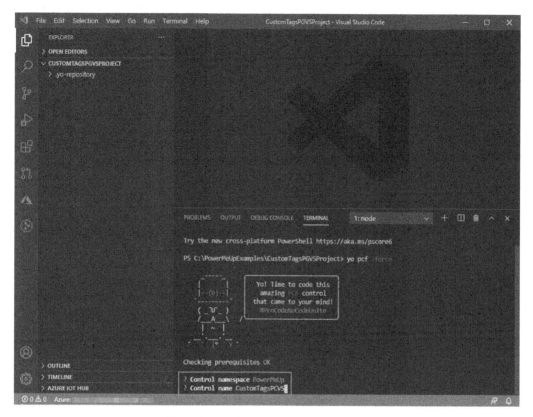

Figure 3.17 – Answering questions part 1

8.   Hit *Enter* when **Field** is highlighted in a blue color:

Figure 3.18 – Selecting the field type

9. Choose **None** from the options provided by using your keyboard's up and down arrow keys:

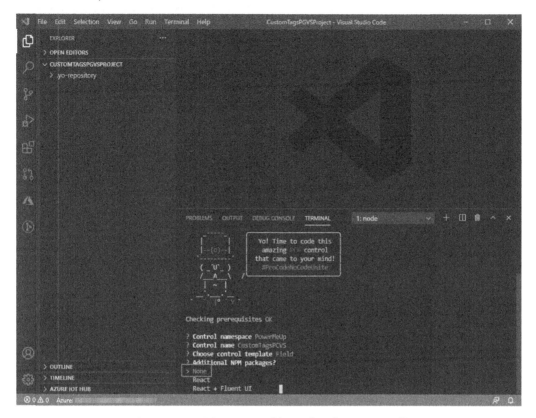

Figure 3.19 – Selecting no additional packages to install

10. Enter the publisher's prefix as pmu.

11. Type `PowerMeUpExercises` in the **Publisher Name** field:

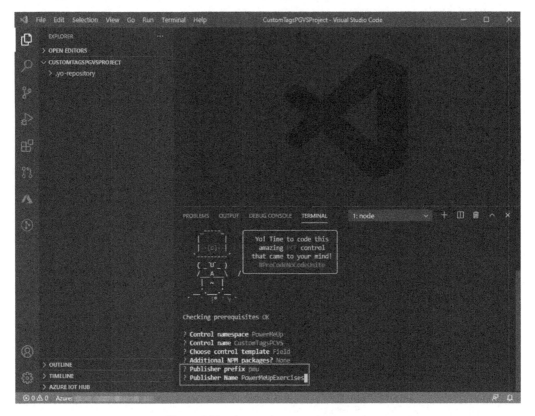

Figure 3.20 – Answering questions part 2

12. Choose **Unmanaged** from the options provided by using your keyboard's up and down arrow keys:

Figure 3.21 – Selecting the solution type to build

13. The final step in the process may involve asking you to overwrite the `ControlManifest` file. You can enter A and then press *Enter*. This will indicate to overwrite the `ControlManifest` file and all other files as necessary:

Figure 3.22 – Overwriting the ControlManifest file

Finally, once execution of all the aforementioned steps is complete, you should see the following output:

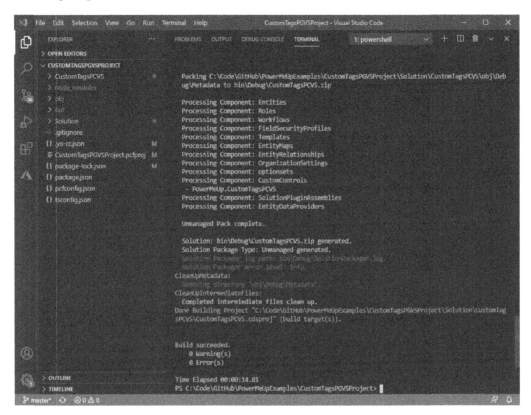

Figure 3.23 – Outcome of executing PCF Generator commands

We have looked at PCF Builder and PCF Generator, two community-built tools that enhance your development experience. Now, let's look at a website that showcases community-built code components.

PCF Gallery

PCF Gallery is a website that hosts a collection of code components built using the Power Apps component framework. The website aims to list the code components created by the Power Platform community. The code components on the website are arranged in a very informative way, displaying a preview image along with the control name. It also shows a number of indicators, such as whether the code component is supported on a canvas app and/or a model-driven app, whether the public repository contains any license for reuse, and whether the repository contains a managed solution package.

The following screenshot gives us a preview of PCF Gallery:

Figure 3.24 – Preview of PCF Gallery

As you can see, there are lot of code components built by the community and nicely presented on PCF Gallery.

Next, let's see how we can use a code component listed on PCF Gallery.

Using a code component from PCF Gallery

To install a code component from PCF Gallery, perform the following steps:

1. Navigate to `https://pcf.gallery`.

2. From the list of code components provided, select your preferred one.

3. On this page, you will see the preview of the code component and, for some controls, you can also see a demo video.

4. You may also see a few indicators if the code components satisfy the conditions for those indicators. The indicator preview is shown in the following screenshot:

Figure 3.25 – List of indicators on PCF Gallery

5. You may also see the **Visit** button, which, when clicked, will take you to the blog post that explains the usage and features of the code component.

6. You will also see a **Download** button, which will take you to the public repository where the control's source code is hosted. On this repository, you can find the managed solution package, which can be downloaded and installed in your environment.

You can download any of your preferred code components for practicing and learning purposes.

Submitting your own code component on PCF Gallery

When you create your code component, and you wish to share it with the Power Platform community, you can submit a form by navigating to `https://pcf.gallery/submit`. Please make sure that the repository for your code component is publicly accessible.

Summary

In this chapter, we looked at two versions of PCF Builder, along with its installation and review process. We initialized a PCF project using both these tools. We also looked at PCF Generator, its installation process, and the way it integrates with PCF Builder. Using these community tools will help you build code components faster and better. We also learned that once you have built your code components, you can share those code components with the community by uploading them to PCF Gallery.

In the next chapter, we will learn the contents of a code component, the structure of the PCF project, and have an overview of the files and folders.

Test your knowledge

1. Which are the two applications where PCF Builder is available? (*100 points*)

   a. VS Code and XrmToolBox

   b. Visual Studio 2019 and Azure DevOps

2. What is the direct link for submitting your own code components on PCF Gallery? (*100 points*)

   a. `https://pcf.gallery/submit`

   b. `https://pcf.gallery/add`

3. How can you skip creation of the Dataverse solution project when initializing a PCF project using PCF Generator? (*200 points*)

   a. `yo pcf --ss yes --force`

   b. `yo pcf --ss true --force`

Further reading

- Source code of PCF Builder for XrmToolBox: `https://github.com/Power-Maverick/PCF-CustomControlBuilder`

- Source code of PCF Builder for VS Code: `https://github.com/Power-Maverick/PCF-Builder-VSCode`

- Source code of PCF Generator: `https://github.com/DynamicsNinja/generator-pcf`

- Community resources: `https://bit.ly/PCFCommunityResources`

4
Project Overview and the Component Life Cycle

In the previous chapter, you learned how to initialize PCF projects. This chapter aims to provide the underlying structure of the PCF project and explain the importance of the files included in the project. We will do a deep dive into how metadata is presented and take a look at the core code file that is provided as a starting point by the framework. At the end of this chapter, you will be introduced to the component life cycle and how events interact with each other.

In this chapter, we are going to cover the following main topics:

- Types of project provided by Power Apps CLI
- Understanding how components are made up
- An overview of the files and the folder structure in a PCF project
- Understanding the `ControlManifest` file
- Exploring the structure of `index.ts`
- Understanding the life cycle of the component

Technical requirements

In order to work through this chapter, you need to install all the prerequisites and download the example library, which will help you with the development process mentioned in *Chapter 1, Introduction to the Power Apps Component Framework*. Download the example library from `https://github.com/PacktPublishing/Extending-Microsoft-Power-Apps-with-Power-Apps-Component-Framework/tree/master/Chapter04`. You will also need to install **XrmToolBox** and **Visual Studio Code**.

The types of project

In *Chapter 2, Power Apps CLI*, we briefly touched upon the types of project that can be initialized by Power Apps CLI, namely PCF, Dataverse solutions, and plugin projects. While working with code components, you will normally only deal with two of the three types of project—PCF and Dataverse solution projects. The PCF project contains all the files and references needed to create one single code component. Dataverse solution projects, on the other hand, create a solution file that can be deployed to any Dataverse environment. You can add one or multiple code components to a single Dataverse solution project. But a Dataverse solution project is not limited to code components and can contain other solution components, such as plugin assemblies. The file extension for a PCF project is `.pcfproj`, and Dataverse solution projects, at the time of writing, have `.cdsproj` as their extension. Each project should be in its own separate folder; they can be nested within each other but should still be separate.

Next, let's learn the different components of a PCF project. This will help you understand the project structure, thus providing you an insight into how these files interact with each other.

The component makeup

Components can be classified into four key areas; the manifest file, component implementation, and any additional resource files that might be needed by the component. This is shown in the following figure:

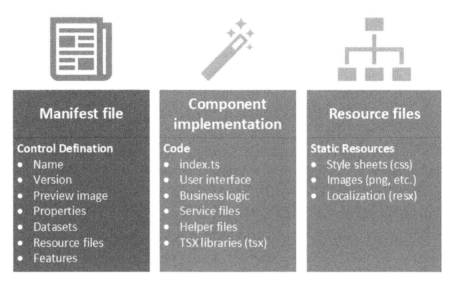

Figure 4.1 – Component makeup

Let's take a look at each one of these in the following subsections.

The manifest file

The manifest file is the metadata file that defines a component. It is an XML document that describes the following:

- The name of the component

- The kind of data that can be configured, either a field or a dataset

- Any of the properties that can be configured when the component is added

- A list of resource files that the component needs

- A list of features that are used by the component

When a user configures a code component, the application uses data in the manifest file to filter out the components so that only valid components are shown for configuration. The properties defined in the manifest file are rendered as configuration fields so that the user can specify the values. These property values are then available to the component at runtime. In later sections, we will be looking at the manifest file in detail.

The framework also allows developers to use certain features. These features need to be defined in the manifest file and can be accessed in the code component. If the code component is not going to use any of the features, then developers can omit them from the manifest file. Features could be using devices such as a camera and a microphone, or access to utility methods provided by the framework such as fetching entity metadata or utilizing Web API methods. The types of feature provided by the framework are shown later in this chapter.

Now that we understand the component makeup, let's take a look at the structure of files and folders provided by the framework when you initialize the PCF project.

The component implementation

Power Apps CLI auto-generates the code file named `index.ts` that has the same class name as the control defined during initialization. This class includes the definitions of functions as described in the code component interface. Developers can implement a component using TypeScript.

The class implements the following methods:

- `init` (*required*)
- `updateView` (*required*)
- `getOutputs` (*optional*)
- `destroy` (*required*)

Each of these methods is described in the *Exploring the index.ts file* section.

The resource files

A code component may utilize one or more resource files to construct its visualization as part of its implementation, and these files are defined in the manifest file. The resources that are not defined in the manifest file but are used in the code component are ignored by the framework when the component is built. So, make sure to add the references in the manifest file of any resources used in the component. Resources can be CSS, images, HTML, or localization files. This excludes TypeScript extension files (`tsx`).

Getting to know the files and the folder structure

In this section, we will look at how to structure your PCF project and what each file means. We will also look at the structure provided by boilerplate code using the PCF Generator.

PCF projects using Power Apps CLI

When you initialize a PCF project, Power Apps CLI will create a few files and folders in the location that you executed your initialization command:

```
pac pcf init -ns Power -n HelloWorld -t field
```

The sample files and folder structure are shown in the following screenshot, which was created by using the preceding command in a folder named `PowerMeUp`:

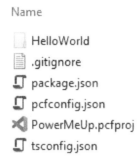

Figure 4.2 – Folder structure when initialized

Let's review the files and folders with respect to the command that was executed:

- `PowerMeUp.pcfproj`: This is the project file and will get its name based on the folder name that you executed in the initialization command. So, remember to name your folder appropriately.

- `tsconfig.json`: This file helps you manage the configuration settings of your TypeScript project.

- `pcfconfig.json`: You will rarely make any changes to this file, but it lets you control your PCF project build process.

- `package.json`: If you have installed any npm packages, they will be listed here as dependencies. It also contains a few npm scripts that can be extended to your preference.

- `.gitignore`: This is a Git file that contains a list of files and folders that need to be ignored when committing the changes to your **Git** repo.

- `HelloWorld`: The command was initialized with a control name of HelloWorld, and that is the reason the CLI created a folder with the same name. This folder will have all the core components to build your single code component.

Inside the `HelloWorld` folder, you will see the following structure. You can call this a code folder because this is where all the components and the code file will reside:

Figure 4.3 – Folder structure inside code folder

Once inside the code folder, let's review each file and folder inside it:

- `ControlManifest.Input.xml`: This is an XML file that contains code component definitions and details such as names, properties, resources, and features.

- `index.ts`: This is the main code file where all the code components' logic will reside.

- `generated`: Any changes that are made to the properties defined in the `ControlManifest.Input.xml` file after compilation get converted into TypeScript defined classes. This class is referred to in the `index.ts` file.

> **Note**
> Both templates (field and dataset) produce the same project structure.

The author's recommended folder structure

Always remember that you can add new files and folders to the project, but references should be added to the `ControlManifest` file in an appropriate section. My recommended folder structure for a PCF project looks like the following:

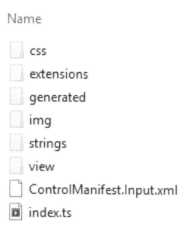

Figure 4.4 – Recommended folder structure

The explanation for each of the folder is as follows:

- `css`: This will host all your style sheet files with the `.css` extension.

- `extensions`: This will store all your classes and interfaces, such as `.tsx` or `.jsx` files.

- `img`: This will contain all the image files used by the code components.

- `strings`: When working with multiple languages, you need to store language code files, and this folder will be used for that. The files will have the `.resx` extension.

- `views`: Sometimes you will need HTML files, and this folder will contain `.html` files.

This is just a recommended folder structure that will segregate different types of files used in your project, making them easier to find. Next, we will look how community tools help you to create these folder structures.

PCF projects using a PCF Generator

When you initialize a PCF project using a PCF Generator or an advanced mode in PCF Builder, you get most of the folder structure defined in the previous section along with the sample files. This is the main reason to use community tools as they provide the recommended boilerplate code with references, so you do not have to spend time setting this structure up.

The following screenshot demonstrates the folder structure inside the code folder when the PCF Generator is used to initialize a PCF project:

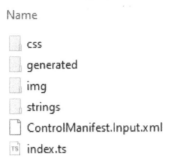

Figure 4.5 – Folder structure when executed using the PCF Generator

As you can see, most of the folder structure defined in the previous section is already generated by the PCF Generator. When you navigate inside each of those folders, you will find that the PCF Generator has added sample `css` and `resx` files in their respective folders with their references added to the `ControlManifest` file. Along with that, it also added a preview image file with a reference in the `ControlManifest` file, saving you the effort of configuring those minor things.

Dataverse solution projects using Power Apps CLI

In *Chapter 8, Introduction to the Dataverse Project*, we will look at the CLI command to create a Dataverse solution project. But let's just assume you have initialized a Dataverse solution project; Power Apps CLI will create a few files and folders in the location that you executed your initialization command. The sample file and folder structure are shown in the following screenshot and was created in a folder named `SampleDvProject`:

Figure 4.6 – Folder structure for Dataverse solution project

Like in a PCF project, the Dataverse solution project file gets its name from the folder name where the initialization command was executed. So, make sure you name your folder correctly, as this would be the name of your solution as well. Inside the `src` folder you will see a folder named `Other`, and inside that folder are the main XML files needed for the creation of the solution:

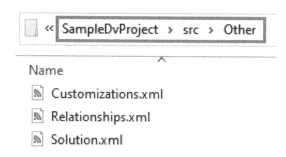

Figure 4.7 – Core XML files for a Dataverse solution project

We will discuss Dataverse solution projects in more detail in *Chapter 8, Introduction to the Dataverse Project*. Let's now look at some of the important files present in a PCF project.

Understanding the ControlManifest file

`ControlManifest` is the metadata XML file that defines a component. It describes the namespace and name of the component, along with some additional information such as the kind of data it can configure (field or dataset), any additional properties that can be configured, a list of resource files that the component needs, and features the component supports.

The file has the following structure:

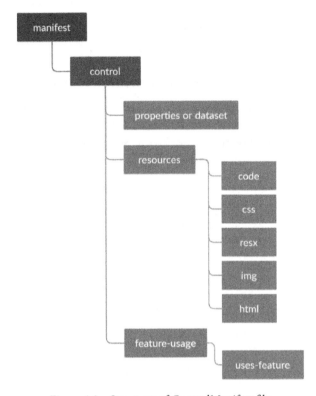

Figure 4.8 – Structure of ControlManifest file

manifest is the root node of the XML manifest file. It has no additional attributes. control is the parent node for all the other nodes in the manifest file. It contains the following attributes:

- namespace: The namespace of the control that shows up when a control is built (*required*).

- constructor: This is the name of your control and the name of the constructor that initializes your component (*required*).

- preview-image: The image that is used when configuring the component. The path to the image is relative to your project location (*not required*).

- version: This defines the version of the component. It uses the semantic versioning scheme (*required*).

- `display-name-key`: This defines the name of the control that is displayed on the UI (*required*).

- `description-key`: This defines the description of the component that will be seen on the UI (*required*).

- `control-type`: It has only one option, `Standard`, and that does not need changing (*required*).

> **Note**
>
> Please note that some of these attributes are required, and if they are not specified you will get build errors.

`property or dataset` is a configurable data or dataset populated during design time, and its value is used by the component during runtime. The type of node to use is defined based on the type of control. We will be looking into this in more detail in the *Dataset type control* sub-section.

The `resources` node in the component manifest refers to the resource files that the component requires to implement its visualization. It contains the following:

- `code`: Refers to the path where the resource files are located. There should be at least one code file.

- `css`: Stylesheets that defines how your UI will render.

- `img`: Any images used within your code component need to be referenced here.

- `html`: To extend your visualization, you can use HTML web resources.

- `resx`: This file provides localization capabilities to your control.

Except for the resource node for `code`, all other resources are optional.

`feature-usage` is a wrapper that defines which features the components will use. Under it, we have `uses-features`, which indicates the feature their components want to use.

If you do not intend to use any of the features, then you can exclude the entire `feature-usage` node.

The following screenshot is an example of a manifest file for a field type code component:

```xml
SampleManifest > ControlManifest.input.xml
  1  <?xml version="1.0" encoding="utf-8" ?>
  2  <manifest>
  3    <control namespace="PowerMeUp" constructor="SampleManifest" version="0.0.1" preview-image="img/preview.png"
  4      display-name-key="SampleManifest" description-key="SampleManifest description" control-type="standard">
  5
  6      <property name="sampleProperty1" display-name-key="Property_Display_Key1" description-key="Property_Desc_Key1"
  7        of-type="SingleLine.Text" usage="bound" required="true" default-value="Sample1" />
  8      <property name="sampleProperty2" display-name-key="Property_Display_Key2" description-key="Property_Desc_Key2"
  9        of-type-group="numbers" usage="bound" required="true" default-value="Sample" />
 10
 11      <type-group name="numbers">
 12        <type>Whole.None</type>
 13        <type>Currency</type>
 14        <type>FP</type>
 15        <type>Decimal</type>
 16      </type-group>
 17
 18      <resources>
 19        <code path="index.ts" order="1"/>
 20        <css path="css/SampleManifest.css" order="1" />
 21        <resx path="strings/SampleManifest.1033.resx" version="1.0.0" />
 22        <img path="img/SampleImage.png" />
 23        <html path="html/SampleHTML.html" order="1" />
 24      </resources>
 25
 26      <feature-usage>
 27        <uses-feature name="Device.captureAudio" required="true" />
 28        <uses-feature name="Device.captureImage" required="true" />
 29        <uses-feature name="Device.captureVideo" required="true" />
 30        <uses-feature name="Device.getBarcodeValue" required="true" />
 31        <uses-feature name="Device.getCurrentPosition" required="true" />
 32        <uses-feature name="Device.pickFile" required="true" />
 33        <uses-feature name="Utility" required="true" />
 34        <uses-feature name="WebAPI" required="true" />
 35      </feature-usage>
 36    </control>
 37  </manifest>
```

Figure 4.9 – Sample manifest file for a field type code component

Now that we understand the `ControlManifest` file structure, let's now look at manifest files for each type of project and see how they differ in the structure.

Manifest file for field type code component

When the control is initialized with the `field` template, we are expecting our control to be bound to one or more fields. For this, we need to define at least one `property` tag. The following is an example of two `property` tags on a sample manifest file:

```
<!--Property with of-type attribute and NOT defined as bound-->
<property name="sampleProperty1" display-name-key="Property_Display_Key1" description-key="Property_Desc_Key1"
  of-type="SingleLine.Text" usage="input" required="true" default-value="Sample1" />

<!--Property with of-type-group attribute and defined as bound-->
<property name="sampleProperty2" display-name-key="Property_Display_Key2" description-key="Property_Desc_Key2"
  of-type-group="numbers" usage="bound" required="false" default-value="Sample2" />
```

Figure 4.10 – Example of two property tags

Let's first look at the different attributes of a `property` tag:

- `name`: The internal name of the property. (*required*)

- `display-name-key`: The control's name that gets displayed on the configuration page. It can also be a key for a localized string. Read more about localization in *Further Reading* section. (*required*)

- `description-key`: The control's description that gets displayed on the configuration page. This string can also be localized and may contain a localization key. (*not required*)

- `of-type`: Defines a single data type for the property. If `of-type-group` is used, then you cannot use `of-type`. (*not required*)

- `usage`: It has two values—`bound` and `input`. If the property is meant to represent an entity attribute that the component can change, then use `bound`. If it will be a read-only value, then use `input`. (*not required*)

- `required`: Defines whether the property is required or not. (*not required*)

- `of-type-group`: Defines a group of data types for the property. If `of-type` is used, then you cannot use `of-type-group`. (*not required*)

- `default-value`: Provides a default value to the component. In model-driven apps, this attribute is only allowed on inputs since the bound parameters expect to have a field associated. (*not required*)

When you use `of-type-group`, you need to define an additional tag called `type-group` that comprises multiple tags named `type` that specify the datatypes the property will support. `type-group` has an attribute called `name`, and this `name` is used on the `of-type-group` attribute mentioned on the property. Let's look at an example to understand this better.

Say we need our property to support single-line text and multiple-line text, which are two different data types. So, we would create a `type-group` tag and name it `mytypes`, and the same name is used on `of-type-group` of the property. The following XML snippet demonstrates this example:

ControlManifest.Input.xml

```
<property name="n1" display-name-key="n1" description
    -key="n1" of-type-group="mytypes" usage="bound" />
<type-group name="mytypes">
    <type>SingleLine.Text</type>
    <type>Multiple</type>
</type-group>
```

Let's take a look at an example of a complete manifest file for a field type control:

1. In the examples library folder, in `Chapter04`, find the `01_FieldExamples` folder.

2. To open the folder in VS Code, navigate to `01_FieldExamples` and right-click anywhere (except on a file).

3. You should see an **Open with Code** option in the Windows context menu (as shown in *Figure 4.11*).

4. Using VS Code, expand `Chapter4Example` from the **EXPLORER** and you should see the following file and folder structure along with the `ControMainfest` file:

Figure 4.11 – Opening the folder in VS Code from Windows Explorer

5. Open and explore the `ControlManifest` file. Compare this file with the definition you learned earlier.

Once you have compared the `ControlManifest` file for the field type code components with the one provided in the example library, and when you've examined the definitions explained earlier and have become familiar with the outline of the file, let's get familiar with the `ControlManifest` file for dataset type code components next.

Manifest file for dataset type code components

When the control is initialized with the **dataset** template, we are expecting our control to be bound to a dataset such as a view, a sub-grid in model-driven apps, or a gallery in canvas apps. For this, we define a `data-set` tag that comprises the following attributes:

- `name`: Internal name of the dataset.

- `display-name-key`: The control's name that gets displayed on the configuration page. This string can also be localized.

- `description-key`: The control's description that gets displayed on the configuration page. This string can also be localized.

- `cds-data-set-options`: This controls the display of the command bar, view selector, and quick find search in the model-driven apps.

The `data-set` tag can also contain child tags named `property-set`. This tag defines an inner configuration that allows you to explicitly configure the columns of your dataset against an attribute of a given type from an entity for which the dataset is configured. It has the same attributes as the `property` tag. Let's look at an example of `property-set`.

Say we have a contact dataset and we are building a component that requires the dataset to always have email addresses. So, we will define this as a `property-set` tag with `required` set to `true`. The following XML snippet demonstrates this example:

ControlManifest.Input.xml

```xml
<data-set name="myDataSet" display-name-key="DataSet Grid"
  description-key="Description">
  <property-set name="myEmail" display-name-key="myEmail"
    description-key="myEmail" of-type="SingleLine.Email"
    usage="bound" required="true" />
</data-set>
```

Let's take a look at an example of a complete manifest file for a dataset type control:

1. In the examples library folder, under `Chapter04`, find the `02_DatasetExamples` folder.

2. Open this folder in VS Code. If you have come here directly, then I explained how to open a folder in VS Code in the previous example for the field type manifest file; please take a look at that.

3. Using VS Code, expand `Chapter4DSExample` from the **EXPLORER** tab, and you should see the file and folder structure along with the `ControlManifest` file.

4. Open and explore the `ControlManifest` file. Compare this file against the definition you looked at earlier.

When you have finished comparing the `ControlManifest` file for dataset type code components provided in the example library with the definitions explained earlier, then also compare it against the `ControlManifest` file for field type code components to identify the differences between the two files. You will see that other than the `property` and `data-set` tags, the rest of the file is pretty much the same.

Now that you are familiar with both types of project, we will get familiar with the data types supported by the framework.

The supported data types

The data types that are currently supported by the framework are as follows:

- `Currency`
- `DateAndTime.DateAndTime`
- `DateAndTime.DateOnly`
- `Decimal`
- `Enum`
- `FP`
- `Multiple`
- `OptionSet`
- `SingleLine.Email`
- `SingleLine.Phone`
- `SingleLine.Text`
- `SingleLine.TextArea`
- `SingleLine.Ticker`
- `SingleLine.URL`
- `TwoOptions`
- `Whole.None`

Eventually, Microsoft is going to add support for more data types, such as entity references and polymorphic lookups. But at the time of writing, these are the only supported data types. You can find a link to the official Microsoft documentation in the *Further reading* section to find more details about supported data types.

The difference between Multiple and SingleLine.TextArea

Both consist of multiple lines of text, but `SingleLine.TextArea` has a limit of 4,000 characters, whereas `Multiple` can contain up to 1,048,576 characters.

Next, we will look at the supported features provided by the framework.

Supported features

Let's look at an overview of the features that are available for the framework; more details on how to work with each of them are provided in *Chapter 10, Diving Deep into the Features Provided by PCF.*

Note

Some of the features may not be supported in canvas apps. Please check the official link provided in the *Further reading* section.

Devices

If you are working with any devices, for example, a camera or a mic, then the framework provides several methods to interact with them. These are listed as follows:

Method	Usage	Description
captureAudio	context.device.captureAudio	Invokes the device microphone to record the audio
captureImage	context.device.captureImage	Invokes the device camera to capture the image
captureVideo	context.device.captureVideo	Invokes the device camera to capture the video
getBarcodeValue	context.device.getBarcodeValue	Invokes the device camera to scan the barcode and retrieve the value
pickFile	context.device.pickFile	Invokes a dialog box to select files from your computer or mobile device
getCurrentPosition	context.device.getCurrentPosition	Fetches the current location using geolocation capability of the device or browser

Figure 4.12 – List of device features

As you can see, your code component can interact with several external devices.

Utility

Utility is a container that provides useful methods. Here are the methods that are encompassed in this container. Currently, these methods are not supported in **Test Harness**:

Method	Usage	Description
getEntityMetadata	context.utils.getEntityMetadata	Returns the entity metadata for a specified entity supplied as a parameter
hasEntityPrivilege	content.utils.hasEnitytPrivilege	Checks if the current user has privilege to a specific entity
lookupObjects	content.utils.lookupObjects	Opens a lookup dialog allowing the user to select one or more records

Figure 4.13 – List of utility methods

These methods provide easy access to some of the regularly used methods in the code component.

Web API

Web API provides a container for **Create, Read, Update, Delete (CRUD)** methods with the **Dataverse** API. Similar to utility methods, these methods are not supported in **Test Harness**:

Method	Usage	Description
createRecord	context.webAPI.createRecord	Creates an entity record
updateRecord	context.webAPI.updateRecord	Updates an entity record
deleteRecord	context.webAPI.deleteRecord	Deletes an entity record
retrieveRecord	context.webAPI.retrieveRecord	Retrieves a single entity record
retrieveMultipleRecords	context.webAPI.retrieveMultipleRecords	Retrieves a collection of entity records as an array

Figure 4.14 – List of Dataverse API methods

Currently, not all API methods that are supported by **Dataverse** are exposed by the Power Apps component framework for consumption. You can find more information in the *Further reading* section.

Now that we have a basic understanding of the `ControlManifest` file for both field and dataset type project, as well as supported data types and features, let's look at the main code file that is provided by the framework.

Exploring the index.ts file

Once you have initialized your PCF project you can find an `index.ts` file in your control folder, as we discussed in the *Getting to know the files and the folder structure* section. This file will have four functions already defined for you, along with an empty constructor. Let's go over the importance of these four functions.

The init function

This is the first function that gets invoked when the control is loaded and is never invoked again until the control is reloaded. For example, when you navigate between records, the control is reloaded. This function can be used to initialize a control's UI. You can also invoke remote server calls and any other initialization that needs to happen when your controls load.

It has four parameters:

- `context`: This is the most important object provided by the framework that gives us access to all the properties and methods that are available in the Power Apps component framework. It also contains the values passed to the control for the property defined in the manifest files; for example, you have bounded your control on a zip code field in a model-driven app, and when you open a record with a zip code value of `12345`, then this value is made available to you in the code via `context`.

- `notifyOutputChanged`: This is a callback method that alerts the framework when the control has a new output ready to be sent to the host asynchronously. This function is only available in `init()`, so it would be good to capture it as a class variable in the `index.ts` file.

- `state`: This enables you to persist the data for a user across multiple renderings of the component within the same session. For example, the user paginates through several pages but then they navigate away and come back to the same form. You could use `state` to load the page that the user was on before they navigated away.

- `container`: The framework's empty container under which you will add your child DOM elements. This enables it to render your control.

The updateView method

This method is used to process any changes external to the code component so that it can be refreshed to reflect the changes. These changes not only include field or dataset items but also encompass the height and width of the component, offline status, or metadata such as label and visibility. For example, you want to make sure your component shows or hides a value based on the visibility of a bounded field.

This method has only one parameter, `context`, which provides all the properties and methods that are available in the Power Apps component framework.

The `updateView` method is always invoked after the `init()` method when the control loads. This method is very important when you need to refresh your component. For example, you have a label as one of your controls in your component and it is bound to a field on a model-driven form; say, **Description**. If the data in the **Description** field changes, you want that to be reflected in your label. The only way this is possible is by using the `updateView` method to fetch the changed data from the **Description** field and reflect this new data on the UI.

The getOutputs method

If the data is changed in your component, you want the component to return the modified data to its host, and that is where the `getOutputs` method plays an important role. You do not need to invoke the `getOutputs` method as it is the framework runtime that invokes it when you call the `notifyOutputChanged` method. This is an optionally defined method that developers need to implement in order for the framework runtime to notify the host of the data changes. Only properties that have usage as `bound` can be returned by the framework. The object(s) returned is based on the nomenclature defined in the manifest file.

For example, you have defined a property called `description` in the manifest file with usage as `bound`. This `description` property value changes in your component; you can return the modified value to its source using the `getOutputs` method.

The destroy method

This method is invoked when the component is to be removed from the **DOM** tree. You can implement this method typically to do code cleanup or release any memory usage, and if you're using React JS then you can use it to unmount your virtual DOMs, cancel remote or Web API calls, remove listeners, and so on. It has no parameters and, unlike `getOutputs`, it can solely be invoked by the framework.

Now that we understand different methods provided to us by the framework, let's take a look at how and when each of these methods interact with each other.

Understanding the component life cycle

The framework invokes different methods described in the previous section at different life cycle stages, and it is crucial to know when these methods will be invoked and how they interact with the host. The host here can be either model-driven or a canvas app, which will contain the component.

Page load

When the page loads, the component invokes the constructor defined in the manifest file. This will create an object for the application to use. When the page is ready, it initializes the component by calling the `init()` method with a set of parameters:

```
init(context: ComponentFramework.Context<IInputs>,
notifyOutputChanged: () => void, state:
ComponentFramework.Dictionary, container:HTMLDivElement)
```

Data changes by the user

When the page loads, the component displays the data until the user interacts with the component to change the data. Once this occurs, you must call the `notifyOutputChanged` method provided in the `init()` method for the framework to invoke the `getOutputs` method. The `getOutputs` method will return the changed values to the host.

Data changes by the app

If the host application changes the data, the component will invoke the `updateView` method and pass the new context object as a parameter. This method should be implemented to refresh the visualization of the component.

The following illustration will help define these processes:

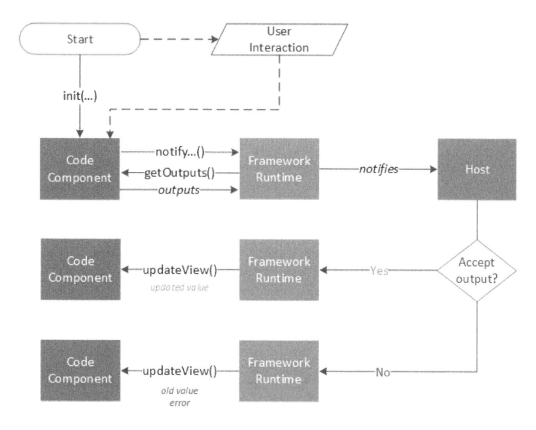

Figure 4.15 – Component event life cycle

In this diagram, we can see the following series of events:

1. `notify...()` refers to the `notifyOutputChanged` method. If your component is interactive, it will be sending data back to the host, so you will need to handle notifications to the host when the output changes by calling `notifyOutputChanged`.

2. The framework runtime will then invoke the `getOutputs` function, which contains all the `bound` properties defined in your manifest files and returns that to the runtime.

3. The runtime will then notify the host of those values, which will perform validation on those values and in the case of a model-driven app, may trigger any `onchange` events registered with the `bound` attributes.

4. If the values are found to be valid, it will then call the updateView method of your component with the new value. If the values are not valid for whatever reason, it will then invoke the updateView method with old values along with the error message.

Let's check out the life cycle using a code component. In the example library, you will find a **Dataverse** solution file in a folder named 3.ComponentLifeCycle. Install this solution like any other solution in your preferred Dataverse environment and perform the following steps:

1. On make.powerapps.com, navigate to **Apps** in the left navigation pane.

2. Under **Apps**, you will find a model-driven app with the name **Component Life Cycle**. Click on this app to open it.

3. The app will load to your default contact view. Open any of the contact records.

4. On the contact record, you will find a field called **Life Cycle Output**. On this field, you will see that the first event triggered was init, followed by the updateView method, as shown in the following screenshot:

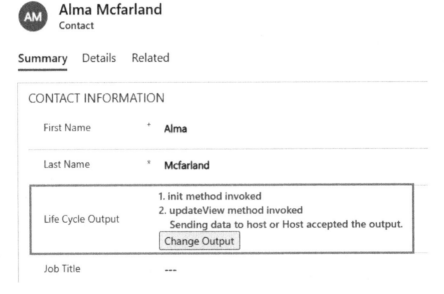

Figure 4.16 – Life cycle when control loads

5. Click on the **Change Output** button, which will notify the *framework runtime* of the changes to the output; this in turn will invoke the getOutputs method enabling the *framework runtime* to send the output to the host.

6. Now, the host invokes any rules defined on the bound field to check if it can accept the output value from the component.

7. If it cannot accept the value from the component, then the framework runtime is notified of the error and sends the error details to the component by invoking the updateView method. This is represented in the following screenshot:

Figure 4.17 – Life cycle when output from component is rejected by the host

8. If it can accept the value from the component, then the updated value is sent back to the component. To test this scenario, click on the **Change Output** button again, which will send the value to the host that gets accepted. This is depicted in the following screenshot:

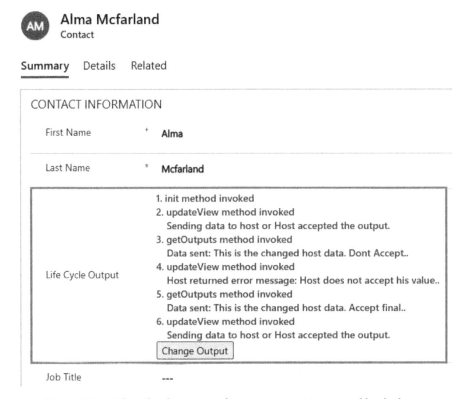

Figure 4.18 – Life cycle when output from component is accepted by the host

This process should help you understand how the component life cycle works. You can check out the source code for this code component in the same example library folder.

Summary

In this chapter, we looked at the PCF project structure, the ControlManifest file, and the index.ts file. We learned the life cycle of code components, which provide insights into how each of the core functions interact with each other. This will help you build better code components. We also briefly looked at the supported data types and features provided by the framework. This provided you with an insight into the entire PCF project, preparing you to start building your code component.

Before we dive into the next chapter, open the folder named 4.TestMe from the example library in VS Code. Start the VS Code integrated terminal and run the following command: npm start. This will initiate a code component built using the Power Apps component framework and provide a glimpse into the possibilities of having different UIs on model-driven and canvas apps.

In the next chapter, you will be building a complete code component for fields and datasets using all the knowledge you have gleaned from the previous chapters.

Test your knowledge

1. Which tool provides the recommended folder structure with minimal effort? (*100 points*)

   a. Power Apps CLI

   b. PCF Generator

2. What are the four functions provided by the framework in the index.ts file? (*100 points*)

   a. initializes, update, output, destroy

   b. init, updateView, getOutputs, destroy

3. Is the following snippet from ControlManifest file for a dataset control correct? (*200 points*)

```
<manifest>
  <control ...>
    <property name="sample1" .../>
    <property name="sample2" .../>
    <data-set name="myDataSet1" ...></data-set>
    <data-set name="myDataSet2" ...></data-set>
  </control>
</manifest>
```

   a. Yes

   b. No

Further reading

- Additional information related to code components can be found in Microsoft's online docs at `http://bit.ly/CodeComponentOverview`.

- Additional information related to supported data types can be found in Microsoft's online docs at `http://bit.ly/PCFDataTypes`.

- Additional information on which app is device features supported can be found in Microsoft's online docs at `https://bit.ly/PCF-Device`.

- Additional information on which app is utility features supported can be found in Microsoft's online docs at `https://bit.ly/PCF-Utility`.

- Additional information on which app is web API features supported can be found in Microsoft's online docs at `https://bit.ly/PCF-WebApi`.

- Additional information related to localization can be found in Microsoft's online docs at `http://bit.ly/PCF-Localization`.

Section 2: Building and Managing Code Components

This second section focuses on creating and building code components. First, we start by building a code component for a field type in Microsoft Dataverse, later followed by building a code component for a dataset type in Microsoft Dataverse. Then we see how to debug a code component in different ways and at different times, such as pre-deployment and post-deployment.

After that, we are introduced to authentication profiles that can help with quick deployments to your preferred Microsoft Dataverse environment. Later, we get introduced to a Microsoft Dataverse solution project that also helps you deploy code components. Lastly, we learn how to configure code components in model-driven and canvas apps for both types of code components.

This section comprises the following chapters:

- *Chapter 5, Code, Test, and Repeat*
- *Chapter 6, Debugging Code Components*
- *Chapter 7, Authentication Profiles*
- *Chapter 8, Introduction to the Dataverse Project*
- *Chapter 9, Configuring Code Components in Power Apps*

5
Code, Test, and Repeat

In the previous chapters, we looked at all the basics of a PCF project and prepared ourselves to build a code component. In this chapter, you will learn many things, from the process itself to initializing a PCF project, to editing the manifest file, and then writing the code to create the components. We will also see how to test and fix issues encountered during testing. Once the code component is ready, we will then learn how to add stylings and preview images. Later, we will look at how to create code components for a view or a sub-grid. This chapter will provide hands-on experience in building two complete code components, one for the field type, which will count the number of characters, and another for the dataset type, which will show the list as cards.

In this chapter, we are going to cover the following main topics:

- Building the code component with a field type template
- Testing the code component that we built
- Adding stylings to the code component using CSS
- Adding a preview image to the code component
- Building the code component with a dataset type template

Technical requirements

In order to work through this chapter, you need to install all the prerequisites and download the example library that will help you with the development process mentioned in *Chapter 1, Introduction to the Power Apps Component Framework*. Download the example library from `https://github.com/PacktPublishing/Extending-Microsoft-Power-Apps-with-Power-Apps-Component-Framework/tree/master/Chapter05`. You will also need to install **Visual Studio Code**.

Building the code component for a field

In the previous chapter, we looked at how to initialize a PCF project, and understood the project and manifest file structures. Now, let's use that knowledge and start building the code component for the field type.

In this section, we will be building a field type code component that will count the characters and display the number of characters left out of the maximum characters that the field can accept. Users will have the ability to define the maximum number of characters the field can accept on the configuration page. We will start by initializing a new project.

Initializing a new PCF project for a field

In order to initialize a new PCF project, perform the following steps:

1. Create a new directory named `MyCharacterCounterProject`, which will be your working directory for building your component. For example, consider the full path, including the directory you created, as `C:\PowerMeUpExamples\MyCharacterCounterProject`.

2. Start VS Code and open the folder location mentioned in *Step 1*.

3. Open the VS Code integrated terminal using *Ctrl + `* and initialize your component project by using the following Power Apps CLI command:

    ```
    pac pcf init --namespace PowerMeUp --name
    MyCharacterCounter --template field
    ```

This will initialize your PCF project and the output will be like that shown in the following screenshot:

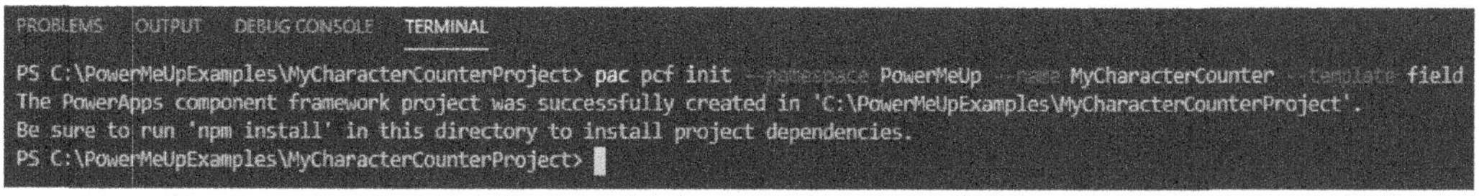

Figure 5.1 – PCF project initialization

4. Now, we need to install the project build tools and dependencies by using the npm install command. You may see some warnings from npm about deprecated packages, but these can be ignored. Once the process is complete, you should see the following output:

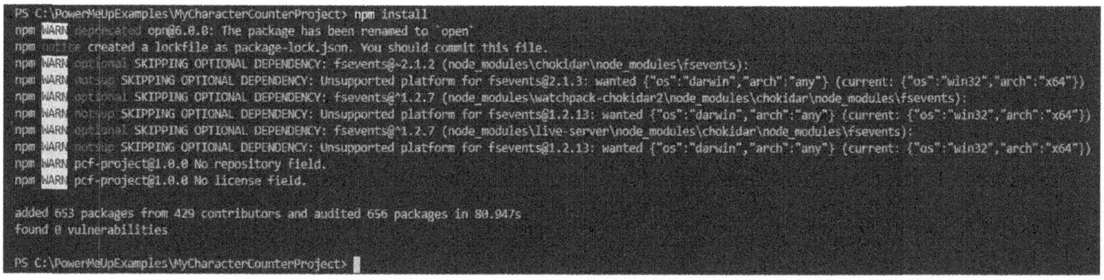

Figure 5.2 – Installing dependencies

All of these steps can easily be achieved using **PCF Builder**. Once these steps have been executed, you should see a PCF project created under the MyCharacterCounterProject folder.

The next step is to test your understanding of the ControlManifest file, which you learned about in *Chapter 4, Project Overview and the Component Life Cycle*.

Updating the control manifest file for a field

After you have initialized your PCF project, you need to update the control manifest file to accurately represent the details of your control. So, expand the MyCharacterCounter folder in the VS Code **EXPLORER** and look for the ControlManifest.Input.xml file.

If you have installed **PCF Builder** for VS Code, then this provides you with the IntelliSense on the control manifest file. All you need to do is invoke IntelliSense by using *Ctrl + Space* on your keyboard.

The following is a list of changes you need to make in your control manifest file:

- Change the following attribute values found on the control tag:

  display-name-key: This powers up the character counter.

  description-key: This counts the number of characters remaining on the control.

- Change the following attribute values on the property tag:

  name: `characterCounterDataInput`.

  display-name-key: This is the data input.

  description-key: This is the control that contains the data from the host where it is bound.

  of-type: Multiple.

  usage: Bound.

  required: True.

- Add another property tag with the following values:

  name: `characterCounterLimit`.

  display-name-key: This is the character limit.

  description-key: This defines the upper limit of characters that a control can accept.

  of-type: `Whole.None`.

  usage: Input.

  required: True.

Once all the changes to the manifest file are complete, save the file and open the VS Code integrated terminal from the **View | Terminal** menu and execute the following command:

```
npm run build
```

Execution of the preceding command will yield the following output:

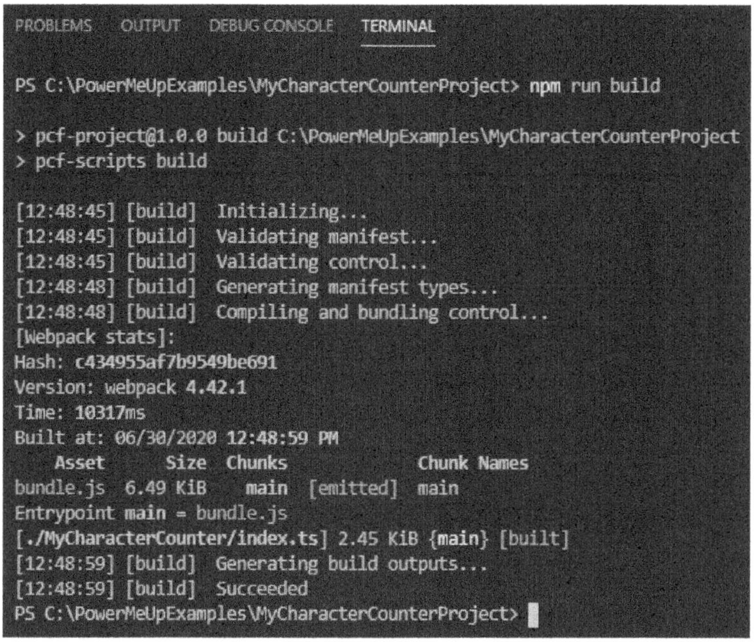

Figure 5.3 – Building a code component project

In this example, we have marked `characterCounterDataInput` as a bound property that will be bound to a field with the `Multiline` data type.

> **Note**
>
> Every time you change the control manifest file or add any property to it, you need to increment the minor version and build your PCF project again.

Once our control manifest file is ready, we can start writing code in the main code file.

Adding logic to the field code component

In the PCF project, the main code file is the `index.ts` file. As seen in the previous chapter, this file comes with four main functions provided by the framework. But before we start adding logic to these methods, we need to declare a number of class properties. These are as follows:

---

index.ts

```
private mainDiv: HTMLDivElement;
private textbox: HTMLTextAreaElement;
private outputLabel: HTMLLabelElement;
private theNotifyOutputChanged: () => void;
private maxCharacterLimit: number;
```

These properties are defined inside the class, but outside of all the methods. The following are the details regarding each of these properties:

- `mainDiv` will be our DOM element that will contain the child textbox and a label.

- `textbox` is our main control that will accept inputs from users.

- `outputLabel` will display the number of characters remaining and the maximum characters allowed by the control.

- `theNotifyOutputChanged` is a parameter-less function variable that will be used to invoke the `getOutputs` method when the user interacts with the textbox control. This was discussed in *Chapter 4, Project Overview and the Component Life Cycle.*

- `maxCharacterLimit` is a variable of the number type that will capture the maximum number of characters this component can accept.

After creating the class properties, we will move on to add logic to the `init` method. The following is the code that will be added to the `init` method:

---

index.ts

```
this.theNotifyOutputChanged = notifyOutputChanged;
this.maxCharacterLimit = context.parameters.
    characterCounterLimit.raw || 0;
//UI
this.mainDiv = document.createElement("div");
this.textbox = document.createElement("textarea");
```

```
this.outputLabel = document.createElement("label");
this.textbox.value = context.parameters.
    characterCounterDataInput.raw || "";
this.textbox.addEventListener("change",
    this.onChange.bind(this));
this.mainDiv.appendChild(this.textbox);
this.mainDiv.appendChild(this.outputLabel);
container.appendChild(this.mainDiv);
this.onChange();
```

Let's now look at the details in terms of how the code in the init method works:

1. As described in an earlier chapter, the init method has four parameters, and one of these is a callback function named notifyOutputChanged. This parameter is only available in the init method, and so we capture this parameter on a class property named theNotifyOutputChanged.

2. To access the value of any property defined in the manifest file, we need to use context, which is supplied as the first parameter to the init method. So, using that, we initialize a variable named maxCharacterLimit with the configuration property value called characterCounterLimit, which will be supplied when the user adds this code component to the host.

3. This is followed by adding logic to create the UI components, beginning with creating our DOM element on mainDiv, and then creating the text area control (textbox) and finally, the label control (outputLabel).

4. Now, let's say we have a record that already contains some data on an attribute where the control will be bound. So, when the code component loads, it should show any existing value. To do that, we need to populate the textbox value with the raw data from the characterCounterDataInput property using context.

5. When the value in the textbox changes, we want that value to be sent back to the source and, in order to make that happen, we need to register an event listener on the change event. This is accomplished by means of the addEventListener function on the textbox control. As we have not defined an onChange method, you will see an error, but this will be resolved by the end of this section.

6.   Once all the requisite elements are ready, we need to add them to the containers in the appropriate order. First, we need to add `textbox` to our `mainDiv`, followed by `outputLabel`. This `mainDiv` needs to be added to the framework's container, which renders all the child elements. Lastly, we will explicitly call the `onChange` event here because the logic to calculate the characters is to be found in this method and we want to calculate the number of characters when the control loads.

Once we have defined the logic in our `init` method, we need to add a definition for the `onChange` method used in the `init` method. The following is the definition of the custom method:

index.ts

```
private onChange(): void
{
    const charRemaining =
        this.maxCharacterLimit - this.textbox.value.length;
    this.outputLabel.innerHTML =
        `${charRemaining}/${this.maxCharacterLimit}`;
    this.theNotifyOutputChanged();
}
```

In the `init` method, we bind the `onChange` method to change the event of the textbox and, when that event occurs, it will invoke this `onChange` method. In this method, we calculate the remaining characters by subtracting the current textbox character length from the maximum character length defined in the `this.maxCharacterLimit` variable, which was captured in the `init` method, and display the data on the label. Finally, we invoke the `theNotifyOutputChanged` method, which, in turn, invokes the `getOutputs` method. The reason for invoking the `theNotifyOutputChanged` method is to notify the framework that the host should pull the latest changed values by calling the `getOutputs` method, where the host can be a model-driven or canvas app.

As we intend to send the changed data back to the host, we now need to define our `getOutputs` method. Any property that has its usage defined as bound will surface in the `getOutputs` method. In our case, `characterCounterDataInput` has its usage defined as bound and so it can return the value back to the host, as shown in the following code block:

index.ts

```
public getOutputs(): IOutputs
{
    return {
      characterCounterDataInput: this.textbox.value
    };
}
```

Whenever the framework invokes the `getOutputs` method, it will notify the host of changes in the values. The host may then perform any validation on the data returned by the code component and, if any events exist on the host, then those events will be invoked.

The code should now be complete and ready to be built and tested. So, let's open the VS Code integrated terminal from the **View** | **Terminal** menu and run the following `build` command:

```
npm run build
```

This will compile your code component and let you know whether there are any errors. At this point, you should not have any errors and you should see that the build was successful. If you encounter any build errors, make sure that all the files are saved before running the `build` command.

Testing the field code component

Let's now take it for a spin by testing the code component in the test harness provided by the framework. To invoke the test harness, you can execute the `npm start` command in the VS Code integrated terminal. However, for a more convenient experience, use the `npm start watch` command, which lets you edit the code while testing it and rebuilds the component if changes are detected in your file without the need to recompile and retest.

When the test harness is up, you will see a textbox and, on the right-hand side panel, you will see the configuration items. Populate the number `100` in the `characterCounterLimit` property. Now, type `My Power Up Character Counter` component in the textbox on the screen and you should observe that the maximum character still shows `0`, meaning that the calculation for the characters remaining is wrong. This is because we are only capturing the maximum character limit in the `init` method, which is invoked when the control loads, and the value at that point in time was `0`. When we changed the value of `characterCounterLimit` from `0` to `100`, the `updateView` method is invoked, which is not defined as yet. The following screenshot shows the test harness screen and inputs:

Figure 5.4 – Test harness for the field type code component

As we have identified an issue when the value is changed, the component doesn't recognize the change and hence, we do not get the proper output. Let's now look at how we can fix the issue.

Fixing the issues observed in the field code component

To fix the issue of when a `characterCounterLimit` value is changed, we would want the value to be reflected in the counting of the characters by the code component. For that, we need to implement the `updateView` method, which gets invoked when a property value changes, in this case, when the maximum character limit or data input changes. If you have used the `npm start watch` command, then, without terminating the `testing` command, start editing your `index.ts` file. If you have used the `npm start` command, then terminate the already running CLI process from the VS Code integrated terminal by using *Ctrl + C* and close the test harness from the browser.

> **Note**
> The remainder of the book will assume that testing is performed using the `npm start watch` command.

Let's now look at the definition of the `updateView` method, which will help us rectify the issue observed:

index.ts

```
public updateView(context: ComponentFramework.
Context<IInputs>): void
{
    const changedCharCounterLimit =
        context.parameters.characterCounterLimit.raw || 0;
    if (this.maxCharacterLimit !== changedCharCounterLimit) {
        this.maxCharacterLimit = changedCharCounterLimit;
        this.onChange();
    }
}
```

As soon as you save the `index.ts` file, the terminal shows the logs that a change was detected, and it recompiles the code component. This will reload the test harness and the issue should be fixed. The following screenshot demonstrates this:

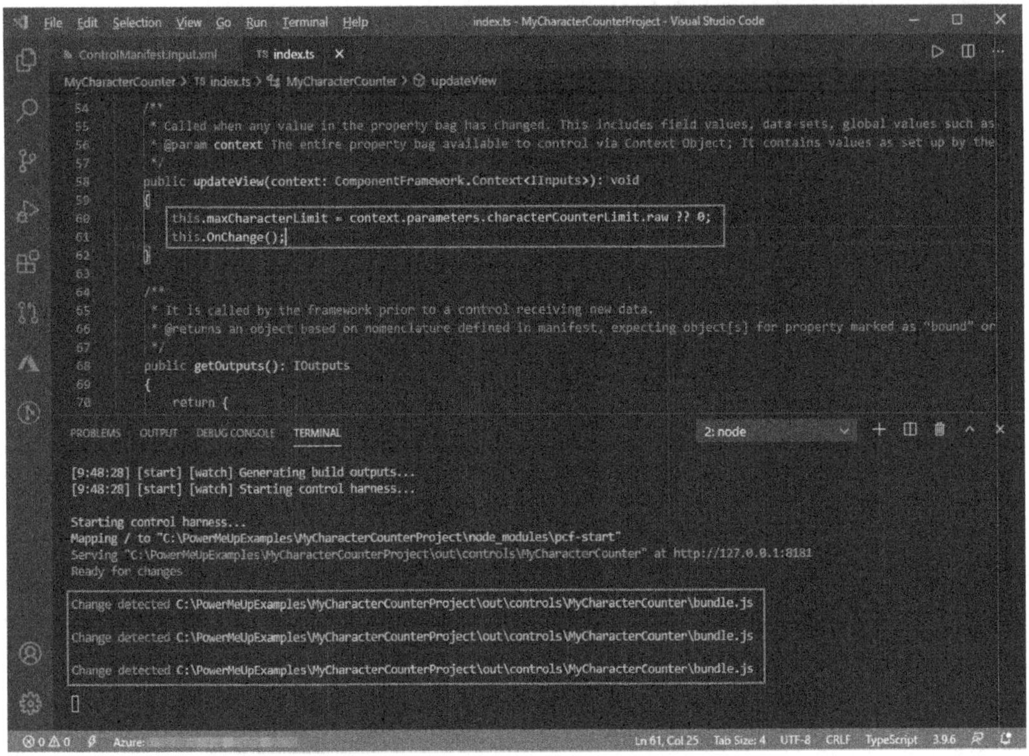

Figure 5.5 – Autorecompile of code when changes are detected

To test whether the issue has been fixed, append `Fixed` to the value in the textbox and it should render a correct count of the characters remaining. Also, observe how the data output section changes as you type in the textbox. This is because of the `getOutputs` method returning the value back to the host, in this case, the test harness. The following screenshot displays this in the test harness:

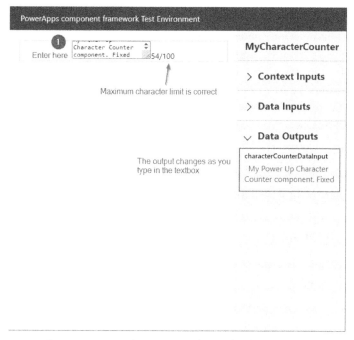

Figure 5.6 – Test harness populating the data outputs

At this point, your first code component should be completely ready. To terminate the test harness, press *Ctrl + C* in the terminal where it is still executing and close the browser.

Now that you have a working code component, you may wish to add some stylings to it. So, let's now take a look at how can we achieve that.

Adding styling to a field code component

Sometimes you may need to add you own styling, such as a hover effect or adding a border. To do so, you can add styling either using a `.css` file or inline styling in the `index.ts` file. The recommended approach is to use the `.css` file for styling, and this is what we will be using in this book.

Also, the class names you have used may contradict the ones that are already used by the host application or, let's say, you want to define explicit styling to all `div` used in your component. As part of the framework when your component is loaded on the host application, the framework adds an explicit class to each of the DOM elements in your code components and the format of that class is `.<namespace>\.<control_name>`. So, in our example, it will be `.PowerMeUp\.MyCharacterCounter`. Using this class in your `css` file, you can define your style context for your elements. Let's create a file under the `.css` folder with the name `MyCharacterCounter.css`. If you have used any of the community tools, you will already be provided with the `css` folder and styling file. In this file, we will be adding the style details for the textbox to show a border and add width. The complete styling is as follows:

MyCharacterCounter.css

```
.PowerMeUp\.MyCharacterCounter .customTextArea {
    resize: none;
    white-space: pre-wrap;
    overflow-wrap: break-word;
    border-width: 1px;
    border-style: solid;
    border-color: transparent;
    border-image: initial;
    padding: 2px;
    width: 96%;
    height: 100%;
}
.PowerMeUp\.MyCharacterCounter .customTextArea:hover {
    border-color: rgb(169, 169, 169);
}
```

As we have defined a class name `customTextArea`, we need to assign it to the control in the `index.ts` file. This is simply done by using a `className` attribute on the HTML elements, as shown next:

index.ts

```
this.textbox.className = "customTextArea";
```

The reference to this new CSS file needs to be added to the control manifest file. The following code shows us how this can be done:

ControlManifest.Inputs.xml

```
<resources>
    <code path="index.ts" order="1"/>
    <css path="css/MyCharacterCounter.css" order="1" />
</resources>
```

Once these changes are complete, you can recompile the code component by using the following command: `npm run build`.

After adding some styling to your code component, let's now look at how to add some preview images to your code component.

Enriching the field code component by using a preview image

When you are on the control configuration page in a model-driven app, you have the ability to see an image associated with the control, along with a display name and description. This is known as a preview image. This helps your users to visualize how your control may look once it is added to the form. This makes it more user-friendly and attractive.

The first thing we need to do is create our image. Once that is complete, you need to add the image to the project so that it can be referenced and captured by the webpack while building. The recommendation is to add it under the `img` folder. If you have used any of the community tools, then you will be provided with an `img` folder and a default preview image. To make this image appear as a preview on the control configuration page, you must use the `preview-image` attribute on the `control` tag, shown as follows:

ControlManifest.Inputs.xml

```
<control namespace="PowerMeUp" constructor="MyCharacterCounter"
version="0.0.1" preview-image="img/PowerUp-PreviewImage.png"
display-name-key="Power Up Character Counter" description-
key="Counts the number of characters remaining on the control"
control-type="standard>
```

As you can see, the `preview-image` attribute contains a relative path to the image that is in the `img` folder inside a root directory. It is that easy, and the preview image, once added, will appear on the configuration box. This is shown in the following screenshot:

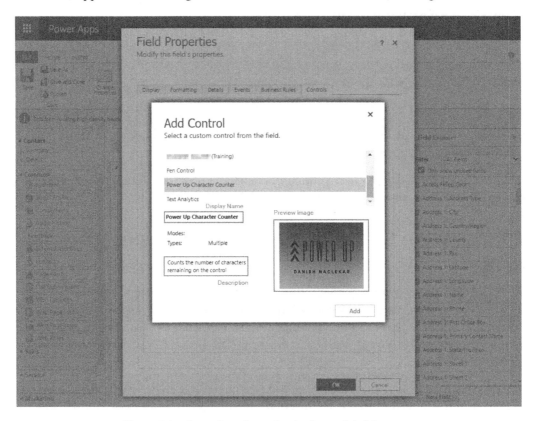

Figure 5.7 – Control configuration in the model-driven app

The preview image container on the configuration page in the model-driven app is a fixed size rectangle of *170 x 130 pixels*, which is in 17:13 aspect ratio. If your image is not of the same ratio, then the image will stretch in both directions to fill the container. The image you add to the preview can either be a `.png`, `.gif`, or `.jpg` file.

This is the last piece of configuration you will need in order to create your complete code component. Let's now look at how different it is to create a code component with a dataset template.

Building a code component for a view or sub-grid

Now that you have learned the process of creating a code component with a field template, let's learn the process of creating a code component with a dataset template. There are a few differences when creating a code component with a dataset template as we are dealing with multiple records rather than a single data object and we will look at those in this section.

In this chapter, we will be building a dataset type code component that will render each contact record in a list as a card. This card will show each column as an item on the card with a value. If the column does not have any data, then it will show a hyphen, (-).

Initializing a new PCF project for a dataset

Similar to the field type code component, we first need to initialize a PCF project. Perform the following steps to create a new component project for a dataset code component:

1. Create a new directory named `MyDataCardProject`, which will be your working directory for building your component. In this sample, consider the full path, including the directory you created, as `C:\PowerMeUpExamples\MyDataCardProject`.

2. Start VS Code and open the folder you created above.

3. Open the VS Code integrated terminal using *Ctrl + `* and initialize your component project by using the following Power Apps CLI command:

   ```
   pac pcf init --namespace PowerMeUp --name MyDataCard
   --template dataset
   ```

4. We need to install the project build tools and dependencies by using the `npm install` command, as we did for the field type code component.

All of these steps can easily be achieved using **PCF Builder**. Once these steps are executed, you should see a PCF project created under the `MyDataCardProject` folder.

Next, we will edit the `ControlManifest` file to provide proper manifest details for our code component.

Updating the control manifest file for a dataset

By now, you should be familiar with the `ControlManifest.Input.xml` file. So, let's move on and edit the file to best represent the control. The following are the changes you will need to make to the manifest file:

- Change the following attribute values found on the control tag:

  display-name-key: This power up the data card.

  description-key: This shows the list of records as cards.

- Change the following attribute values found on the dataset tag:

  name: `datasetGrid`

  display-name-key: `Data Cards`

As we saw while editing the manifest file for the field type code component, every time we edit the manifest file, we must build our PCF project. So, let's open the VS Code integrated terminal from the **View** | **Terminal** menu and type the following command:

```
npm run build
```

When building a code component for a dataset, the `data-set` tag is the equivalent of the `property` tag, where you bind your view or sub-grid. In this example, it is called `datasetGrid`.

Once our control manifest file is ready, we can start writing code in the main code file.

Adding logic to a dataset code component

Let's start by declaring global constants outside the class below the `import` statements. These constants will be explained and used later in the code:

index.ts

```
const buttonStyleHidden: string = "customButtonHidden";
const gridRowRecordId: string = "powerupRowRecId";
```

These constants are used as follows:

- `buttonStyleHidden` contains the class name that will be used to show and hide the **Load More...** button.
- `gridRowRecordId` contains the name of the attribute that will be added to each record in the grid with the record ID as its value.

Now, like the field code component, declare the class properties as follows:

index.ts

```
private mainDiv: HTMLDivElement;
private gridDiv: HTMLDivElement;
private loadMoreButton: HTMLButtonElement;
private theNotifyOutputChanged: () => void;
private theContext: ComponentFramework.Context<IInputs>;
```

These properties are defined inside the class but outside all the methods. The following are the details regarding each of these properties:

- mainDiv is our DOM element that will contain all our custom elements.

- gridDiv is our main control that will render the cards.

- loadMoreButton will give users the ability to load more records upon the click of a button.

- theNotifyOutputChanged is a parameter less function variable that will be used to invoke the getOutputs method when the user interacts with the button control.

- theContext will give you access to all the properties and functions that are provided by the framework.

After creating the class properties, we will move on to add logic to the init method. The following is the code that will be added to the init method:

index.ts

```
context.mode.trackContainerResize(true);
this.theContext = context;
this.theNotifyOutputChanged = notifyOutputChanged;
this.mainDiv = document.createElement("div");
this.mainDiv.className = "main";
this.gridDiv = document.createElement("div");
this.gridDiv.className = "grid";
this.loadMoreButton = document.createElement("button");
this.loadMoreButton.innerHTML = "Load More..."
this.loadMoreButton.classList
```

```
    .add(buttonStyleHidden, "customButton");
this.mainDiv.appendChild(this.gridDiv);
this.mainDiv.appendChild(this.loadMoreButton);
container.appendChild(this.mainDiv);
```

Let's look at the details in terms of how the code in the `init` method works:

1. The `trackContainerResize` method helps to determine the height and width allocated to the component.

2. We will require access to `context` and `notifyOuputChanged` further on in the code, so we capture these in the `init` method and assign it to class properties.

3. Now, we start adding the logic to create the UI components, starting with our wrapping div element (`mainDiv`), followed by the grid div element (`gridDiv`) and a button with a **Load More...** label, which will help us to load more data, thereby giving us the ability to paginate. We have assigned some classes to these elements. These will be defined later in the stylesheet.

4. Once all the necessary elements are ready, we need to add them to the containers in the appropriate order. First, we add `main grid div`, followed by the button, to our wrapping `div` element. This wrapping `div` is then added to the framework's container that renders all the child elements.

As you can see in the preceding code, the `init` method only initializes the elements and does not render the UI with data. The logic for that will be added in the `updateView` method, as shown in the following code:

index.ts

```
this.toggleLoadMoreButton(context.parameters.datasetGrid);
    if (!context.parameters.datasetGrid.loading) {
        // Get sorted columns on the view
        const columnsOnView =
            this.getSortedColumnsOnView(context);
        if (!columnsOnView || columnsOnView.length === 0) {
            return;
        }
        // Remove all existing elements
        while (this.gridDiv.firstChild) {
            this.gridDiv.removeChild(this.gridDiv.firstChild);
```

```
            }
        this.gridDiv.appendChild(
            this.createGridBody(columnsOnView,
            context.parameters.datasetGrid));
}
```

After you have added the preceding code to the updateView method, let's see how it will work. This is described as follows:

1. toggleLoadMoreButton will be a custom method that we will define later in this section. You will see an error, but once you define the method, this error should go away.

2. In the if statement, we check whether the grid or view has completed its loading operation and only then do we start building the UI. This loading method is part of the framework.

3. Inside the if statement, we fetch the columns in a sorted order. The getSortedColumnsOnView method is a custom method that will be defined later in this section.

4. If no columns are found, then we terminate the rendering process, otherwise we remove all existing elements from the main grid div element. If we do not remove all existing elements from main grid div, and if updateView is invoked due to container changes or for any other reason, it will keep adding repeated data to the main grid div element. Once the code is complete, to understand how the DOM works, you can comment out this line and test how the component behaves.

5. Once all the existing elements are removed, we will now append new elements to the main grid div element. To do so, we invoke a custom method named createGridBody, which takes in a list of all the columns, and the dataset parameter named datasetGrid, which we defined in the manifest file.

Let's now define our custom methods, starting with toggleLoadMoreButton, followed by the getSortedColumnsOnView and createGridBody methods.

The following is the code for the `toggleLoadMoreButton` method:

index.ts

```
private toggleLoadMoreButton(gridParam: DataSet): void {
  if (gridParam.paging.hasNextPage &&
    this.loadMoreButton.classList.contains(buttonStyleHidden))
  {
      this.loadMoreButton.classList.remove(buttonStyleHidden);
  }
    else if (!gridParam.paging.hasNextPage &&
      !this.loadMoreButton.classList.contains(buttonStyleHidden))
    {
        this.loadMoreButton.classList.add(buttonStyleHidden);
    }
}
```

Basically, this function shows the **Load More...** button if the dataset has a next page to load, or hides the button if there are no more pages to load. Hence, it is named `toggle`.

The following is the definition of the `getSortedColumnsOnView` method:

index.ts

```
private getSortedColumnsOnView
    (context: ComponentFramework.Context<IInputs>)
    : DataSetInterfaces.Column[] {
        if (!context.parameters.datasetGrid.columns) {
            return [];
        }
        const columns =
            context.parameters.datasetGrid.columns.filter(
            function (columnItem: DataSetInterfaces.Column) {
                return columnItem.order >= 0;
            });
        // Sort columns so that it will be rendered in order
        columns.sort(
            function (a: DataSetInterfaces.Column
                , b: DataSetInterfaces.Column) {
                    return a.order - b.order;
```

```
            });
        return columns;
}
```

In this method, we first check that the columns in the dataset are not undefined. If they are undefined, we skip further processing. If data is present in the columns, then we filter out the columns whose display order is less than zero as these columns are supplementary and do not necessarily need to be shown on the UI. This is followed by the code to sort the columns in their display order.

The createGridBody method is the core method that renders the entire UI of the code component and is defined as follows:

index.ts

```
private createGridBody(columnsOnView: DataSetInterfaces.
Column[], gridParam: DataSet): HTMLDivElement {
    const gridBody: HTMLDivElement =
        document.createElement("div");
    if (gridParam.sortedRecordIds.length > 0) {
        for (let currentRecordId of
                gridParam.sortedRecordIds) {
            const gridRecord: HTMLDivElement =
                this.createCard(columnsOnView, gridParam,
                currentRecordId);
            gridBody.appendChild(gridRecord);
        }
    }
    else {
        const noRecordLabel: HTMLDivElement =
            document.createElement("div");
        noRecordLabel.innerHTML = "No records found";
        gridBody.appendChild(noRecordLabel);
    }
    return gridBody;
}
```

The following explains how the `createGridBody` method works:

1. We begin by creating the `gridBody`, which will hold all the cards.

2. We then loop through all the records (let's call it a *record loop*) and initialize a `div` element named `gridRecord` that will hold the contents of the current record in the loop by assigning the response from a supporting method called `createCard`. The `createCard` method will be used to format all the row data into a card.

3. The `div` element with the name `gridRecord` is then appended to `gridBody`.

4. The `else` block defines how the component should behave when no data is found.

5. Finally, return the entire DOM as `gridBody`.

Let's now look at the `createCard` supporting method:

index.ts

```
private createCard(columnsOnView: DataSetInterfaces.Column[],
    gridParam: DataSet, currentRecordId: string):
    HTMLDivElement {
    const gridRecord: HTMLDivElement =
        document.createElement("div");
    gridRecord.className = "gridItem";
    gridRecord.setAttribute(gridRowRecordId,
        gridParam.records[currentRecordId].getRecordId());
    columnsOnView.forEach(colItem => {
        gridRecord.appendChild(this.createCardItems(gridParam,
            currentRecordId, colItem));
    });
    return gridRecord;
}
```

Let's understand the `createCard` supporting method:

1. We begin by creating a `div` element named `gridRecord` and setting a record ID and a class name that will be defined in the CSS stylesheet.

2. We need to loop through all the column values (let's call it a *column loop*) and create the required UI elements that will hold the column name and values. The creation of UI elements is performed by another supporting method named `createCardItems`. This method returns a `div` element with all the required UI elements as a child.

3. The elements returned by `createCardItems` are added to `gridRecord`, which is then returned to the calling method.

As we have used the `createCardItems` supporting method, let's take a look at its definition:

index.ts

```ts
private createCardItems(gridParam: DataSet, currentRecordId:
        string, columnItems: DataSetInterfaces.Column):
        HTMLParagraphElement {
    const para = document.createElement("p");
    const label = document.createElement("span");
    label.className = "gridLabel";
    label.innerHTML = `${columnItems.displayName}:`;
    const content = document.createElement("span");
    content.className = "gridText";
    if (gridParam.records[currentRecordId].getFormattedValue(
      columnItems.name) != null &&
      gridParam.records[currentRecordId].getFormattedValue(
      columnItems.name) != "") {
        content.innerHTML =
          gridParam.records[currentRecordId].
          getFormattedValue(columnItems.name);
    } else {
      content.innerHTML = "-";
    }

    para.appendChild(label);
    para.appendChild(content);
    return para;
}
```

The following is an explanation of how the `createCardItems` method works:

1. Create a paragraph tag that will act as the parent for all the other elements we will be creating.

2. This is followed by the creation of a span element that will act as a label that should display the column name.

3. The next step is to create another span element that will act as content that should display the row value for a particular column.

4. Both of these elements are then added to the paragraph element, which is returned to the calling method.

Now that the core logic to render the UI with data is complete, let's focus our attention on styling the many `div` elements to look like a card.

Adding styling to a dataset code component

Throughout the code, we have used lots of classes and we need to define the styles for those elements. Similar to the styling we learned in the previous section, we will use the `.PowerMeUp\.MyDataCard` classes to define the styles on our code component. Let's create a file under the `css` folder named `MyDataCard.css`. The following is the important style definition of the dataset component. For a complete style definition, please refer to the project on GitHub:

MyDataCard.css

```css
.PowerMeUp\.MyDataCard .grid {
    background-color: transparent;
    border: solid thin lightgray;
    display: inline-block;
}
.PowerMeUp\.MyDataCard .gridItem {
    background-color: #1fc8db;
    background-image:
linear-gradient(141deg, #9fb8ad 0%, #1fc8db 51%, #2cb5e8 75%);
}
.PowerMeUp\.MyDataCard .gridLabel {
    color: lightcyan;
}
```

```
.PowerMeUp\.MyDataCard .gridText {
    color: midnightblue;
}
```

As we have added a new styling file, we need to add its reference to the manifest file, which can be done by adding a css tag under the resources tag as follows:

ControlManifest.Inputs.xml

```
<resources>
        <code path="index.ts" order="1"/>
        <css path="css/MyDataCard.css" order="1" />
</resources>
```

This will ensure that when you build the component, the framework will compile the code file along with the styling file when creating the bundle.

Once the control is built using the npm run build command, the dataset code component should be ready for testing.

Testing the dataset code component

We can test the dataset code component by using the framework's test harness. To invoke the test harness, you need to execute the npm start command in the VS Code terminal. You can also use npm start watch for a more convenient experience. When the test harness loads, on the right-hand panel, you will see configuration items and, under **Data Inputs**, you can select your test data, which expects a comma-separated values (.csv) file. So, to test our component, let's create a .csv file, as shown next:

CSV test data

```
Super Hero Name,Creator,Date of Birth
Iron Man,Stan Lee,May 29 1970
Capitan America,Jack Kirby,July 4 1918
Thor,Stan Lee,
Hulk,Stan Lee,
Spider Man,Stan Lee, August 10 2001
```

Some of the columns in the test data have intentionally been left blank.

> **Note**
> You can find this file in the example library on GitHub.

Select the `.csv` file you just created using the **Select a file** button from the right-hand pane. The following screenshot shows the result in the test harness:

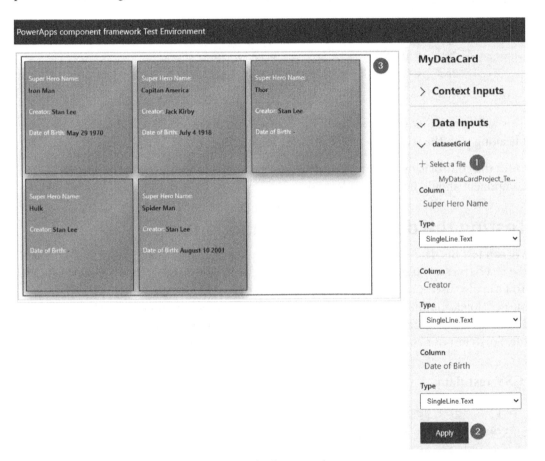

Figure 5.8 – Testing the dataset code component

After uploading the `.csv` file to the test harness, select proper data types from the dropdowns on each of the column values and click **Apply**. This will render the values on the data card as shown in the preceding screenshot.

Summary

In this chapter, we learned how to edit the manifest file for both field and dataset code components. We also built a fully functioning code component and learned how to style it and add a preview image. This chapter will help you to better understand the manifest file, which provides details in terms of how the code component should be rendered and configured on the host. With the help of the code components built in this chapter, you should be able to build your own code components for fields and datasets.

In the next chapter, we will learn about debugging skills at different stages in both model-driven and canvas apps.

Testing your knowledge

1. What is the command to initiate a test harness and rebuilds if any of the file changes? (*100 points*)

   a. `npm start`

   b. `npm start watch`

2. Which is the correct command to initiate a PCF project to build a code component for a view or sub-grid? (*100 points*)

   a. `pac pcf init --namespace PowerMeUp --name Sample --template dataset`

   b. `pac pcf init --namespace PowerMeUp --name Sample --template view`

3. Which file extension is acceptable by the test harness to test a code component for dataset? (*100 points*)

   a. File with extension `.csv`

   b. File with extension `.xlsx`

4. Select the correct statement from the following: (*200 points*)

   a. PCF project can contain multiple components.

   b. SCSS file is unsupported in PCF project.

Further reading

- Additional information on building code components can be found in the Microsoft documentation at `https://bit.ly/BuildPCF`.

- Look at the video on how to build a field type code component at `http://bit.ly/VideoBuildPCF`.

- Download sample components from `https://aka.ms/PCFSampleControls` and learn how to use the sample components by referring to the following link: `http://bit.ly/UseSampleComponents`.

6
Debugging Code Components

In the previous chapters, we created two code components, looked at the process for testing code components, applied styles, and added a preview image.

As you begin to develop more complex code components, you might come across a need to debug them to either resolve a bug or to understand the flow of data within a code component. In this chapter, you will learn how to debug code components in a more interactive way, which can help you identify bugs and build better code components. By the end of this chapter, you will be able to debug any code component, whether it's local or hosted in an app.

In this chapter, we are going to cover the following main topics:

- Overview of the test harness
- Debugging using the test harness
- Debugging components hosted in model-driven apps
- Debugging components hosted in canvas apps

Technical requirements

In order to work through this chapter, you need to install all the prerequisites and download the example library mentioned in *Chapter 1, Introduction to the Power Apps Component Framework*. You will also need to install **Visual Studio Code**, **Fiddler Classic**, which is provided by **Telerik**, and **Google Chrome**.

Overview of the test harness

The **test harness** is a utility built by Microsoft that helps you quickly render a component in a local environment, helping you to test and debug the code component. We have already seen parts of this utility in the previous chapter. Let's understand the different aspects of the test harness; we'll start the test harness from within a PCF project. The command to start the test harness is either npm start or npm start watch.

After the test harness has started, the component will be displayed in a browser window. Observe the following screenshot – the panel on the right has three main sections: **Context Inputs**, **Data Inputs**, and **Data Outputs**:

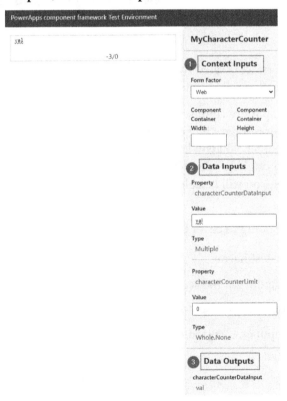

Figure 6.1 – Overview of the test harness

Let's analyze each of those sections in detail:

- **Context Inputs**: Within the test harness, you can provide various inputs to specify how the component will be rendered. You can select the form factor, such as **Web**, **Tablet**, or **Phone**. You can also provide an explicit width and height to see how the component will render with various dimensions. The latter is useful to test the responsiveness of your code component.

- **Data Inputs**: The data inputs help to ensure that the component functions as expected when different data parameters are provided and allows you to determine how the component will render based on the type specified in a given field. If the component is of the dataset type, you can load a CSV file with mock data. This file can be exported from your target environment or you can build a new one. Whenever the inputs change, the `updateView` method is invoked.

- **Data Outputs**: The data outputs ensure that the component is returning the correct data when different parameters are provided or different scenarios are performed on the component. This is only rendered when the component's `getOutputs` method is invoked.

Now that we understand the different sections of the test harness, next, we will look at debugging the field type code component we built in *Chapter 5, Code, Test, and Repeat*.

Debugging using the test harness

Most modern browsers have a variety of built-in debugging capabilities. Microsoft Edge, Google Chrome, Mozilla Firefox, and Apple Safari each have built-in developer tools that allow interactive debugging. You can use any browser you would prefer, but the examples and screenshots in this book are based on Google Chrome.

While the test harness is running in a browser, press *Ctrl + Shift + I* on your keyboard to launch **DevTools**. Let's first start with understanding how to use **DevTools** to inspect the elements that make up a code component.

Inspecting elements in a code component

In **DevTools**, the first tab, named **Elements**, shows the elements panel, which provides you with a way to view the HTML that is rendered on the page. You can access your elements on the UI by using the **Inspect** functionality, which can be accessed in one of the following two ways:

- Highlight the element using your mouse and right-click an element on your page, then select **Inspect**, as shown in the following screenshot:

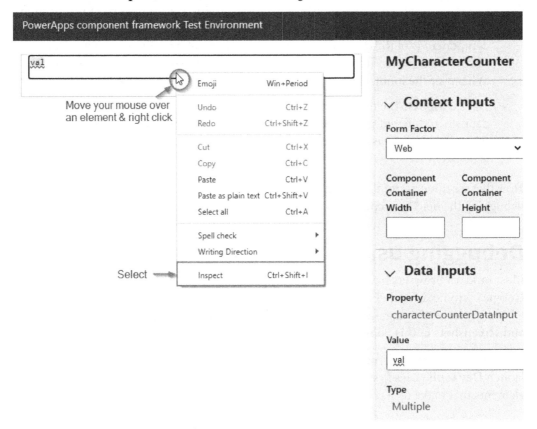

Figure 6.2 – Using Inspect from DevTools

This is the easiest way, but sometimes, due to overlapping DOM elements, it can be hard to select it directly by right-clicking on it. Hence, there is another way.

- Turn on **Element Inspector** in **DevTools** and hover over an element; it will become highlighted. Select an element and a corresponding source will be populated in the **Elements** tab as shown in the following screenshot:

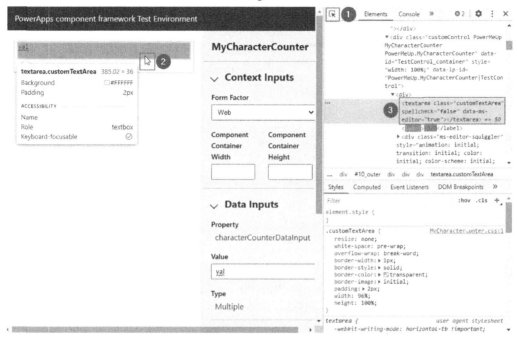

Figure 6.3 – Using Element Inspector from DevTools

So, now that you are familiar with how to inspect elements in your code component, let's look at how to use console logs to evaluate scripts.

Inspecting console logs to evaluate scripts

A common way to get debug context within a client script is to use the `console.log()` method. If you want to provide logging inside your component, you can use this method. These logs are displayed in the **DevTools** console panel whenever they are executed, which provides a valuable way to trace logic as it runs within your component.

The following screenshot shows an example of a couple of logs that were written by the test harness:

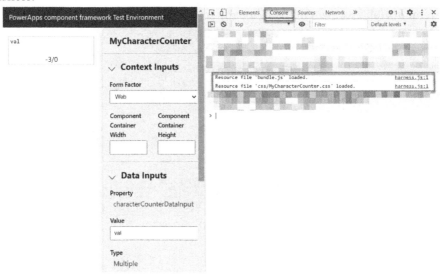

Figure 6.4 – Example of console logs in DevTools

You also can run your own script from within the console if you are in the right context of the script execution. This method can be valuable for testing various method executions and logic from within the context of a live environment.

The following screenshot demonstrates a script that retrieves the value of an element called `customTextArea`:

Figure 6.5 – Evaluating the script in a console log

This method is used to perform quick debugging, but sometimes there is a need to perform deeper debugging of the logic. So, let's look at how to perform deeper debugging of logic using the test harness.

Debugging using breakpoints

One of the most valuable utilities in **DevTools** is the ability to set debugger breakpoints in your code so that you can inspect variables and the flow of your method's implementation. The **Sources** tab provides you with the source code for all corresponding files of the current page.

The following screenshot shows how to find the index.ts file:

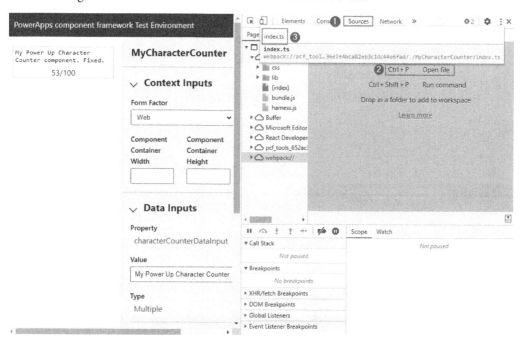

Figure 6.6 – Finding the index.ts file in DevTools

Now, do the following:

1. Once you find the `index.ts` file, look for the `onChange` method and set a breakpoint on the first line in that method.

    > **Insights**
    >
    > This strategy only works when you have source maps available. The webpack configuration adds add source maps when building in debug mode, and the code might look slightly different as it is transformed using Babel.

2. Now, to invoke the debugger, type any string in the textbox and focus out of it; this will hit the breakpoint, providing you with the ability to manually step through the logic of the event handler.

3. Additionally, you can inspect values, such as those that have changed, by hovering your mouse on the variables.

4. This can also work when evaluating them in **Console**, as shown in the following screenshot:

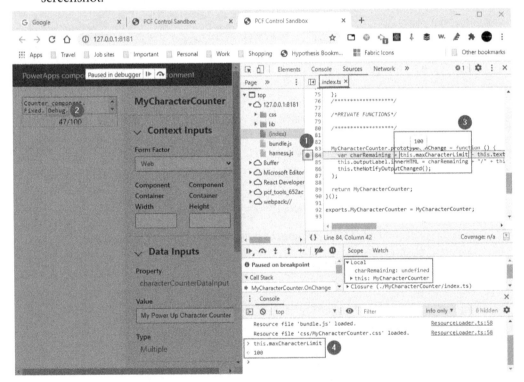

Figure 6.7 – Stepping through debugging in DevTools

The test harness allows you to test most scenarios without the need to deploy the code component in its host environment. But currently, there are some features that do not work in the test harness, such as the web API, because all those features are environment-dependent and we are in a localized environment that is unaware of the Dataverse environment and its metadata. That brings us to our next topic: debugging in a development environment on the Power Platform.

Debugging in model-driven apps

In certain scenarios, you will want to deploy your code component to a model-driven app. The deployment and configuration of code components are covered in *Chapter 8, Introduction to the Dataverse Project*, and *Chapter 9, Configuring Code Components in Power Apps*, and this section assumes that you have configured code components in model-driven apps. So, we will look at how to debug a code component once it is deployed and configured. For this tutorial, we will be using `AutoResponder` in **Fiddler Classic**, which is a tool that allows us to perform web debugging for any process that logs and inspects all HTTP(S) traffic between your computer and the internet. The process can be for a standard browser or a desktop application; if there is traffic between your computer and the internet, then the tool allows you to perform a multitude of operations on those requests and responses. Let's see how to go about it.

Installing and configuring Fiddler Classic

You can download and install Fiddler Classic at `https://www.telerik.com/download/fiddler`.

Once Fiddler Classic is installed, you need to configure it to capture and decrypt HTTPS traffic. This can be done by navigating to the **Tools | Options... | HTTPS** tab; check the **Capture HTTPS CONNECTs** and **Decrypt HTTPS traffic** checkboxes. This is shown in the following screenshot:

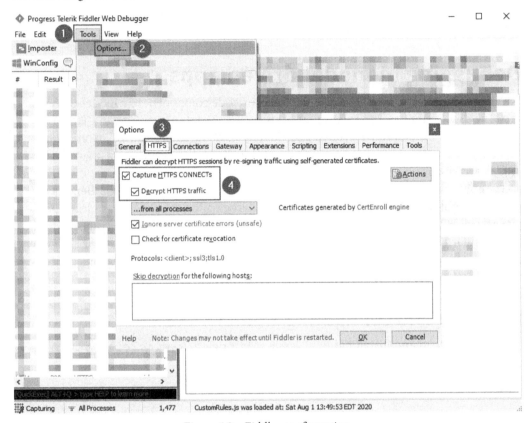

Figure 6.8 – Fiddler configuration

You may get a warning that Fiddler Classic will install a certificate so that it can suppress security warnings. Depending on whether you have permissions and you are willing to do so, you can click on either **Yes** or **No**.

At this point, Fiddler should be configured and prepared for debugging. Next, let's look at how to use **AutoResponder** to debug a code component.

Debugging using AutoResponder

To debug with **AutoResponder**, we need to perform the following steps:

1. In the right pane of Fiddler, select the **AutoResponder** tab.

2. Then, check the **Enable rules**, **Accept all CONNECTs**, and **Unmatched requests passthrough** checkboxes, if not already checked.

3. Click on **Add Rule** in the **Rule Editor**.

4. Then, in the first textbox, enter the following regex, `regex:(?insx).+.<controlname>/bundle.js`, but replace `controlname` with the appropriate control name. In the second textbox, enter the path of your code component's `bundle.js` file from the **out** directory and click **Save**.

    Here we are continuing our example of the character counter developed in the previous chapter, so the final version should look as shown in the following screenshot:

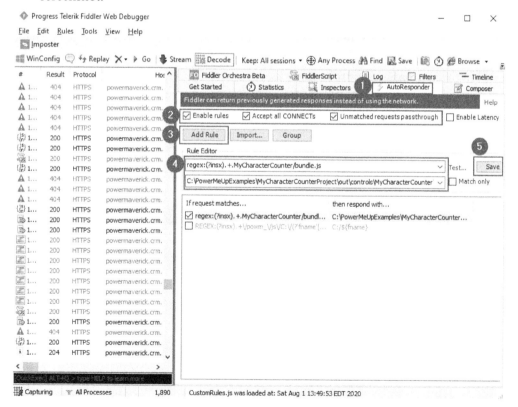

Figure 6.9 – Using Fiddler's AutoResponder

5. Now, open the form where the control is configured in the model-driven app. Press *F12* on the keyboard to launch **DevTools** and make sure the **Disable cache (while DevTools is open)** option under the **Network** section is checked. This is shown in the following screenshot:

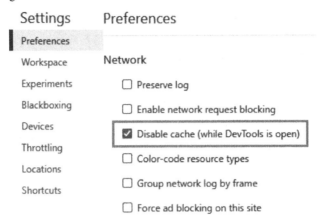

Figure 6.10 – Hard reloading in Chrome

6. Now, using **DevTools**, open the index.ts file by pressing *Ctrl + P*, which provides you with a search box; type index.ts to search for the file and select the one that has the appropriate control name:

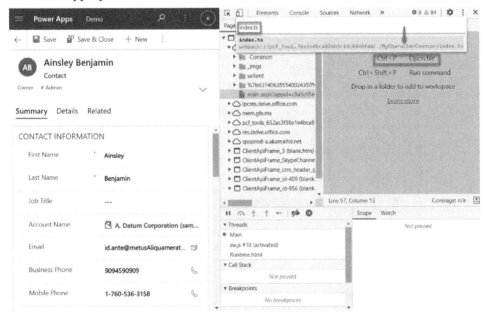

Figure 6.11 – Finding the index.ts file in DevTools

7. Once you have located your `index.ts` file, apply a debugger in the file as we saw in the previous section. Type any string in the textbox and focus out of it; this will hit the breakpoint, providing you with the ability to manually step through the logic of the event handler.

You can also do some code updates in your local file, followed by building the project. Once the project build is successful, refresh the browser to reflect your changes from local files in the model-driven app. Using the same example of the character counter, let's add a line of code in the `updateView` method in the `index.ts` file as follows:

```
console.log("This line of code appear in MDA because of
Fiddler");
```

8. Let's now build the project by using the `npm build` command. Once the build is successful, refresh the browser where the code component resides, and you will see the new changes to the source code of the `index.ts` file in **DevTools**, as shown in the following screenshot:

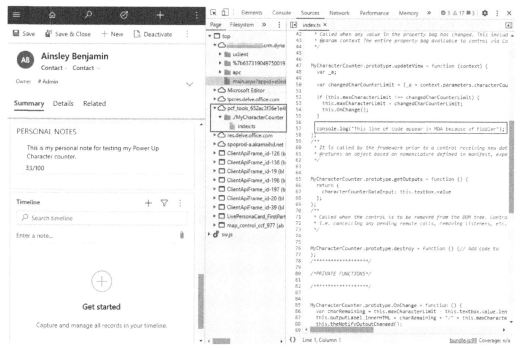

Figure 6.12 – Changes reflected in the live source code

Using the same process, you can debug any code component deployed to a model-driven app with the help of **AutoResponder**. Let's now look at the process for debugging canvas apps.

Debugging in canvas apps

Similar to the previous section, this section assumes that you have deployed and configured code components using canvas apps as described in *Chapter 8*, *Introduction to the Dataverse Project*, and *Chapter 9*, *Configuring Code Components in Power Apps*. Once you have configured the code component on an individual screen, we will focus on understanding the process of debugging a code component that's added to a canvas. In this example, we are going to work with the character counter code component, assuming it is already added on a screen in a canvas app. There are two ways you can debug a code component from a canvas app: using **DevTools** and using **AutoResponder**. We will be looking into each of these options.

Debugging using DevTools

Let's start **DevTools** by pressing *Ctrl + Shift + I* to perform debugging. First, you need to make sure you open the canvas app for editing in the maker portal. Once the app is open for editing, navigate to the screen that hosts the code component and from the browser menu, open **DevTools**, click on the **Source** tab, and search for the index.ts file using the search box.

When you have the index.ts file open, refer to the following screenshot and the steps that follow it, which will guide you through the process of debugging a code component in a canvas app:

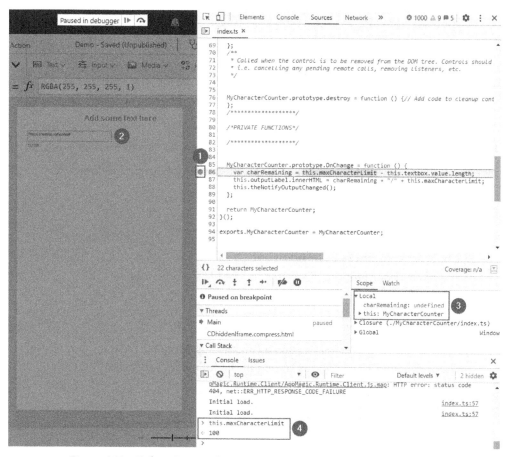

Figure 6.13 – Debugging a code component in a canvas app using DevTools

1. Set your breakpoint on the first line of the code in the onChange method of your
    index.ts file.

2. Type a string in the textbox and focus out of it; a breakpoint will be hit, providing
    you with the ability to manually step through the logic.

3. You can also check the **Scope** section, which will show you the values of the
    variables that are local to the scope of the function you are in and some global
    variables if you have any.

4. Once your debugger is inside the function, you can even inspect the values of the
    variables within the scope of that function.

When using this approach, you are always testing against the codebase from when the
component was first deployed. If any code changes have happened since the deployment,
then you will need to redeploy the code component.

Debugging using AutoResponder

As stated in an earlier section, by using Fiddler's **AutoResponder** functionality you can point your component to utilize the codebase of your local machine. This avoids you having to redeploy your component and perform unit testing every time there are code changes. The following steps will help you understand the process for debugging a code component in a canvas app:

1. Open **Fiddler** and in the right pane, select the **AutoResponder** tab.

2. Check the **Enable rules, Accept all CONNECTs**, and **Unmatched requests passthrough** checkboxes, if not already checked.

3. Click on **Add Rule** in the **Rule Editor**.

4. In the first textbox, enter the following: `Resources0Controls0PowerMeUp.MyCharacterCounter.bundle.js?sv=`, and in the second textbox, enter the path of your code component's `bundle.js` file from the **out** directory.

5. Next, save the configuration by clicking **Save**.

6. Open **ScriptEditor** in **Fiddler Classic** by pressing *Ctrl + R*.

7. Search for the `OnBeforeResponse` function by using *Ctrl + F* and modify this method with additional code as shown in the following screenshot:

```
static function OnBeforeResponse(oSession: Session) {
    if (m_Hide304s && oSession.responseCode == 304) {
        oSession["ui-hide"] = "true";
    }
    if (oSession.oRequest.headers.Exists("Host") && oSession.oRequest.headers["Host"].EndsWith("windows.net")) {
        if (oSession.oResponse.headers.Exists("Access-Control-Allow-Origin")){
            oSession.oResponse.headers["Access-Control-Allow-Origin"] ="*";
        }
        else{
            oSession.oResponse.headers.Add("Access-Control Allow-Origin","*");
        }
    }
}
```

Figure 6.14 – Preview of the OnBeforeResponse method in ScriptEditor of Fiddler Classic

The scripts served from Power Apps are from a different domain, so *Step 7* is needed to configure Fiddler Classic to accept responses from a different origin than the request.

8. Once the code is added to the `OnBeforeResponse` method, click on **File | Save** in **ScriptEditor** and close the window.

Now that Fiddler Classic is configured for debugging, let's continue our example of the character counter; the final version should look as shown in the following screenshot:

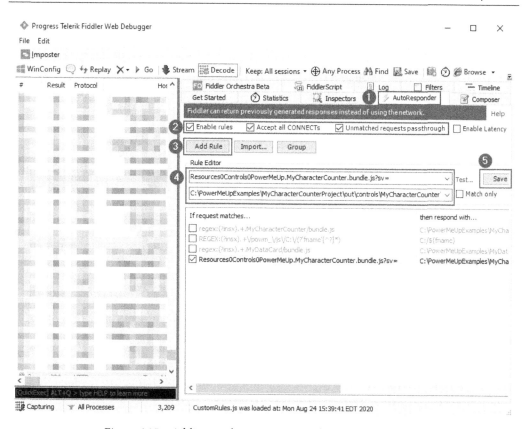

Figure 6.15 – Adding a rule in AutoResponder for the canvas app

If the canvas app was already open, then close and reopen the app. You can perform some code updates in your local file. Once all the changes are performed, build the project, and after the successful completion of the build process, refresh the browser to reflect your changes from local files in the canvas app.

Summary

In this chapter, we learned about several different ways that a code component can be debugged; we started with the test harness, followed by **DevTools**, and we later learned how to use **Fiddler Classic's AutoResponder** for both model-driven and canvas apps. This helps you debug and resolve any issues you might face with code components that you build, whether they are local or hosted in an app.

In the next chapter, we will learn how to connect with a CDS instance and perform some quick deployments to a live environment to test the scenarios that cannot be tested using the test harness.

Test your knowledge

1. What is the regex that needs to be populated in the first textbox of the **Rule Editor** in **AutoResponder** when debugging a code component named *MyControl* in a model-driven app? (*100 points*)

   a. `regex:(?control).+.MyControl/bundle.js`

   b. `regex:(?insx).+.MyControl/bundle.js`

2. What is the entry that needs to be populated in the first textbox of the **Rule Editor** in **AutoResponder** when debugging a code component named *MyCharacterCounter* that has a namespace of *PowerMeUp* in a canvas app? (*100 points*)

   a. `Resources0Controls0PowerMeUp.MyCharacterCounter.bundle.js?sv=`

   b. `ResourcesControls.PowerMeUp.MyCharacterCounter.bundle.js?sv=`

3. What are the missing sequences here, where we are debugging a code component deployed to a model-driven app? (*200 points*)

   Configure **AutoResponder** > Open the form where the code component is deployed > Perform a hard reload > **?** > Make some code changes to the local file > **?** > Refresh the browser

   a. Add debug point in index file | Build PCF project

   b. Clear cache | Start watch

Further reading

Additional information related to using Fiddler's **AutoResponder** can be found in the Microsoft documentation at `https://bit.ly/FiddlerAutoresponder`.

7
Authentication Profiles

In the previous chapters, we learned several techniques to inspect and debug a code component, and at this point, you should be able to create your own code components. In this chapter, we are going to learn all about authentication profiles. We will look at how to create and manage them along with the process of doing a quick deploy using authentication profiles. By the end of this chapter, you should be able to create and deploy code components to a Dataverse environment.

In this chapter, we are going to cover the following main topics:

- Understanding authentication profiles
- Creating authentication profiles
- Managing authentication profiles
- Deploying code components using authentication profiles

Technical requirements

In order to work through this chapter, you need to install all the prerequisites and download the example library mentioned in *Chapter 1, Introduction to the Power Apps Component Framework*. You will also need to install **Visual Studio Code**, **PCF Builder**, and **Google Chrome**.

Understanding authentication profiles

Let's first understand what authentication profiles are. Authentication profiles are connections that have been verified by a Microsoft authentication service to a particular Dataverse environment and are saved on your local machine in the form of JSON files. These connections are machine-specific, so if you change your machine, you will have to re-create the profiles.

Now let's understand why these authentication profiles are needed. In previous chapters, we discussed that some of the capabilities provided by the Power Apps component framework cannot be tested using the test harness, and we need to deploy code components to a live Dataverse environment in a very streamlined, quick, and reliable way. Authentication profiles provide that ability. This makes it easier for us to perform our end-to-end testing of code components.

So, let's look at how to create these profiles.

Creating authentication profiles

Power Apps CLI provides a command to create authentication profiles, but you can also leverage a graphical interface provided by the **PCF Builder** for XrmToolBox to create your authentication profiles.

Let's look at both methods, starting with using the command provided by Power Apps CLI.

Creating profiles using Power Apps CLI

The command to create an authentication profile provided by Power Apps CLI is as follows:

```
pac auth create --url UrlReplace
```

Let's now begin with the steps for this:

1. Open a Command Prompt and using the provided command, replace `UrlReplace` with the actual URL for your Dataverse environment, which will look something like `https://xyz.crm.dynamics.com`.

2. When you hit *Enter*, the system will prompt you with a login screen, where you need to enter your credentials pertaining to that environment.

3. Once you have successfully logged in, the system will show a message on the console stating **Authentication successfully created**. This is shown in the following screenshot:

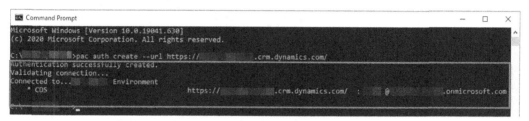

Figure 7.1 – Creating a profile using the Power Apps CLI command

As can be seen from the screenshot, after being given the correct credentials, the system creates an authentication profile on the machine.

If you like a graphical user interface, then you can use PCF Builder, which we are going to cover next.

Creating profiles using PCF Builder

Even though PCF Builder uses the same syntax as the Power Apps CLI command, it is nice to create and manage things using a graphical interface, and that is exactly what PCF Builder helps us to do.

To create an authentication profile using PCF Builder, perform the following steps:

1. Open **XrmToolBox** and start the **PCF Builder** tool. For this activity, you can opt not to connect to a Dataverse environment.

2. From the PCF Builder toolbar provided by the tool at the top of the screen, click on **Authentication Profiles**; this will reveal two options: **Create Profile** and **List Profiles**.

3. Clicking on **Create Profile** will show an input box where you need to enter your complete Dataverse environment URL, which will be something like `https://xyz.crm.dynamics.com`; then click on the **OK** button. This will prompt you with a login screen where you need to enter your credentials. The following screenshot shows where the tool displays the input box, where you can enter the Dataverse environment URL:

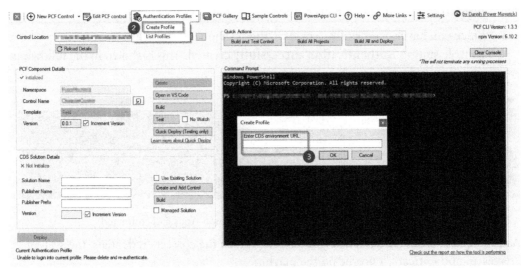

Figure 7.2 – Creating a profile using PCF Builder

4. Once you have successfully logged in to the system, the console on the PCF Builder tool will show a message stating **Authentication successfully created**. This is shown in the following screenshot:

```
Windows PowerShell
Copyright (C) Microsoft Corporation. All rights reserved.

PS C:\
                                    pac auth create --url https://            .crm.dynamics.com
Authentication successfully created.
Validating connection...
Connected to...Developer Environment
    *          CDS   https://            .crm.dynamics.com   :
    @                .onmicrosoft.com
```

Figure 7.3 – Profile successfully created using PCF Builder

As can be seen from the screenshot, after being given the correct credentials, the system creates an authentication profile on that machine.

Let's look at how to manage these profiles.

Managing authentication profiles

Once you have connected to several Dataverse environments, you might need to see which environments you have configured; you may also want to switch between them or delete one that you do not want. Each of these various functions has separate commands provided by Power Apps CLI. But these profiles can also be managed in **PCF Builder**. In this section, we will first take a look at all the commands provided by Power Apps CLI and later the process provided by **PCF Builder**.

Changing profiles using Power Apps CLI

If you want to check all the authentication profiles you are connected to, you need to run the following command in the command prompt:

```
pac auth list
```

The console will show you a list of all the profiles with an index number along with a star (*), followed by the type of environment, the URL, and the authenticated username. Refer to the following screenshot:

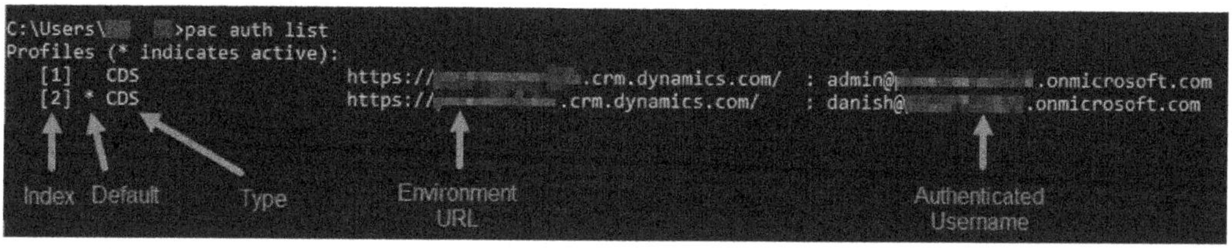

Figure 7.4 – List of profiles created on a machine

The index number is used for further managing the list, whereas * denotes that a particular environment is the selected environment for deployments; the type is always CDS.

Once you have the list of all the profiles that are connected to a Dataverse environment, you will want to change the selected environment for deployments from time to time. This can be done by running the following command in the command prompt:

```
pac auth select --index <index of the profile>
```

The index of the profile needs to be provided based on the indexes shown when you execute the `pac auth list` command. If the change was successful, the system will notify you with a message that reads **New default profile**, and then it will show the URL of the profile you selected. The following screenshot shows how to provide the index to the command in order to change the selection:

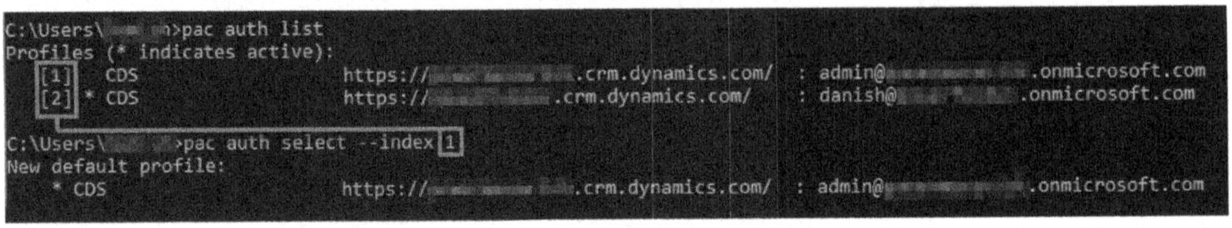

Figure 7.5 – Changing the selected profile

From the preceding screenshot, we can observe the following:

- We first executed the `pac auth list` command to get a list of all the available profiles on the machine, and then we executed the `pac auth select` command with the profile index number **1** as it was not the currently selected profile.

- The execution resulted in the console showing the message that the new default profile was changed, and we provided a URL with the username to confirm the change.

Now that we know how to get a list of the authenticated profiles on a machine and change the selected profile, let's learn how to perform deletes.

Deleting profiles using Power Apps CLI

If for some reason you do not want to see a specific profile previously created on your machine, then you can delete the profile from the machine by using the following command:

```
pac auth delete --index <index of the profile>
```

Similar to how we changed the selected profile using the index number, we need to select a number based on the indexes shown after executing the `pac auth list` command and supply that index number to the `delete` command. If the change was successful, then the system will notify you with a message that reads **Deleted profile**. The following screenshot shows how to provide an index to the command in order to delete a profile:

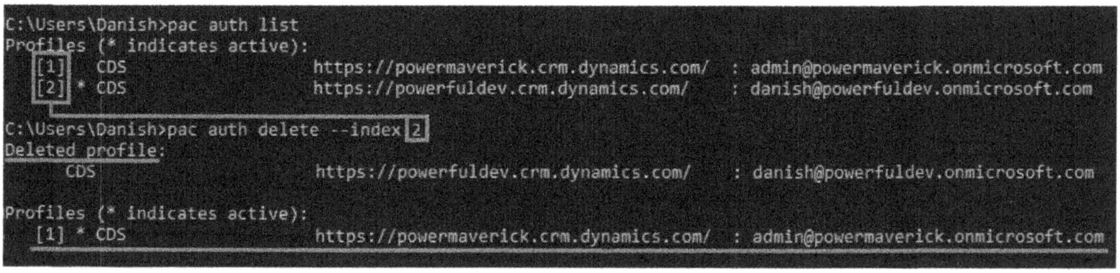

Figure 7.6 – Deleting a profile from a machine

Observe that when the profile that is currently selected is the one that is being deleted, the system will choose the first profile listed in the index from the available profiles to be the new default profile after that profile is deleted. If the deleted profile is not currently selected, then the default profile remains intact.

In cases where you want to delete all the profiles from a machine, you can clear the authentication profiles by using the following command:

```
pac auth clear
```

The authprofile.json file contains information on all the profiles created on a machine, and each authentication token is stored in a token cache file on that machine. The action to clear all the profiles completely deletes the authprofile.json file and the token cache file from the machine.

So far, you have learned how to view a list of profiles and how to change or delete a specific profile. Let's learn one more handy command that will provide you with organization details.

Retrieving the details of a selected profile using Power Apps CLI

Using the pac auth list command, you can find out the URLs and usernames that you have authenticated on your machine, but if you would like to know the details of the currently selected profile, then you will have to use the following command:

```
pac org who
```

This command will not only provide you with the URL and username of the currently selected profile but will also provide more details such as the ID, unique name, and friendly name of the organization. These details can be helpful before you execute a quick deploy, which we will be learning about in the *Deploying using authentication profiles* section.

Now that we are familiar with all the commands used to manage authentication profiles using Power Apps CLI, let's look at how PCF Builder provides a graphical interface without us having to write any of those commands.

Managing profiles using PCF Builder

In the previous section, we saw that we need to execute either `pac pcf list` or `pac org who` commands to identify the currently selected profile. But PCF Builder provides that information without any effort.

As soon as you start PCF Builder, the first command that gets executed is `pac org who`, and the information retrieved from this command is displayed in the tool under the **Current Authentication Profile** section, as shown in the following screenshot:

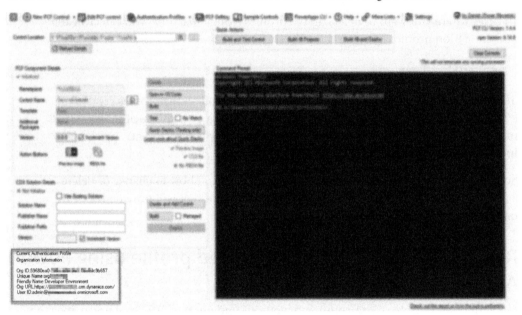

Figure 7.7 – Current authentication profile in PCF Builder

This information is displayed without any effort, so you always find out which authentication profile is currently selected. This saves you a lot of effort, especially when using a quick deploy, which we will be looking at in the *Deploying using authentication profiles* section.

Now let's see how easy it is to create and manage profiles. As PCF Builder is already loaded in XrmToolBox, click on the **Authentication Profiles** option in the toolbox; this will reveal two options: **Create Profile** and **List Profiles**. Clicking on **List Profiles** will display a list of all the profiles created on the machine; internally, it will run the `pac auth list` command and show the details in a tabular format that is easy to read and manage. This is shown in the following screenshot:

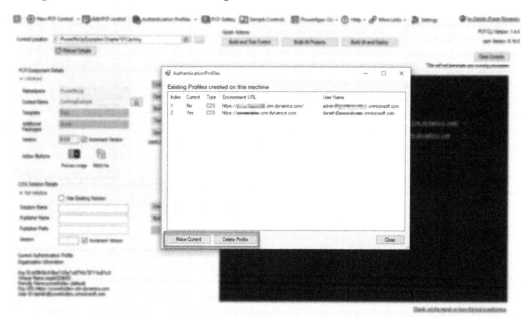

Figure 7.8 – List of profiles created on a machine in PCF Builder

Now you can select any of the profiles and click on the **Make Current** button to change the default profile or even click on **Delete Profile** to delete the selected profile from the machine. Whichever profile and option you choose, the tool will then run a specific command based on the selection, and you can see the command execution in the console provided by the tool.

In this example, we will change the default profile as shown in the following figure:

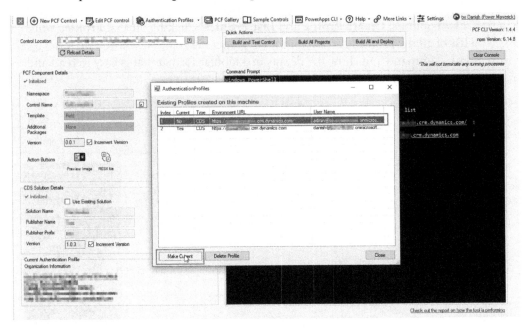

Figure 7.9 – Changing the currently selected profile in PCF Builder

When you click on the **List Profiles** menu option, you are provided with a list of all the authentication profiles on the machine. You can select the profile that you want to make the default profile and click on **Make Current**. This will execute the `pac auth select` command with a proper index number provided. You can also select **Delete Profile**, which will execute the `pac auth delete` command with a proper index number provided. When the command is executing, you can see the output in the console provided by the tool, as shown in the following screenshot, where we made the first profile the current profile:

Figure 7.10 – The change profile command's output displayed in the console

As you can see, PCF Builder makes it easy to manage authentication profiles.

Now that you are familiar with creating and managing the authentication profiles, let's look at how to quickly deploy code components into a Dataverse environment using profiles.

Deploying using authentication profiles

After you have successfully created an authentication profile, you can start publishing your code components to a Dataverse environment with all the latest changes. This is possible due to the push command provided by the framework. The push command speeds up the development cycle because it bypasses the code component versioning requirement and does not require that you build your solution project (cdsproj) to import the code component.

We will first look at the approach for deployment using Power Apps CLI and later look at the deployment process using PCF Builder.

Deploying using Power Apps CLI

Power Apps CLI provides us with a command that allows us to deploy our code component to a Dataverse environment. When the command is executed, the tool builds the component project that generates the `bundle.js` file in the *out* directory, followed by building a temporary solution that contains the code component, which is then deployed to the Dataverse environment using the solution import feature.

The following steps will help you deploy a single code component:

1. Ensure that you have a valid authentication profile created or selected from an existing profile.

2. Navigate to the root directory where the code component project is created.

3. Run the following command:

```
pac pcf push --publisher-prefix <your publisher prefix>
```

Using this command, we will deploy the `MyCharacterCounter` code component that we created in *Chapter 5, Code, Test, and Repeat*. We will be deploying this code component to a Dataverse environment configured on the selected authentication profile by executing the following command in the directory where we have the PCF project file with the `.pcfproj` extension:

```
pac pcf push --publisher-prefix powm
```

This command will deploy the character counter code component to the Dataverse environment defined by the selected authentication profile, and you should see the following output produced on the console:

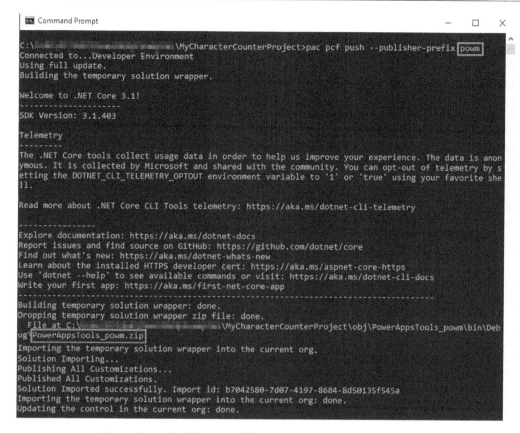

Figure 7.11 – Deploying a code component using Power Apps CLI

When using the `pac pcf push` command, the Power Apps CLI tool will start the build process followed by packaging the code component into a temporary solution wrapper ZIP file. The name of the temporary file will be a constant `PowerAppsTools_` appended with the prefix you provided in the command. Considering the command that was executed earlier, you can observe that the filename generated by the tool was `PowerAppsTools_powm`, where `powm` was the prefix provided in the command.

If you have used the same prefix to deploy more than one code component, then all those code components can be found in a single solution in the Dataverse environment. For example, if you deployed the `MyDataCardProject` code component using the same command and prefix, then after successful deployment, you will find both the code components in the same solution in the Dataverse environment as shown in the following screenshot:

Solutions > **PowerAppsTools_powm**

Display name ∨		Name	Type ∨
powm_PowerMeUp.MyCharacterCounter	···	powm_PowerMeUp.MyCharacterCounter	Custom control
powm_PowerMeUp.MyDataCard	···	powm_PowerMeUp.MyDataCard	Custom control

Figure 7.12 – Two code components in same the Dataverse solution using the pac pcf push command

> **Caution**
>
> Using a temporary solution generated by the framework through the `push` command is not recommended for the deployment of code component to other environments. You should add the code component to a solution with your other customizations, so they are released as part of your standard application life cycle management process.

When adding a code component to another solution, you must make sure that the prefix of the code component matches the prefix of the solution to which you are adding it. If there is a mismatch in the prefix, then you will get an error while importing the solution in another environment.

Now, let's look at the process of deploying code components using PCF Builder.

Deploying code components using PCF Builder

When your code component is ready for testing in a live environment, you can utilize the **Quick Deploy** feature of PCF Builder to deploy the code component to your currently selected profile. As we saw in an earlier section, PCF Builder displays the currently selected profile information as soon as you start the tool, ensuring that you are aware of the profile that is currently selected. Similar to the other commands, you do not need to write any commands in PCF Builder; you just need to click the **Quick Deploy** button, which will initiate the deployment of the code component to the environment that is currently selected.

Also, you do not have to ensure that you are in the correct folder because PCF Builder will do that for you, making the deployment process much smoother. The following screenshot shows the console log that is displayed by the tool when you click the **Quick Deploy** button and enter powm as the publisher prefix:

Figure 7.13 – Deploying a code component using the Quick Deploy feature in PCF Builder

As PCF Builder internally uses the same command as provided by Power Apps CLI, it behaves the same way as we discussed in the previous section.

Summary

In this chapter, we learned how to create and manage authentication profiles using both Power Apps CLI and PCF Builder. We also learned how to quickly deploy code components to a desired Dataverse environment using both Power Apps CLI and PCF Builder. This chapter should help you to manage and deploy authentication profiles easily.

In the next chapter, we will look at how to use Dataverse projects and the key differences between authentication profiles and Dataverse projects in terms of deployments.

Test your knowledge

1. What is the command used to check all the details of the currently active profile? (*100 points*)

    a. `pac org who`

    b. `pac auth list`

2. What is the correct requirement when specifying the publisher prefix for the `pac pcf push` command? (*100 points*)

    a. Cannot contain numbers

    b. Cannot be more than 5 characters

3. Let's assume you have deployed a code component using the `pac pcf push` command with the `pmu` prefix. Now, you want to deploy a new code component using the same command and prefix. What will be the outcome? (*200 points*)

    a. You will get an error stating that you cannot add a code component with the same publisher prefix.

    b. The new code component will be deployed in the same solution that the first code component was deployed in.

Further reading

*   Additional information on creating and managing authentication profiles can be found in the Microsoft documentation at `http://bit.ly/Connect-Environment`.

*   Additional information on deploying code components using authentication profiles can be found in the Microsoft documentation at `http://bit.ly/Deploy-Environment`.

8
Introduction to the Dataverse Project

In the previous chapters, we learned about the process of deploying code components quickly during the development cycle. In this chapter, we will learn about the process of packaging your code components as a solution from scratch or using an existing solution file. By the end of this chapter, you should be able to package your code components and deploy that package to your desired Dataverse environment, or even distribute it for other teams so that they can use your solution file.

In this chapter, we are going to cover the following main topics:

- Overview of the Dataverse solution project
- Initializing the solution project and adding a code component
- Building a Dataverse project and obtaining the output
- Deploying new code components to an existing solution
- Exporting the solution's ZIP file using Power Apps CLI commands
- Understanding the complete development cycle

Let's get started!

Technical requirements

To work through this chapter, you will need to install all the prerequisites mentioned in *Chapter 1, Introduction to the Power Apps Component Framework*. Download the example library from `https://github.com/PacktPublishing/Extending-Microsoft-Power-Apps-with-Power-Apps-Component-Framework/tree/master/Chapter08`. This will help you with the development process described in this chapter. You will also need to install **Visual Studio Code**, **PCF Builder**, and **Google Chrome**.

Overview of the Dataverse solution project

Before we look at the overview of the Dataverse solution project, we need to familiarize ourselves with the solutions in Dataverse. A solution can be defined as a container that is used to track changes that are made to one or more components, and then transports them from one environment to another. There are various types of components, such as tables, processes, and web resources. Apps are also considered a type of component in the solution. A solution also enables us to implement the **Application Life Cycle Management (ALM)** process for any customizations that are added to Dataverse.

In the previous chapter, you looked at a deployment method using the `pac pcf push` command. Though that is one way of deployment, it deploys only a single code component using a temporary solution, and code components are always built using the debug mode. The Dataverse solution project on the other hand creates a solution file. This is not only limited to PCF code components, but it can also contain any kinds of components that are supported by the Dataverse solution file (such as web resources and plugin assemblies). For now, you can only add project references that are limited to PCF and the Plugin project. You can create a Dataverse project by using the **Power Apps CLI** command, which generates a project structure with a Dataverse project file that has a `.cdsproj` extension.

> **Note**
> The Dataverse project file extension will change to align with the product being renamed.

We also need to become familiar with the managed and unmanaged solution types. When you create a solution in the Power Apps maker portal, the solution type will be unmanaged. This is because unmanaged solutions can be exported as both unmanaged as well as managed, whereas managed solutions cannot be exported. Unmanaged solutions can be edited, whereas managed solutions cannot be edited. Additional components can be added to unmanaged solutions but that is not the case with managed solutions. Another important point to note is that unmanaged solutions are recommended to be used in development environments, while managed solutions should be used in non-development environments. There are many other differences between these two types of solutions. More information about these solution types can be found in the *Further reading* section.

Now that we know more about solutions and the Dataverse solution project, let's look at how to initiate a solution project and add the code component to it.

Initializing the solution project and adding a code component

The Power Apps CLI provides us with a set of commands we can use to initialize a Dataverse solution project and add references to the component project. To start initializing your first Dataverse solution project, perform the following steps:

1. Create a folder that will serve as your workspace for bundling your code components into a solution file.

2. Start VS Code. Then, within VS Code, navigate to the folder that you just created.

3. Open an integrated terminal for VS Code; the default command to open the terminal in VS Code is *Ctrl +* `.

4. For initializing the Dataverse project, you will have to run the following Power Apps CLI command in the terminal:

```
pac solution init --publisher-name <publisher name>
--publisher-prefix <prefix>
```

When providing your publisher name or prefix, you cannot use spaces or any special characters. There is a character limit of 5 for the publisher prefix; if you specify more than 5 characters, then you will get an error.

At this point, a new project should be created in your workspace, and one of the file should have a `.cdsproj` extension. First, let's understand the structure of this project.

Let's say you have created a folder named `PowerMeUpDataverse` and executed the following command:

```
pac solution init --publisher-name Me --publisher-prefix pmu
```

The following is the file and folder structure that is generated by the Power Apps CLI:

Figure 8.1 – File and folder structure for the Dataverse solution project

As you can see, the tool generated a project file called `PowerMeUpDataverse.cdsproj` because the command where it was executed had that folder name. So, you must always remember to name your solution folder correctly because that will be the name of your project, as well as your Dataverse solution file.

Upon navigating inside `src > Other`, you will see the following structure, which is where all the XML files exist:

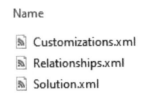

Figure 8.2 – Solution XML files inside src > Other

Once you're inside this folder, you can open each of the files within it. The `Customizations.xml` and `Relationships.xml` files with contain empty templates. The `Solution.xml` file will also have a default template, but there will be some tags inside it. The tags that stand out in this file are as follows:

- **Description**: This will contain the description of your solution that is shown during the import process. It provides the user with insight into the solution when they're importing it into a specified Dataverse environment.

- **Version**: This is the version of your solution file. A solution version has the following format: *major.minor.build.revision*. When you're adding new capabilities, it is always recommended to increment this version.

- **Managed**: This tag defines which type of solution file will be generated by the project, and it takes in a numeric value. A value of 0 is for unmanaged, a value of 1 is for managed, and a value of 2 is for generating both managed and unmanaged solution files.

- **Publisher > UniqueName**: This specifies the unique name of the publisher. Each environment has unique publishers. If you define a publisher name that exists in the environment where the solution will be imported, it will overwrite it with the details you provide in this Dataverse solution file.

- **Publisher > Description**: This provides a description for your publisher only.

- **Publisher > EmailAddress**: This provides an email address for the publisher.

- **Publisher > SupportingWebsiteUrl**: If you want to provide the URL of your website on a publisher profile, then you can provide it here.

- **Publisher > CustomizationPrefix**: A unique publisher prefix that distinguishes your component from others. As we mentioned earlier, this must be 1-5 characters in length and can include numbers.

- **Publisher > CustomizationOptionValuePrefix**: This will be auto generated for your publisher when you initialize the Dataverse solution project and only contains numbers. It is used when you add options to choices and provides you with an indicator of which solution was used to add the option.

You can edit the data for any of the tags, but remember to follow the conventions we discussed earlier.

Another file that you may wish to review is the solution project file itself. When you open the `.cdsproj` file in VS Code, you should see an output similar to the following:

```xml
PowerMeUpDataverse.cdsproj
1   <?xml version="1.0" encoding="utf-8"?>
2   <Project ToolsVersion="15.0" DefaultTargets="Build" xmlns="http://schemas.microsoft.com/developer/msbuild/2003">
3     <PropertyGroup>
4       <PowerAppsTargetsPath>$(MSBuildExtensionsPath)\Microsoft\VisualStudio\v$(VisualStudioVersion)\PowerApps</PowerAppsTargetsPath>
5     </PropertyGroup>
6
7     <Import Project="$(MSBuildExtensionsPath)\$(MSBuildToolsVersion)\Microsoft.Common.props" />
8     <Import Project="$(PowerAppsTargetsPath)\Microsoft.PowerApps.VisualStudio.Solution.props"
9       Condition="Exists('$(PowerAppsTargetsPath)\Microsoft.PowerApps.VisualStudio.Solution.props')"/>
10
11    <PropertyGroup>
12      <ProjectGuid>52742b8d-088f-47a2-b7a1-4ed962815771</ProjectGuid>
13      <TargetFrameworkVersion>v4.6.2</TargetFrameworkVersion>
14      <!--Remove TargetFramework when this is available in 16.1-->
15      <TargetFramework>net462</TargetFramework>
16      <RestoreProjectStyle>PackageReference</RestoreProjectStyle>
17      <SolutionRootPath>src</SolutionRootPath>
18    </PropertyGroup>
19
20    <!-- Solution Packager overrides, un-comment to use: SolutionPackagerType (Managed, Unmanaged, Both)
21    <PropertyGroup>
22      <SolutionPackageType>Managed</SolutionPackageType>
23    </PropertyGroup>
24    -->
25
26    <ItemGroup>
27      <PackageReference Include="Microsoft.PowerApps.MSBuild.Solution" Version="1.*"/>
28    </ItemGroup>
29
30    <ItemGroup>
31      <ExcludeDirectories Include="$(MSBuildThisFileDirectory)\.gitignore"/>
32      <ExcludeDirectories Include="$(MSBuildThisFileDirectory)\bin\**"/>
33      <ExcludeDirectories Include="$(MSBuildThisFileDirectory)\obj\**"/>
34      <ExcludeDirectories Include="$(MSBuildThisFileDirectory)\*.cdsproj"/>
35      <ExcludeDirectories Include="$(MSBuildThisFileDirectory)\*.cdsproj.user"/>
36      <ExcludeDirectories Include="$(MSBuildThisFileDirectory)\*.sln"/>
37    </ItemGroup>
38
39    <ItemGroup>
40      <None Include="$(MSBuildThisFileDirectory)\**" Exclude="@(ExcludeDirectories)" />
41      <Content Include="$(SolutionPackageZipFilePath)">
42        <CopyToOutputDirectory>PreserveNewest</CopyToOutputDirectory>
43      </Content>
44    </ItemGroup>
45
46    <Import Project="$(MSBuildToolsPath)\Microsoft.Common.targets" />
47    <Import Project="$(PowerAppsTargetsPath)\Microsoft.PowerApps.VisualStudio.Solution.targets"
48      Condition="Exists('$(PowerAppsTargetsPath)\Microsoft.PowerApps.VisualStudio.Solution.targets')"/>
49
50  </Project>
```

Figure 8.3 – Solution project file

We don't need to take action on this file yet, but we will come back to this file again once we've added the PCF project reference.

> **Note**
> Currently, the Dataverse solution project references *.Net Framework 4.6.2.*

Now that you understand the structure of the project, let's learn how to add the code component to the project. Pick the *MyCharacterCounter* code component you built earlier in this book and copy the full path to the PCF project. For example, let's assume that the *MyCharacterCounter* project is at C:\MyCharacterCounterProject. Then, in VS Code, we will execute the following command in our terminal:

```
pac solution add-reference --path C:\MyCharacterCounterProject
```

Once you have executed this command, the output should say that the project reference was successfully added to the solution project, as follows:

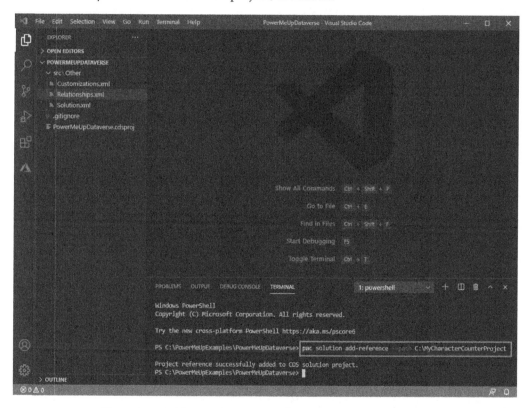

Figure 8.4 – Adding a PCF project reference to the solution project

Now, let's open the solution project file and review the changes that took place as we added the reference to PCF project. The following screenshot shows the solution project file once the reference was added to the PCF project:

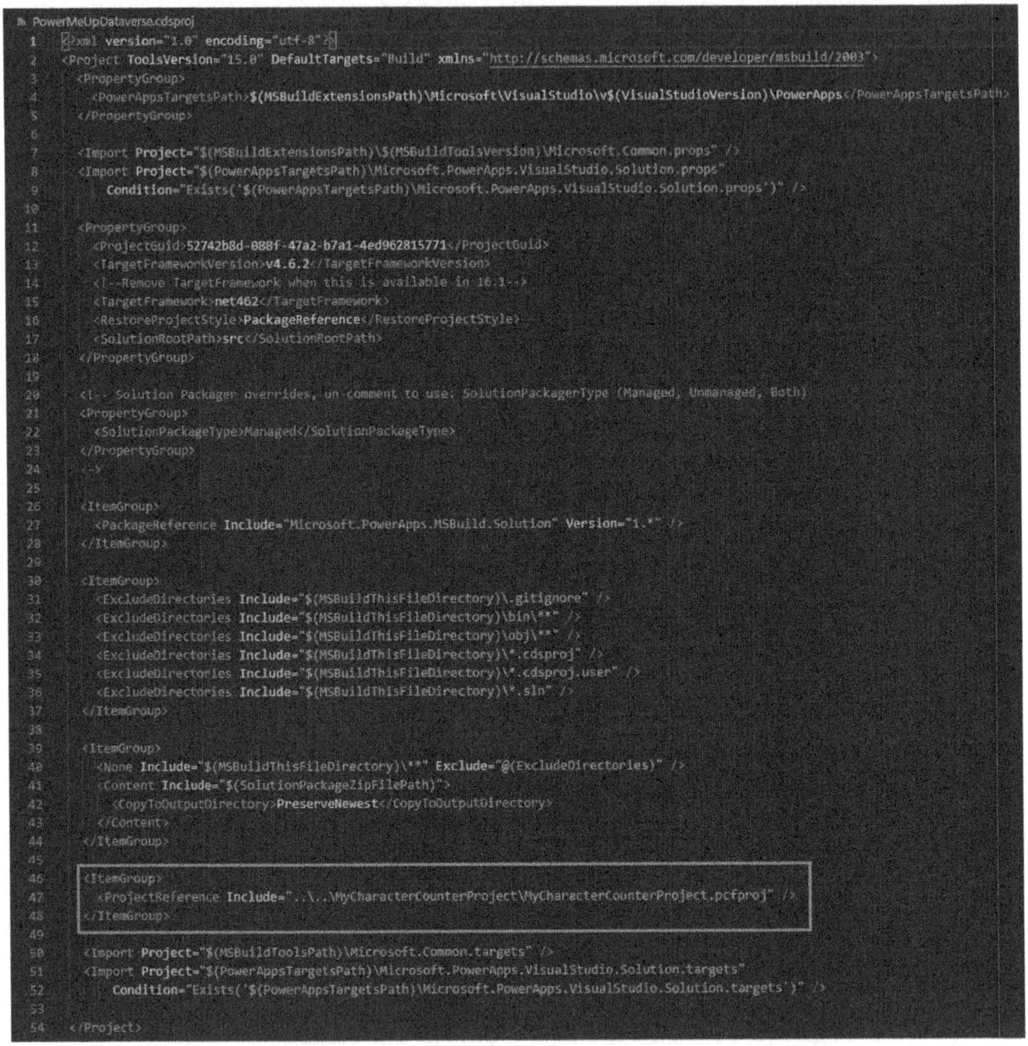

Figure 8.5 – The solution project file after adding a reference to the PCF project

As you can see, a new `ItemGroup` was added with a reference to the PCF project. No changes were made to any of the other files.

> **Note**
>
> Always make sure your solution name is unique and is not the same as any of the PCF project references you have added.

PCF Builder for **XrmToolBox** provides you with an easy user interface for creating the Dataverse solution project and adding the reference to the PCF project with a single button click.

Now that you have made sure everything is correct, we can start to understand the build process for the solution project.

Building a Dataverse project and obtaining the output

Before we understand the build process, you need to ensure that your local development machine is configured properly. If you plan on using VS Code for building the Dataverse project, then you need to confirm that the MSBUILD path has been registered on the system environment user variable. Usually, the MSBUILD executable file can be found under your latest Visual Studio folder. If you are unsure of where to find the MSBUILD executable file, then start **PCF Builder** for XrmToolBox and open the **Settings** window. You will be able to see **MS Build Path** on the settings window; copy this path. Perform the following steps to confirm or add the copied MSBUILD executable file path to your environment variable:

1. From your VS Code terminal, execute the following command. This will open **System Properties** window:

    ```
    SystemPropertiesAdvanced
    ```

2. Click on **Environment Variables**.

3. Under the **User variables** section, select and double-click on **Path** to open it.

4. Check if you can find any of the values pointing to MSBUILD.

5. If you have found a path to MSBUILD, then you can skip the rest of these steps; otherwise, continue in order to add the path to the environment variable.

6. Click the **New** button and paste the path that you copied earlier.

7. Click the **Ok** buttons on all the open windows.

This should set the MSBUILD path on the environment variables. You might want to restart your computer for these changes to take effect.

Now that **VS Code** is all set up to run our MSBUILD commands, we can continue to understand the process of building the solution project.

Understanding the default build process

First, you need to make sure you are in the project directory, which is where your .cdsproj file is located, before executing the build command. If you are continuing with our Dataverse solution project from earlier, then you should already be in the correct project directory in VS Code; that is, your PowerMeUpDataverse folder. Using your VS Code terminal, execute the following command:

```
msbuild /t:build /restore
```

When building the project for the first time, it is recommended that you run the preceding command with /restore switch. However, when you're rebuilding the solution project, you should use the following command:

```
msbuild /t:rebuild
```

The rebuild command makes sure that the project output is cleaned and built again, thereby producing a fresh output.

Once the solution project has been successfully built, you can find the solution file that was generated in the \bin\debug folder. It will have the filename equivalent of the Dataverse solution project's filename. This command will generate a solution file of the unmanaged type.

Next, we'll learn how to generate a solution file that is the managed or both type and the managed and unmanaged type at the same time.

Generating different types of solution packages

In order to generate a solution package of type managed, we will have to open the .cdsproj file in edit mode using VS Code and add the following section to the XML file:

PowerMeUpDataverse.cdsproj

```
<PropertyGroup>
    <SolutionPackageType>Managed</SolutionPackageType>
</PropertyGroup>
```

`SolutionPackageType` can contain one of the three distinct values: `Unmanaged`, `Managed` and `Both`. If this section does not exist, then, by **default**, the tool will generate an *unmanaged* type of solution file. When you provide `Both` as an option in the **SolutionPackageType**, then the tool will generate two files: one will be unmanaged, while the other will be managed. The managed file will be appended with `_managed` in the solution filename to distinguish it from the two type of files. The file generation occurs only when you execute the `msbuild` command with any of the attributes provided by the command.

Continuing our example, once you have edited the `PowerMeUpDataverse.cdsproj` file with **SolutionPackageType** as `Managed`, it will generate only the managed type solution file, where the filename is the same as that of the Dataverse solution's project file. The solution file these is generated in the `\bin\debug` folder and is always a *non-production* version. Next, we will look at how to generate a production version and its benefits.

Creating a production version

When you use the `msbuild` command to build the solution project that references a PCF project, the code component's bundled file that gets generated is not minified and contains source maps. This enables you to debug the code once it's been deployed on the host environment. However, the size of such a bundled file can become large when lots of dependencies are added to your code. Such code components are non-production versions. When you create production version code components, the tool generates a minified bundled file that reduces the size of the bundled file, as well as the overall solution file. Hence, it is recommended to create a production version code component for your *Test* and *Production* instances. Instead of using the `build` command we discussed earlier, use the following command:

```
msbuild /t:rebuild /p:configuration=Release
```

The /p:configuration=Release switch tells the tool to generate the solution file as a production version in the \bin\release folder. During this process, it will minify the code component bundled file, and the overall size of the solution file will be reduced. Let's test this using our PowerMeUpDataverse solution project. Using your VS Code terminal in your project, execute the preceding command with the release configuration. Now, head on over to the \bin\release folder and take note of the size of the solution file. To compare it against the non-production version, open the \bin\debug folder and take note of the size of the solution file. You will see that there's a difference of 1 KB, as shown in the following screenshot:

PowerMeUpDataverse › bin › Debug				
Name	Date modified	Type	Size	
PowerMeUpDataverse.zip		Compressed (zipp...	29 KB	
PowerMeUpDataverse_managed.zip		Compressed (zipp...	29 KB	
SolutionPackager.log		Text Document	3 KB	

PowerMeUpDataverse › bin › Release				
Name	Date modified	Type	Size	
PowerMeUpDataverse.zip		Compressed (zipp...	28 KB	
PowerMeUpDataverse_managed.zip		Compressed (zipp...	28 KB	
SolutionPackager.log		Text Document	3 KB	

Figure 8.6 – Solution file size comparison between the non production version and the production version

In this example, there isn't any drastic reduction in the size of the solution file. This is because the code component is not using too many dependencies, and it is a very simple code component with not too many lines of code. But when you create complex code components with many dependencies and import statements, your code component bundled file will become large, and when you use the production version, you will see a drastic improvement in the size of the solution file.

Let's also check if the code component's bundled file was minified. To do this, follow these steps:

1. Extract the contents of the `PowerMeUpDataverse.zip` file into the `\bin\release` folder.

2. Navigate to `PowerMeUpDataverse\Controls` and open the `pmu_PowerMeUp.MyCharacterCounter` folder, as shown in the following screenshot:

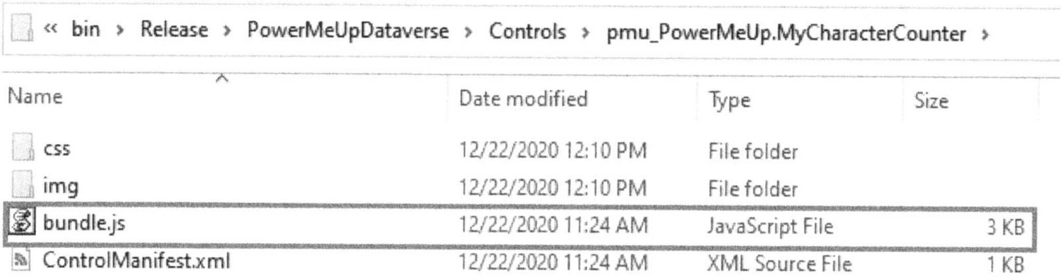

« bin › Release › PowerMeUpDataverse › Controls › pmu_PowerMeUp.MyCharacterCounter ›			
Name	**Date modified**	**Type**	**Size**
css	12/22/2020 12:10 PM	File folder	
img	12/22/2020 12:10 PM	File folder	
bundle.js	12/22/2020 11:24 AM	JavaScript File	3 KB
ControlManifest.xml	12/22/2020 11:24 AM	XML Source File	1 KB

Figure 8.7 – Navigating to the code component inside the solution file

3. Open the `bundle.js` file using Visual Studio Code. Observe that its contents has been minified.

You can also compare the `bundle.js` file's non-production version with its production version.

Now that you know how to build different solution projects, generate a production version, and how to obtain the solution file that can be deployed to any Dataverse environment, let's understand the process of adding multiple code components to a single solution file.

Adding multiple code components to a single Dataverse solution

Unlike the PCF project, which can contain only one component, the Dataverse solution project can contain references to multiple code components and different file paths. As we discussed at the beginning of this chapter, solutions are containers that can have multiple components – in this case, multiple code components. So, let's learn how to add multiple code components to our `PowerMeUpDataverse` solution project. We've already added the `MyCharacterCounter` code component to this project. Now, we are going to add the `MyDataCard` code component that we built during the course of this book. Consider `C:\MyDataCardProject` as the full path of this code component. Here, we will be executing the following command in VS Code, which is where the `PowerMeUpDataverse` solution project is open:

```
pac solution add-reference --path C:\MyDataCardProject
```

Once you've executed this command, the output should say that the project reference was successfully added to the solution project, like so:

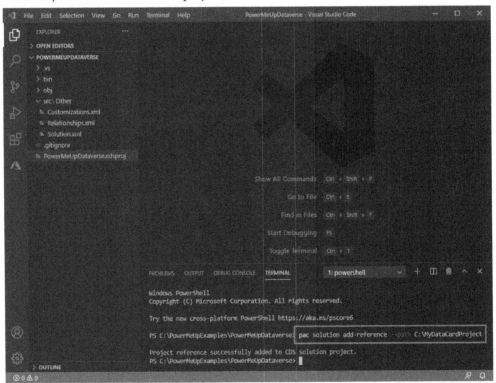

Figure 8.8 – Adding another PCF project reference to the Dataverse solution project

This action will change the solution project file. We can see these changes in the following screenshot:

```xml
PowerMeUpDataverse.cdsproj
1   <?xml version="1.0" encoding="utf-8"?>
2   <Project ToolsVersion="15.0" DefaultTargets="Build" xmlns="http://schemas.microsoft.com/developer/msbuild/2003">
3     <PropertyGroup>
4       <PowerAppsTargetsPath>$(MSBuildExtensionsPath)\Microsoft\VisualStudio\v$(VisualStudioVersion)\PowerApps</PowerAppsTargetsPath>
5     </PropertyGroup>
6
7     <Import Project="$(MSBuildExtensionsPath)\$(MSBuildToolsVersion)\Microsoft.Common.props" />
8     <Import Project="$(PowerAppsTargetsPath)\Microsoft.PowerApps.VisualStudio.Solution.props"
9       Condition="Exists('$(PowerAppsTargetsPath)\Microsoft.PowerApps.VisualStudio.Solution.props')" />
10
11    <PropertyGroup>
12      <ProjectGuid>52742b8d-088f-47a2-b7a1-4ed962815771</ProjectGuid>
13      <TargetFrameworkVersion>v4.6.2</TargetFrameworkVersion>
14      <!--Remove TargetFramework when this is available in 16.1 -->
15      <TargetFramework>net462</TargetFramework>
16      <RestoreProjectStyle>PackageReference</RestoreProjectStyle>
17      <SolutionRootPath>src</SolutionRootPath>
18    </PropertyGroup>
19
20    <!-- Solution Packager overrides, un-comment to use: SolutionPackagerType (Managed, Unmanaged, Both)
21    <PropertyGroup>
22      <SolutionPackageType>Managed</SolutionPackageType>
23    </PropertyGroup>
24    >
25    <PropertyGroup>
26      <SolutionPackageType>Both</SolutionPackageType>
27    </PropertyGroup>
28
29    <ItemGroup>
30      <PackageReference Include="Microsoft.PowerApps.MSBuild.Solution" Version="1.*" />
31    </ItemGroup>
32
33    <ItemGroup>
34      <ExcludeDirectories Include="$(MSBuildThisFileDirectory)\.gitignore" />
35      <ExcludeDirectories Include="$(MSBuildThisFileDirectory)\bin\**" />
36      <ExcludeDirectories Include="$(MSBuildThisFileDirectory)\obj\**" />
37      <ExcludeDirectories Include="$(MSBuildThisFileDirectory)\*.cdsproj" />
38      <ExcludeDirectories Include="$(MSBuildThisFileDirectory)\*.cdsproj.user" />
39      <ExcludeDirectories Include="$(MSBuildThisFileDirectory)\*.sln" />
40    </ItemGroup>
41
42    <ItemGroup>
43      <None Include="$(MSBuildThisFileDirectory)\**" Exclude="@(ExcludeDirectories)" />
44      <Content Include="$(SolutionPackageZipFilePath)">
45        <CopyToOutputDirectory>PreserveNewest</CopyToOutputDirectory>
46      </Content>
47    </ItemGroup>
48
49    <ItemGroup>
50      <ProjectReference Include="..\..\MyCharacterCounterProject\MyCharacterCounterProject.pcfproj" />
51      <ProjectReference Include="..\..\MyDataCardProject\MyDataCardProject.pcfproj" />
52    </ItemGroup>
53
54    <Import Project="$(MSBuildToolsPath)\Microsoft.Common.targets" />
55    <Import Project="$(PowerAppsTargetsPath)\Microsoft.PowerApps.VisualStudio.Solution.targets"
56      Condition="Exists('$(PowerAppsTargetsPath)\Microsoft.PowerApps.VisualStudio.Solution.targets')" />
57
58  </Project>
```

Figure 8.9 – The solution project file after adding a second reference to the PCF project

As you can see, a new **ProjectReference** tag was added, along with a reference to the *MyDataCard* PCF project. Similarly, you can add more PCF projects to this solution project. Once you are done adding references to your PCF projects, you can build the solution project, which will generate the solution ZIP file. This can be imported into any Dataverse environment, and it will have multiple code components listed in it.

> **Insights**
>
> You can import the solution ZIP file created from this process to your preferred Dataverse environment as the code components within this solution file will be used in the next chapter.

Next, we will look into the process of using an existing solution project to add more code components to it.

Deploying new code components to an existing solution

What if you already have a solution created in your Dataverse environment and you want to add the new code components to an existing Dataverse solution. There are couple of ways you can achieve that; either using Power Apps CLI or using PCF Builder for XrmToolBox.

Let us first understand the process of using an existing solution to add a new code component using Power Apps CLI.

Using the solution clone command of the Power Apps CLI

The Power Apps CLI provides us with a command that enables us to create a Dataverse solution project from an existing solution in the Dataverse environment. To create the solution project, the tool needs to connect to your Dataverse environment, which is why it uses the authentication profile for the same.

Before you start creating a solution project from an existing solution, you need to make sure you are connected to a proper Dataverse environment. Execute the following command that we learned about in *Chapter 7, Authentication Profiles*, which will identify the currently selected profile:

```
pac org who
```

If the currently selected Dataverse environment is not correct, then make sure to switch profiles or create a new one, as we learned in *Chapter 7, Authentication Profiles*. We will be using two dummy PCF projects, both of which are available in the example library, called `CLIDummyOneProject` and `CLIDummyTwoProject`. Once you have connected to your desired Dataverse environment, follow these steps:

1. Create a dummy solution in your Dataverse environment. Name it `DummyCLISolution` with whatever publisher you prefer.

2. Optionally, you can add a few components inside `DummyCLISolution` using the Power Apps maker portal.

3. In VS Code, open the folder where you want the solution project to reside.

4. Execute the following command in VS Code to clone your solution project:

   ```
   pac solution clone --name DummyCLISolution
   ```

   This will create a new directory that will contain your solution project, along with any existing components from the Dataverse solution.

5. Execute the following command to navigate inside this new directory:

   ```
   cd DummyCLISolution
   ```

6. Copy the path of the `CLIDummyOneProject` PCF project.

7. Add the `CLIDummyOne` code component to this solution project by executing the following command, which will add a reference to the PCF project:

   ```
   pac solution add-reference --path "C:\PowerMeUpExamples\
   CLIDummyOneProject"
   ```

8. Also, add the `CLIDummyTwo` code component to this solution project. Copy the path of the `CLIDummyTwoProject` PCF project and execute the following command:

   ```
   pac solution add-reference --path "C:\PowerMeUpExamples\
   CLIDummyTwoProject"
   ```

9. Make sure `CLIDummyOneProject` and `CLIDummyTwoProject` have been built successfully. You might want to run `npm install` to fix any missing references and rebuild these projects.

10. Build the solution project using the following command:

    ```
    msbuild /t:build /restore
    ```

At this point, you should have a solution ZIP file that contains all the existing components, along with two new additional code components that can be imported into the Dataverse environment.

A similar result can also be achieved but with less effort by using PCF Builder for XrmToolBox.

Using PCF Builder to add new components to an existing solution

PCF Builder for XrmToolBox makes it easy to add a new code component to an existing solution. This enables us to package all our code components in a single solution, which can be easier for sharing, distributing, or even deploying to different environments using the ALM process. We will be using a dummy control that's available in the example library named MyDummyControlOneProject and the MyDummyControlTwoProject PCF project. The following steps showcase the process of bundling all the code components into an existing solution:

1. Start by creating a dummy solution in your Dataverse environment. Let's name it Dummy Existing Solution.

2. Open PCF Builder in XrmToolBox and connect to your Dataverse environment.

3. Populate the location of the MyDummyControlOneProject PCF project in **Control Location** and click on **Reload Details**.

4. Click on **Open in VS Code**, and open VS Code's integrated terminal using *Ctrl + T*.

5. Run the following command in the integrated terminal of VS Code:

   ```
   npm install
   ```

6. Close and return to **PCF Builder** in XrmToolBox.

7. Inside the **CDS Solution Details** section, click on the **Use Existing Solution** checkbox. This should load all the solutions from your Dataverse environment.

8. Find Dummy Existing Solution from the **Solution Name** drop-down. **Publisher Name**, **Publisher Prefix**, and **Version** will be auto-populated.

9. Click on the **Export and Add Control** button. This command will export the solution file from your Dataverse environment to your local machine.

10. Click the **Build** button to build the project and generate the solution ZIP file, which can be deployed to your Dataverse environment. Wait until you see that the build is successful.

11. At this point, if you want to deploy this solution to your Dataverse environment, you can click the **Deploy** button.

To confirm if this process was a success, you can navigate to your solution in your Dataverse environment and check if the code component exists in this solution. Now, repeat these steps but for the `MyDummyControlTwoProject` PCF project. Once you have successfully built the Dataverse solution project for the `MyDummyControlTwoProject` PCF project, you should see the following output:

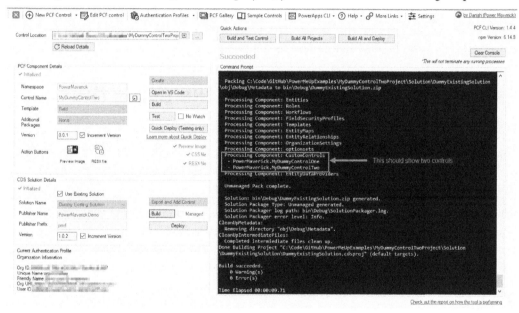

Figure 8.10 – Two components contained in a single solution file

Observe that both the `MyDummyControlOne` and `MyDummyControlTwo` controls exist in a single solution file. Once you've deployed this solution to your Dataverse environment, you will see two code components in it, as shown in the following screenshot:

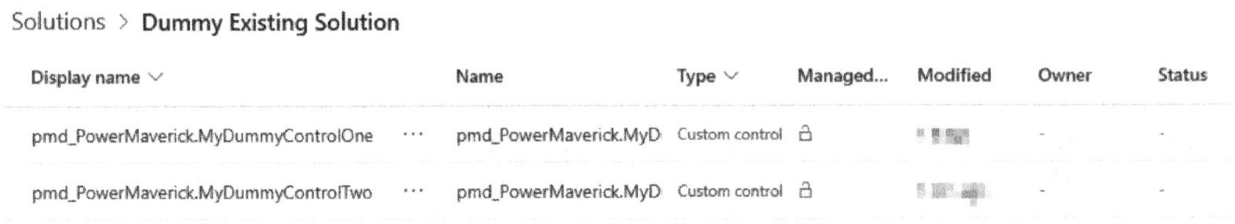

Solutions > **Dummy Existing Solution**

Display name ∨		Name	Type ∨	Managed...	Modified	Owner	Status
pmd_PowerMaverick.MyDummyControlOne	···	pmd_PowerMaverick.MyD	Custom control	🔒		-	-
pmd_PowerMaverick.MyDummyControlTwo	···	pmd_PowerMaverick.MyD	Custom control	🔒		-	-

Figure 8.11 – The existing solution in our Dataverse environment with two imported solutions

As you can see, we can reuse an existing Dataverse solution to add all our newly built code components, which can ease the deployment process. Next, we'll learn about a few more Power Apps CLI commands that pertain to solutions.

Exporting the solution's ZIP file using the Power Apps CLI commands

The Power Apps CLI provides us with an additional command that will export a solution ZIP file from a Dataverse environment. This command is a step forward for the ALM story.

When exporting a solution from a Dataverse environment, you need the ability to specify how the solution should be exported. Hence, the command `pac solution export` provides different attributes that help you get the solution export you desire. The following are the attributes that are provided by the Power Apps CLI for exporting the solution:

Attribute	Required?	Description
path	Yes	Path and name of the file where solution zip file will reside.
name	Yes	Name of the solution in the Dataverse environment.
managed	No	Specifies whether the file should be exported as managed.
targetversion	No	Specifies the version of the file that will be exported.
include	No	Settings that should be included with the exported file. Valid values are: autonumbering, calendar, customization, emailtracking, externalapplications, general, isvconfig, marketing, outlooksynchronization, relationshiproles, sales
async	No	If true then exports the solution file asynchronously.
max-async-wait-time	No	Specifies the maximum wait time until erroring out when exporting the solution file asyncronolusly. If this attribute is not specified then the default value is 60 minutes.

Figure 8.12 – Attributes of the solution export command

So, assuming we want to export the DummyCLISolution solution from a Dataverse environment, we need to follow these steps:

1. Identify a folder where you want to export the solution ZIP file and open that folder in VS Code.

2. Using your VS Code terminal, execute the following command:

```
pac solution export --path DummyCLIExport.zip --name
DummyCLISolution
```

Here, we have specified the path as DummyCLIExport.zip, which indicates the tool that will be used to export the solution ZIP file. This will be done at the location where the command is executed. DummyCLIExport will be used as the name of the exported solution ZIP file. We also specified DummyCLISolution, which is the name of the solution in the Dataverse environment.

This process should provide you with a file named DummyCLIExport.zip, which will contain all the components that exist in the DummyCLISolution solution in your Dataverse environment.

Understanding the complete development cycle

So far, we have learned about few ways a code component can be deployed to a Dataverse environment. But the biggest question is, which strategy should we use and when? Thanks to **Scott Durow**, who helped me with the following flow chart that explains the complete development and deployment process that's involved when you're building a code component:

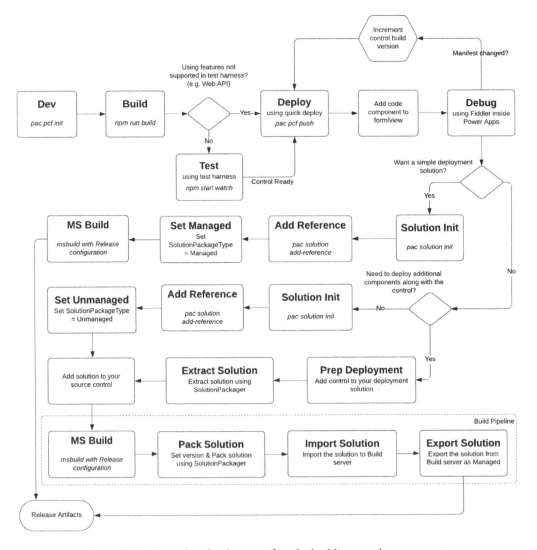

Figure 8.13 – Complete development flow for building a code component

As you can see, we have used different deployment strategies throughout this process. We also used Solution Packager to extract and pack the solution that allows incremental *pack and unpack functionality*, which can be used during the automated build and release pipelines providing full application life cycle management for your Power Platform.

> **Remember**
>
> Whenever you change the control manifest file, you will have to increment the versions in the `manifest` file of the PCF project, as well as `solution.xml` file of the Dataverse solution project, before you can build the projects.

It is recommended to always keep non-production versions in your development environment so that you can continue to test your code component. However, rest of the non-development environments should have a production version of your code component. Sometimes, if your code component is too large to be imported into your development environment, then you will have to import a production version containing minified code into your development environment.

> **Note**
>
> The flow chart provided in this section is just a recommendation to help you make a better and more informed decision.

Summary

In this chapter, we learned about the basics of a solution project, learned how to create a solution project, and added a reference to a PCF project. Later, we learned how to build the project and obtain some output. We also learned how to generate different solution types, how to create a solution file that can be deployed to production, and how to add multiple code components to a single solution project. Lastly, we looked at the process of adding new code components to an existing solution, which can help in simplifying the deployment process, before learning how to export a solution using the Power Apps CLI. This chapter should have helped you learn how to generate solution files and package code components that can be distributed and deployed to any Dataverse environment.

In the next chapter, we will do a deep dive into some of the features that are provided by the Power Apps Component Framework that can help us create more complex code components.

Test your knowledge

1. What command cleans and builds the solution project? (*100 points*)

    a. `msbuild /t:build /restore`

    b. `msbuild /t:rebuild`

2. Which project can contain references to multiple code components? (*100 points*)

    a. Dataverse solution project

    b. PCF project

3. Select the correct sentence. (*200 points*)

    a. We can easily debug a code component that has been packaged using its production version.

    b. Solution files that are deployed using the `pac pcf push` command will have a solution name prefixed with `PowerAppsTools_`.

Further reading

- Additional information on packaging a code component can be found in Microsoft's documentation at `http://bit.ly/ImportPCF`.

- Additional information on the `pac` commands for your solution can be found in Microsoft's documentation at `http://bit.ly/PacSolution`.

- An overview of Power Apps Solutions can be found in Microsoft's documentation at `http://bit.ly/PowerAppsSolutions`.

- Additional information about the difference between managed and unmanaged solutions can be found in Microsoft's documentation at `http://bit.ly/SolutionManagedUnmanaged`.

- More information about the SolutionPackager can be found in Microsoft's documentation at `http://bit.ly/SolutionPackager`.

9
Configuring Code Components in Power Apps

In the previous chapters, we learned how to create a deployable bundle using the Dataverse solution project. In this chapter, we will learn how to configure both field and dataset code components on model-driven as well as canvas apps. By the end of this chapter, you will be able to configure any code components on both model-driven and canvas apps.

In this chapter, we are going to cover the following main topics:

- Adding a field type code component to a model-driven app
- Configuring a dataset type code component in a model-driven app
- Adding a code component to a canvas app

Let's get started!

Technical requirements

To work through this chapter, you will need to install the *MyCharacterCounter* and *MyDataCard* code components in your Dataverse environment. These code components were created in *Chapter 5, Code, Test, and Repeat*, and can be found in this book's example library at `https://github.com/PacktPublishing/Extending-Microsoft-Power-Apps-with-Power-Apps-Component-Framework/tree/master/Chapter05`. For details on how to download the example library, please read the process mentioned in *Chapter 1, Introduction to the Power Apps Component Framework*.

Adding a field type code component to a model-driven app

When a code component of the field type is deployed to a Dataverse environment, you can add it to your preferred form in a model-driven app. This transforms a regular field that traditionally contains text into a visualization provided by your code component.

We will be using the *MyCharacterCounter* code component that we built in *Chapter 5, Code, Test, and Repeat*, and will configure it on a form. First, you need to deploy this code component in your Dataverse environment; the deployment process was discussed in the *Adding multiple code components in a single Dataverse solution* section in the previous chapter. Now, using the following steps, we will change a default label and multi-line text box field into a character counter code component on the *Contact* entity.

At the time of writing this book, we are unable to use Power Apps Maker portal to add code components to a form. Due to this, we will be using a traditional interface instead. Let's get started:

1. Navigate to **Settings** > **Customization**. Click **Customize the System**. Optionally, you can open an existing solution that contains the **Contact** entity.

2. Expand **Entities** and expand the entity that you want; in this case, the **Contact** entity.

3. Select **Forms**, and then open a form such as the *Main* form.

4. In the form editor, double-click the field where you want to add a code component; in this case, the **Description** field. You can use any other field you like.

5. On the **Field Properties** page, select the **Controls** tab, and then select **Add Control**.

6. On the **Add Control** page, select the component that you want – in this case, the **Power Up Character Counter** component – and select **Add**. This can be seen in the following screenshot:

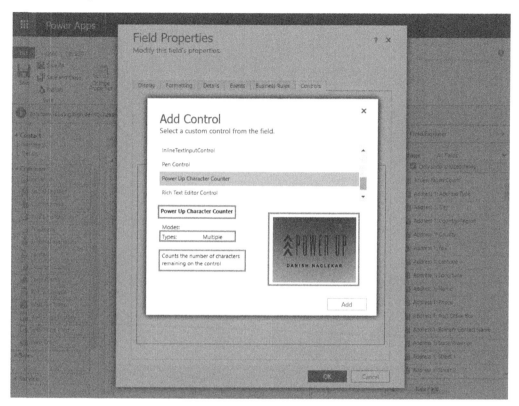

Figure 9.1 – Control details and previewing the Add Control page of a field

7. Choose the client where you want the component to appear. There are three options: **Web**, **Phone**, or **Tablet**. We will discuss the difference between each of them later in this section. For now, select all these options.

8. Select the *pencil* icon next to the properties to configure the code component. In this case, edit **Character Limit** to set a static value or bind it to an existing field. Let's set a static value of **100** and click on **OK**.

9. Optionally, you can check **Hide Default Control**, which will hide the component so that neither the component nor the data is displayed in any of the clients that do not support the code component. This can be seen in the following screenshot:

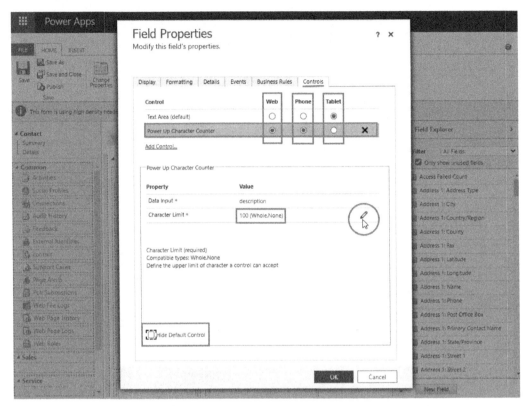

Figure 9.2 – Configuring the control on the Field Properties page

10. Select **OK** to close the **Field Properties** page.

11. Activate customization on the entity form by selecting **Save** and clicking on **Publish**. Close the form editor when publishing is complete.

Similar steps can be performed on any field on any form. Now, go to the **Contact** entity form where you configured your control and check if it renders properly and works correctly.

During *step 7*, we saw three different options presented by the application: **Web**, **Phone**, and **Tablet**. You need to select **Web** when you want your code component to render on a web browser. When you want your code component to render on *Dynamics 365 for phones* or *Power Apps*, you will need to select the **Phone** option. In order to enable the code component on tablet device that are running *Dynamics 365 for tablets*, you will need to select the **Tablet** option next to the component.

This should help you configure any code component for a field on a model-driven app. Next, we'll learn how to configure a dataset code component on a table in a model-driven app.

Configuring a dataset code component in a model-driven app

A dataset code component can be configured on various visualizations, such as a view, sub-grid, or a dashboard. Each of them has a different configuration process. First, we will look how to add a code component to a specific view of a table.

Adding a code component to a specific view of a table

A table can contain multiple views, and the application provides us with a way to set different visualizations using code components on different views of a table. This enhances the usability of the application. For example, you can have a calendar control on one view and a card control on another view for the same table.

The following steps will change the visualization of the **My Active Contact** view on the **Contact** table to a card view using the *MyDataCard* code component, which is of the dataset type, that we created in *Chapter 5, Code, Test, and Repeat*:

1. Navigate to **Settings** > **Customization**. Click **Customize the System**. Optionally, you can open an existing solution that contains the **Contact** entity.

2. Expand **Entities** and expand the entity that you want; in this case, the **Contact** entity.

3. Expand **Views** and select the view that you want to configure the code component on; in this case **My Active Contact**.

4. From the menu, select, **More Actions** > **Edit**. This will pop up a new window with the selected view.

5. Under the **Common Tasks** section, click on **Custom Controls**. A custom control properties window will appear. Then, click on **Add Control**. This can be seen in the following screenshot:

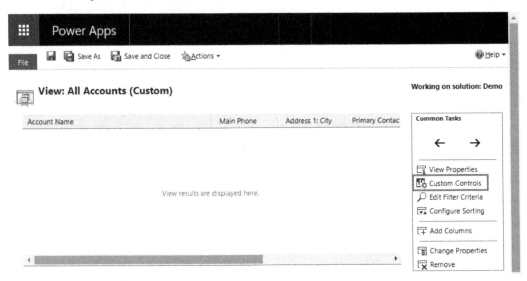

Figure 9.3 – View editor page for adding a custom control to a specific view

6. On the **Add Control** page, select the component that you want – in this case, the **Power Up Data Card** component – and then select **Add**.

7. Choose the client where you want the component to appear. In this case, you can select all the available options.

8. If the code component needs more configurations, then select the *pencil* icon next to the fields that are available to configure them; otherwise, click on **OK**:

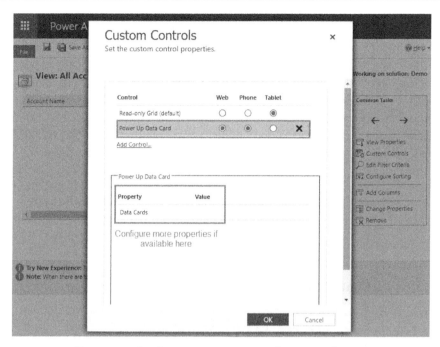

Figure 9.4 – Configuring a custom control on a specific view

9. Activate the customization by clicking **Save and Close**, followed by clicking the
    Publish button on the entity.

Similar steps can be performed on any view with different code components. Now, go
to a model-driven app and navigate to the **My Active Contacts** view on a **Contact** table.
Check that the view is rendered with the code component. If you navigate to a different
view on a *Contact* table, you will not see the data card visualization.

Now, let's learn how to add a code component that will set up a custom visualization on all
the views of the home page for a table.

Adding a code component to a table

Sometimes, you may want to set a custom visualization on all your views. It would take lot of repetition to configure all the views using the previously discussed method to configure the code component on a specific view. There is an easy way to set the code component on a table that will render all the views with the visualizations provided by the configured code component. If no code component is configured on the table, then it will show the default visualization. In this section, we will be configuring the *Power Up Data Card* code component, which we created in *Chapter 5, Code, Test, and Repeat*. The following steps describe this process:

1. Navigate to **Settings** > **Customizations** and click on **Customize the System**. Optionally, you can open an existing solution that contains the **Contact** table.

2. Expand **Entities** and choose the entity to which you want to add the code component; in this case, the **Contact** table.

3. Click on the **Controls** tab and click on **Add a control**.

4. On this page, select the component that you want – in this case, the **Power Up Data Card** component – and select **Add**:

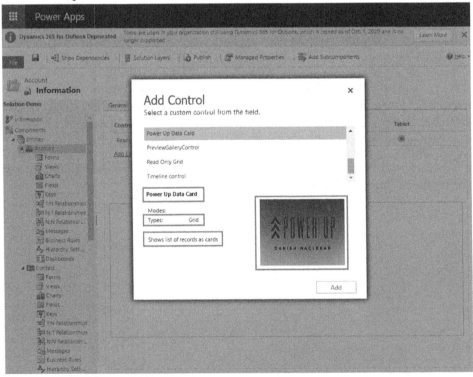

Figure 9.5 – Dataset control preview on the Add Control page of a table

5. Choose the client where you want the component to appear. In this case, you can select all the available options.

6. If the code component needs more configurations, then select the *pencil* icon next to the fields available for configuration.

7. Activate the customization process by clicking **Save**, followed by clicking **Publish**.

The final configuration page should look as follows:

Figure 9.6 – Dataset configuration settings of a table

Similar steps can be performed on any entity. Now, go to the home page of the *Contact* entity and check if the view is being rendered with the code component. Remember that this will set all the available views to render with the configured code component.

Next, we'll learn how to add a code component to a sub-grid. This will set the custom visualization on a form where the sub-grid is displayed.

Adding a code component to a sub-grid

A sub-grid in a model-driven app is an out-of-the-box visualization where data is presented in a tabular format. This visualization is added to the form of a table that displays data from a related table. For example, if we want to show all the related contacts of an account, then we need to add a Contacts sub-grid that displays all related contacts on an account form. The application allows us to add a custom visualization for these sub grids using code components, thus enhancing the user interface.

We will be using the *Power Up Data Card* code component we created in *Chapter 5, Code, Test, and Repeat*, to display contact cards on an account form. The following steps define this process:

1. Navigate to **Settings** > **Customizations** and click on **Customize the System**. Optionally, you can open an existing solution that contains the **Account** and **Contact** tables.

2. Expand **Entities** and choose the entity where the sub-grid exists on a form – in this case, the **Account** table.

3. Select **Forms** and open a form, such as the **Main** form.

4. In the form editor, double-click the sub-grid where you want to add a code component; in this case, **Contact** sub-grid.

5. On the **List or Chart Properties** page, select the **Controls** tab, and then select **Add Control**.

6. On the **Add Control** page, select the component that you want – in this case, the **Power Up Data Card** component – and select **Add**, as shown in the following screenshot:

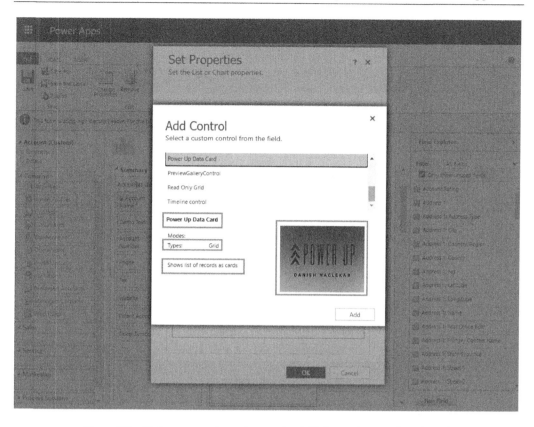

Figure 9.7 – Dataset control preview on the Add Control page of a sub-grid

7. Choose the client where you want the component to appear. In this case, you can select all the available options.

8. If the code component needs more configuration, then select the *pencil* icon next to the fields that are available for configuration:

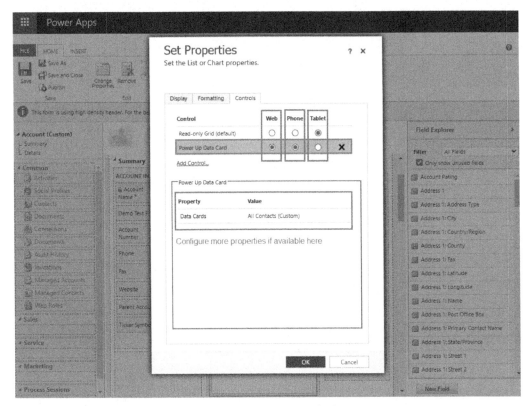

Figure 9.8 – Configure dataset control on the list properties page

9. Select **OK** to close the **Set Properties** page.

10. To activate customization on the entity form, select **Save**, and then select **Publish**.

11. Close the form editor.

To confirm if the configuration is correct, go to the **Account** form where you configured the sub-grid and validate that the sub-grid has been rendered with the visualizations from the code component. In this case, no matter which view you select, the sub-grid will always show the visualization from the code component.

Code components of the dataset type can also be configured on a dashboard. Let's learn how to configure a code component on a dashboard in a model-driven app.

Configuring a code component on a dashboard

Dashboards provide different visuals that is a combination of various data that is important to a user. A dashboard contains a combination of view, chat, and web resources and an iframe to a website using a URL. Since dashboards can contain views, these views can be displayed with different visualizations using code components.

We will be using the *Power Up Data Card* code component we created in *Chapter 5, Code, Test, and Repeat*, to display contact cards on an account form. The following steps define this process:

1. Navigate to **Settings** > **Customizations** and click on **Customize the System**.
2. Click on **New** > **Dashboard** to create a new dashboard. Optionally, you can use any of the existing dashboards that have list components. If you're using an existing dashboard, then go to *step 5*.

3. Select any layout; for instance, **3-column focused dashboard**. Then, click **Create**.

4. Provide a name for your dashboard, such as PCF Dashboard.

5. In the first block, add a list component for the **Contact** table with the **My Active** *Contacts* view; in the rest of the blocks, you can add any component. The following screenshot shows an example of a dashboard being configured:

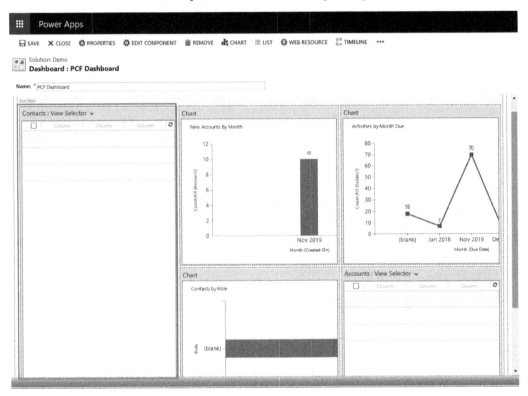

Figure 9.9 – Example of the dashboard getting set up

6. Now, select the first block where you added a list component for the **Contact** table with the *My Active Contacts* view. From the menu, click on **Edit Component**, followed by the **Controls** tab. Then, select **Add Control**.

7. On the **Add Control** page, select the component that you want – in this case, the **Power Up Data Card** component – and select **Add**.

8. Choose the client where you want the component to appear. In this case, you can select all the available options.

9. If the code component needs more configuration, then select the *pencil* icon next to the fields that can be configured:

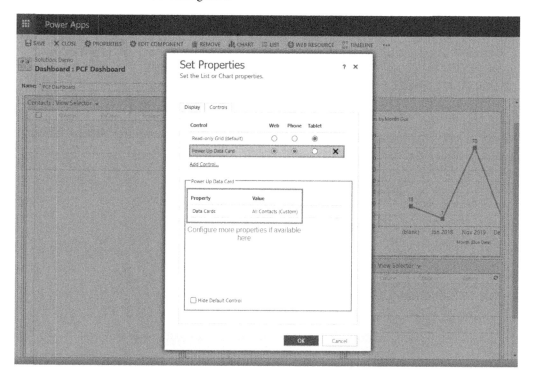

Figure 9.10 – Dashboard view being set up with a code component

10. Select **OK** to close the **Properties** page.

11. Once you've finished configuring the dashboard, click **Save** and **Close**.

12. To activate customization on the dashboard, select the dashboard and click **Publish**.

Let's go to our dashboards and select the dashboard where we made our configurations; in this case, **PCF Dashboard**. Check if the first block is now rendered with the visualization from the code component, as shown in the following screenshot:

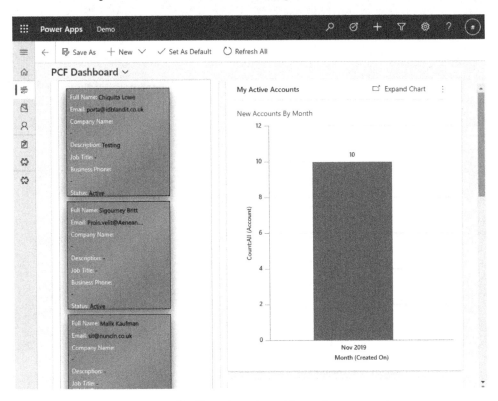

Figure 9.11 – Dashboard preview with a code component

Now that we've learned how to configure a dataset on different components in a model-driven app by providing enhanced visualizations, let's learn how to configure code components in canvas apps.

Adding a code component to a canvas app

There are multiple types of components available in canvas apps, and one of the types is code components. In model-driven apps, code components need to be bound to a field or a dataset, which can either be a view or a sub-grid. But in canvas apps, code components do not need any bindings. Hence, they work differently than the code components we configured in our model-driven app. When you're building code components, always keep in mind which app they will support. If you decide that your code component will support both type of apps, then you must make sure that they will work on both apps.

Before you can start adding code components to canvas apps, you need to make sure you enable the feature on an environment that allows you to add code components to canvas apps. This feature can only be enabled by the administrators for a specific environment. The following steps describe how to enable this feature:

1. Log into the Power Apps admin center using the following URL: `https://admin.powerplatform.com`.

2. Select the environment where you want to enable this feature.

3. Click the **Settings** option on the top ribbon.

4. Expand **Product** and click on **Features**.

5. From the list of available features, set the switch for **On** under **Power Apps component framework for canvas apps** and click **Save**. This is shown in the following screenshot:

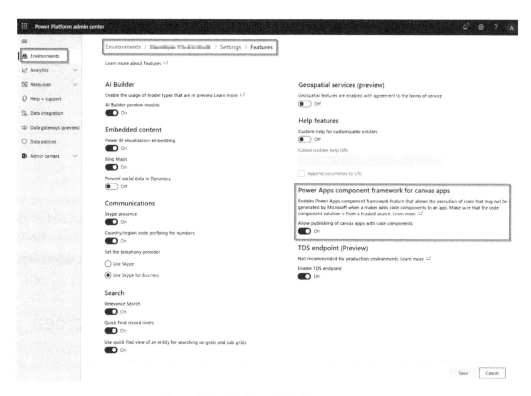

Figure 9.12 – Enabling PCF for canvas apps

After enabling this feature, if you open any canvas app in the Maker portal for editing and click on **Insert** > **Custom** > **Import component**, you should be able to see an additional tab called **Code**. This will contain all the code components that are available to you, as shown in the following screenshot:

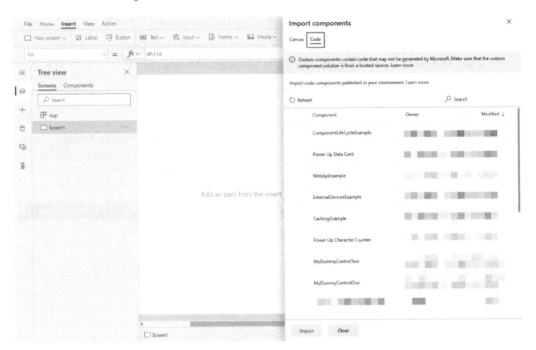

Figure 9.13 – A tab named Code when importing a component from the Custom menu option

On the **Code** tab, you should see all the code components that have been installed in that environment. For this section, make sure the *MyCharacterCounter* and *MyDataCard* PCF controls have been imported into the environment where you will be creating your canvas app.

Now, let's learn how to add and configure a code component on a screen in a canvas app.

Configuring a field type code component on a screen

Canvas apps contain multiple screens, and you can add a code component to a specific screen by performing the following steps:

1. Navigate to the Power Apps Maker portal at `https://make.powerapps.com`.

2. Select the appropriate **Environment**.

3. Create a new canvas app or edit an existing app that you want to add a code component to.

4. On the canvas app designer, select the screen that you want to add the code component to.

5. Go to **Insert** > **Custom** > **Import component** and select the **Code** tab.

6. Select a component from the list – in this case, the **Power Up Character Counter** component – and click **Import**.

7. Now, from the left menu pane, select the insert button, indicated by the + symbol, and expand the **Code components** section. Select the **Power Up Character Counter** code component to add it to the selected screen, as shown in the following screenshot:

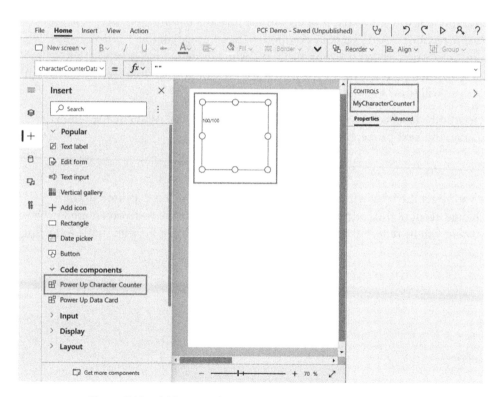

Figure 9.14 – Adding a code component to a screen in canvas apps

8. Configure the code component by selecting the **Advanced** tab from the property pane on the right.

9. Under the **DATA** section, you can find few properties that may need configuring. In this case, set **characterCounterLimit** to 100.

Now, when you preview the app using the play button on the top ribbon, you will see that the code component is rendered with a text box and a label displaying the remaining characters. If you enter some text in the text box, the label will show the number of characters left from the maximum allowed characters. But since this component is not bound, changing the text has no effect on anything, and any text that's typed into the text box will be lost. To capture the text that is the data output of the code component, we need to implement the **OnChange** event, which is provided by the app. So, for this example, we will capture the text from the code component in a variable. Enter the following formula into the **OnChange** event of the code component you added. This should be called `MyCharacterCounter1`:

```
Set(Desc, MyCharacterCounter1.characterCounterDataInput);
```

If a code component is being used on a property defined as bound, then the code component will show that property in the formula bar. In this case, the `MyCharacterCounter` code component has a usage on the `characterCounterDataInput` property, which is defined as bound. That is the reason why when you type in the name of the code component, followed by a dot symbol, IntelliSense will show you the name of the property.

Now, let's add a label component to the same canvas app and populate the following formula on the **Text** property of that label:

```
Desc
```

Once you've set the label with the value of the variable that was captured in the **OnChange** event of the code component, you will see that the text you entered in the code component will be reflected on this label as you type. This can be seen in the following screenshot:

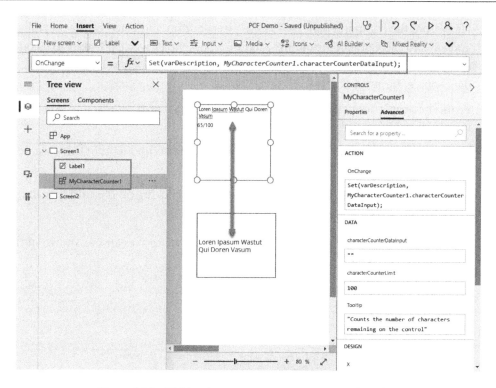

Figure 9.15 – Field code component on canvas apps in action

Now that you've learned how to configure a field type code component on a screen, let's learn how to configure a dataset type code component on a screen.

Configuring a dataset type code component on a screen

As the name suggests, dataset code components are reliant on a dataset. Unlike field code components, dataset code components need to be bound to a list of items. Hence, when you add a dataset code component, the app recognizes it and automatically provides you with an option to select your data source. The following steps will help you configure the code component for a dataset:

1. In the canvas app designer, select the screen where you want to add the code component.

2. Go to **Insert** > **Custom** > **Import component** and select the **Code** tab.

3. Select a component from the list – in this case, the Power Up Data Card component – and click **Import**.

4. Now, from the left menu pane, select the insert button, indicated by the + symbol, and expand the **Code components** section. Select the **Power Up Data Card** code component to add it on the selected screen. The app will suggest that you select your data source; for now, skip this part.

5. From the properties pane on the right, click on **Data Cards(Items)** and select the Contacts table.

6. Now, select the view you want to render on this code component. In this case, select **My Active Contacts**.

7. Optionally, you can also choose your own fields by clicking on the **Edit** link in front of **Fields**.

This should render the **Data Cards** code component in your canvas app, as shown in the following screenshot:

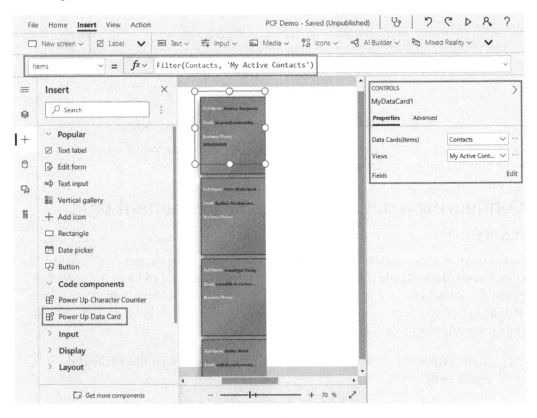

Figure 9.16 – Adding a dataset code component to a canvas app

As with all the properties in canvas apps, **Items** can contain a formula that produces a table. So, let's try to change the **Items** property with the following formula:

```
FirstN(
    Filter(
        Contacts,
        'Contacts (Views)'.'My Active Contacts'
    ),
    10
)
```

This formula will only show the top 10 records. As you can see, once you add this formula, the list will change and only display the top 10 records from the contact table. Similar to the field code component, the dataset code component also has an **OnChange** event, but it also has an additional event called **OnSelect**. This is triggered when one of the items from the dataset is selected.

Now that we know how to configure code components on a screen in a canvas app, let's learn how to configure a code component in a gallery component.

Adding a code component to a gallery component

A gallery component in a canvas app is the most versatile component that can contain other components as child components. In this section, we are going to learn how to utilize both the field and dataset code components in a gallery. Follow these steps to add the character counter and data card code components to a single gallery component:

1. On the canvas app designer, add a new screen where you want to configure the gallery with a code component.

2. Add a gallery component and populate **Data source** with the **Contacts** table and **Views** with **My Active Contact**.

3. Change **Template Size** to 220.

4. Click the *pencil* icon on the gallery to enter edit mode for the gallery.

5. Now, from the left menu pane, select the insert button, indicated by the + symbol, and expand the **Code components** section. Select the **Power Up Character Counter** and **Power Up Data Card** code components to add them to the selected gallery.

6. Drag and place the **Power Up Character Counter** code component below the subtitle.

7. Drag and place **Power Up Data Card** next to the title and subtitle. Select **Accounts** as a data source.

8. The placements should look similar to the following:

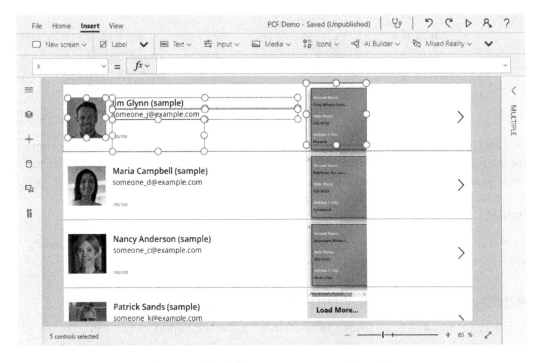

Figure 9.17 – Placements for different components inside a gallery component

9. Using **Tree View**, select **MyCharacterCounter2** and configure the **characterCounterDataInput** to `ThisItem.Description` and set **characterCounterLimit** to `100`.

10. Select **MyDataCard2** and configure **Data Cards(Items)** with the following formula:

```
First(
    Filter(
        Accounts,
        'Primary Contact'.Contact = ThisItem.Contact
    )
)
```

11. On **MyDataCard2**, click on **Fields** from the property pane and remove the **Primary Contact** card, if it exists.

This should render the gallery in your canvas app like so:

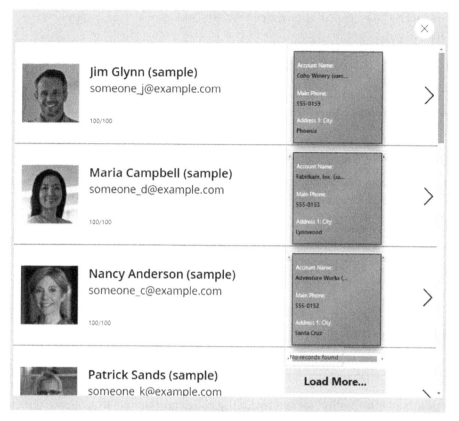

Figure 9.18 – App preview with a code component inside a gallery component on a canvas app

As you can see, we can use a combination of the field and dataset code components in a gallery to enhance the user interface in canvas apps.

Summary

In this chapter, we learned how to configure field and dataset type code components in a form, view, sub-grid, and dashboard in a model-driven app. We also learned about the different ways in which the code component can be configured in canvas apps. Finally, we learned that we can use both the field and dataset type code components in a gallery. This chapter should have helped you learn how to configure code components in any app.

In the next chapter, we will do a deep dive into some of the features that are provided by the Power Apps component framework that can help us create more complex code components.

Test your knowledge

1. On which Dataverse component can we not configure a code component? (*100 points*)

    a. View

    b. Chart

2. Which of the following is the correct statement? (*100 points*)

    a. Both the field and dataset code components can be configured in the same canvas apps gallery component.

    b. The field and dataset code components cannot be configured in the same canvas apps gallery component.

3. An out-of-the-box canvas apps component contains code components – true or false? (*200 points*)

    a. True

    b. False

Further reading

- Additional information related to adding code components to a model-driven app can be found in Microsoft's documentation at `http://bit.ly/AddPcfMDA`.

- Additional information related to adding code components to a canvas app can be found in Microsoft's documentation at `http://bit.ly/AddPcfCanvasApps`.

Section 3: Enhancing Code Components and Your Development Experience

This last section provides guidelines to enhance your code components and improve your development experience. First, we focus heavily on understanding the different events and methods provided by the Power Apps component framework. Using these events and methods, we build several tiny code components.

After that, we learn advanced techniques that are helpful when building a code component for a dataset. These include sorting, paging, opening a record from a selection, and interacting with the command ribbon provided by model-driven apps.

Then, we see how to make our development experience better by using Lint and Prettier. We also learn the technique to set up a testing framework. Lastly, we are introduced to React and Fluent UI, which will help you enrich the user interface of code components.

This section covers the following topics:

- *Chapter 10, Diving Deep into the Features Provided by PCF*
- *Chapter 11, Creating Advanced Dataset Code Components*
- *Chapter 12, Enriching Your Dev Experience*

10
Diving Deep into the Features Provided by PCF

In the previous chapters, we learned about several techniques we can use to create, test, inspect, debug, and configure a code component. At this point, you should be able to create your own code components. However, the Power Apps component framework provides additional features that enable you to build complex code components. In this chapter, we will look at some of them in depth by examining their usage with some examples. By the end of this chapter, you will be aware of most of the capabilities the Power Apps component framework has to offer.

In this chapter, we are going to cover the following main topics:

- Understanding the context
- Exploring the `updateView` method
- Understanding the importance of the `getOutputs` method
- Inspecting the caching mechanism

- Working with external devices
- Exploring the Web API

Let's get started!

Technical requirements

To work through this chapter, you will need to install all the prerequisites that will help you with the development process. These were mentioned in *Chapter 1, Introduction to the Power Apps Component Framework*. Download the example library from https://github.com/PacktPublishing/Extending-Microsoft-Power-Apps-with-Power-Apps-Component-Framework/tree/master/Chapter10. There are different folders for each section; so, make sure you are using the right project for the right section by checking the folder's name. You will also need to install **Visual Studio Code** and **Google Chrome**.

Understanding the context

The core property of the Power Apps component framework is its **context**. It provides access to all the other properties and methods available in the framework.

We used the Power Apps component framework's context in *Chapter 5, Code, Test, and Repeat*, to access the values of the properties defined in the manifest file. Apart from this, it also provides access to several other features. This is shown in the following diagram:

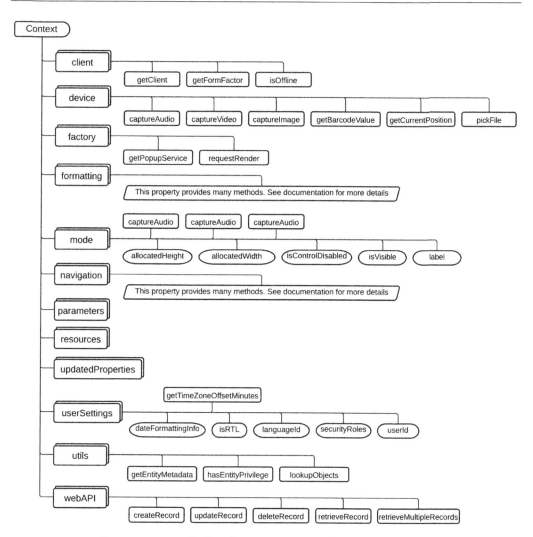

Figure 10.1 – Methods and properties provided by the framework

Each of these properties and methods can be used to create complex code components. Since context is the core module of the framework, it is available in both the `init` and `updateView` methods. If you need to utilize any of the properties or methods from outside this context, then you can pass the reference as a parameter. But when it comes to using context in different helper files other than `index.ts`, I would recommend against passing the entire context to those files. Instead, pass only the required information and return the relevant information; this will ensure your business logic is abstracted when you're using the MVVM pattern.

When you're building complex code components, `updateView` plays an important role since when the data gets updated, the framework communicates that data back to the host. Now, let's explore the `updateView` method.

Exploring the updateView method

Before we begin exploring the `updateView` method, let's revise some of the things we learned about in *Chapter 4, Project Overview and the Component Life Cycle*. We learned that, during the component life cycle, `updateView` is invoked whenever the value is changed by the host. We also learned that `updateView` is invoked when a bound property defined in the manifest file is changed by the user. There are other reasons why we would wish to invoke the `updateView` method, so we will be exploring some of those reasons to better understand the importance of the `updateView` method.

Using the example library in the *1.UpdateView-GetOutputs* folder provided for this chapter, build the PCF project and start the test harness. Let's go through some scenarios that will help you understand how the `updateView` method works:

1. **First-time load**

    When the code component initially loads, we know that the `init` method has been invoked. This is followed by the `updateView` method being invoked. This is because the definition of `updateView` states that this method is invoked when any value of property bag changes or any global value changes. During `init`, all these aspects are changing, which is why the `updateView` method is invoked. This is depicted in the following screenshot:

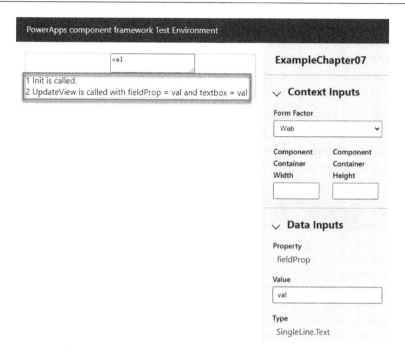

Figure 10.2 – Exploring Update View when it's initialized

As you can see, after the `init` method was invoked, the `updateView` method was invoked. The `updateView` method was supplied with the property value, which was populated in the text box of the code component. Hence, the values of `fieldProp` and `textbox` are the same.

2. **Change the text in the text box provided by the code component**

Now, let's change the text in the text box that's available on the UI provided by the code component. Just entering a single character will invoke an OnChange method, which, in turn, will call the notifyOutputChanged method. This method will invoke the getOutputs method, which returns the data to the host. Meanwhile, since we changed the fieldProp property, this invoked the updateView method. The data that was returned to the host gets validated by the host and if it's accepted, the code components receive the updated data in the context properties. This can be seen in the following screenshot:

Figure 10.3 – Exploring Update View when the UI changes

As you can see, updateView gets invoked twice; first with the old value in fieldProp and then with the updated value in fieldProp. Always remember that when any UI changes occur and if the notifyOutputChanged function is *not* invoked, the getOutputs method will *not* be called, which also means that the updateView method will not be invoked.

3. **Change the text in the Data Inputs section of the test harness**

When you change the text in the **Data Inputs** section of the test harness, the value was changed in the host. This means that any property value changes will invoke the updateView method. Consider, for example, that the code component has been deployed to a model-driven app on an account number field, but it also has a property that is bound to the account name field. When the data is updated in the account name field, this will invoke the updateView method as the property value changes. This is shown in the following screenshot:

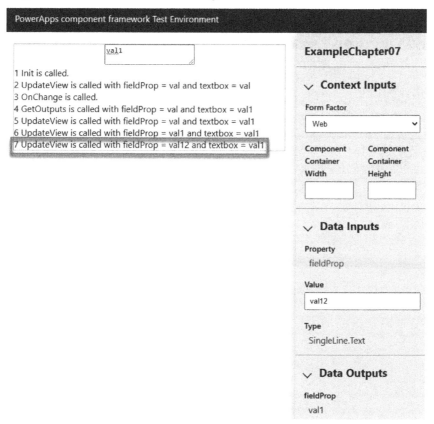

Figure 10.4 – Exploring Update View when the value is changed by the host

In this case, appending *2* to the text for the `fieldProp` property invokes the `updateView` method. However, note that this is not reflected in the text box of the code component. This is because when the new value is provided to the `updateView` method, the code does not update the text box value. It is up to the developer to decide on how to handle the new values that are provided to the control. The same scenario also occurs when the field on the host changes visibility or toggles enable/disable.

4. **Change the form factor from Context Inputs**

    Form factor is the type of display device where the code component is getting rendered. This does not frequently change in real time, but when you develop your code components, you will want to ensure that they render properly on every device. This is where the test harness comes in handy. You can change the form factor, which will invoke the `updateView` method. This is shown in the following screenshot:

Figure 10.5 – Exploring Update View when the form factor is changed

The properties will remain unchanged, but you can use the `context.client.getFormFactor()` method to identify which of the display device is being used. This allows you to make proper adjustments to the control layouts.

5. **Change height and width from Context Inputs**

    As the definition for `updateView` method goes, it also gets invoked when the height or the width of the component container changes. This can happen frequently when users are trying to resize the window of the host. Based on that, the host might try to resize the containers to fit them accordingly on the UI. When this happens, you will want your code component to realign as per the height and width of the container itself. The test harness provides us with the ability to test such scenarios by changing the height and width of the component's container. This is shown in the following screenshot:

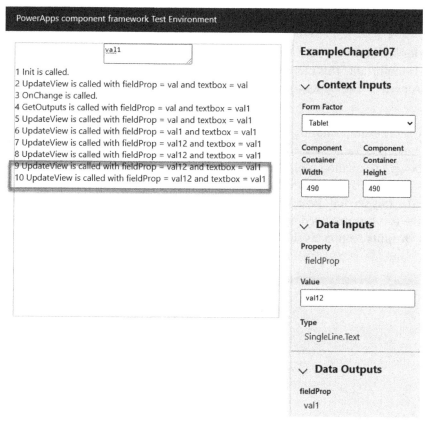

Figure 10.6 – Exploring Update View when the height and width of the component container are changed

When you change the height and width even by a single digit, this will invoke the updateView method. So, if you typed three digits into the width text box of the test harness, that will invoke updateView three times.

You will have to be extra careful if auto-saving has been turned on in your model-driven app, as this might complicate the process. This is because there will be frequent data transfers between the host and the component. However, sometimes, the values might not be accurate, which might cause your control to lose current values and use old values instead.

Now that we understand the intricacies of the updateView method, let's look at the importance of the getOutputs method.

Understanding the importance of the getOutputs method

Since we looked at the getOutputs method briefly in the previous section, we will look at why it is important. This method is invoked when the component has modified the **bound** properties. The values for such properties should be communicated back to the host.

Using the same example library we used previously, observe that we are returning an updated textbox value back to the host via fieldProp, which is a bound property in the getOutputs method. This can also be validated by using the **Data Output** section of the test harness. If any updated value is returned to its host, then you should see such values under this section. When you initiate a test of the example library and change the value in the text box provided by the component, you can observe the changed value in the **Data Outputs** section, as shown in the following screenshot:

Figure 10.7 – Observing the Data Outputs section in test harness

If you do not wish to return any updates back to the host, which might be the case for read-only components, then the return block will be empty. To try this out, let's edit the `index.ts` file in the example library by commenting the code within the `return` block. Before you do this, make sure that any running testing processes have been terminated and that you've close the tab on your browser where the test harness was running:

index.ts

```
public getOutputs(): IOutputs {
    return {
        //fieldProp: this.textbox.value
    };
}
```

Once you have commented the code, as highlighted in the preceding code snippet, you need to build and initiate the test of the code component. When the test harness is up and running, you can perform the same activity by entering a character in the text box provided by the component. But this time, you will notice that the **Data Outputs** section is not populated, as shown in the following screenshot:

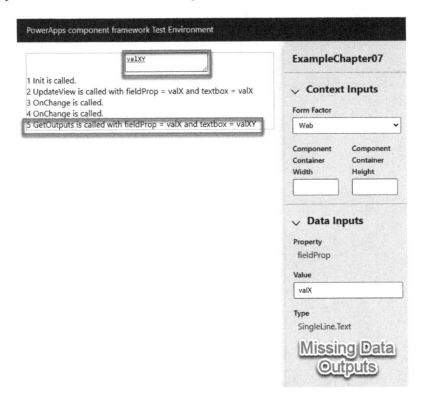

Figure 10.8 – No data returned from the component to the host

This is because nothing is returned from the component. Also, observe that in *Figure 10.7*, under **Data Inputs**, fieldProp was updated but in *Figure 10.8*, the value of fieldProp does not get updated. Since no data is being returned by the component to the host, the host is unaware of any changes that have been made to the property value.

Next, we'll learn how to return a null value from the code component to the host.

Setting a null value on the field

When we want to set a null value on the field that is bound to a code component, we have to return the property with an `undefined` value to the host, as highlighted in the following code:

---

index.ts

```
public getOutputs(): IOutputs {
    return {
        fieldProp: undefined
    };
}
```

When testing this change in the test harness, the **Data Outputs** section will show the returned bound value as undefined. This is shown in the following screenshot:

Figure 10.9 – Returning null to the host from the component

To test this change, after initiating the test for the code component in the test harness, you can enter a letter into the text box provided. This will invoke the OnChange event. This calls the notifyOutputChanged function, which, in turn, invokes the getOutputs method. Inside this method, the component returns **undefined** back to the host.

You won't always want to return null values to the host; sometimes, you may only want to return null values based on certain conditions. Let's look at how we can achieve that.

Setting values on the field based on a condition

Using the same example library that we used previously, consider that if the user removes all the characters from the text box, you will want the value of the field that's being sent to the host to be null. We can use complex logic to set a value that will be returned to the host by including an if-else or a switch statement. In the following code, we used if-else to set the value to null when the value in the text box is empty:

index.ts

```
public getOutputs(): IOutputs {
    if(this.textbox.value === "")
    {
        return {
            fieldProp: undefined
        };
    }
    else
    {
        return {
            fieldProp: this.textbox.value
        };
    }
}
```

This can be tested in the test harness, as shown in the following screenshot:

Figure 10.10 – Setting values based on conditions

The text box value is empty but the value that is returned to the host is **undefined**.

In the next scenario, we will learn how to omit returning values from certain properties to the host and what this means.

Omitting updates to a field

Sometimes, you may come across a requirement where you have a code component with multiple bound fields, but you do not want to send updates to a particular field in the getOutputs method. If you assign **undefined** to that field, it will still send updates to the host as a null value, thus invoking any event that is registered for that field on the host and calling the updateView method. But if you do not include the bound property in the getOutputs return statement, then you can omit the updates to that property. Doing this will not trigger any events that have been registered for that field on the host, and the updateView method will also not invoke.

When the user changes the value in the text box, you do not want that value to be reflected by the host. However, if the user removes all the characters from the text box, you would want the value of the field being sent to the host to be null. We will continue editing the same code we used previously, as follows:

index.ts

```
public getOutputs(): IOutputs {
    if(this.textbox.value === "")
    {
        return {
            fieldProp: undefined
        };
    }
    else
    {
        return {
            //fieldProp: this.textbox.value
        };
    }
}
```

Observe that the highlighted code has been commented out, which is why we've omitted the changes being sent to the host for that condition. This can be tested in the test harness, as shown in the following screenshot:

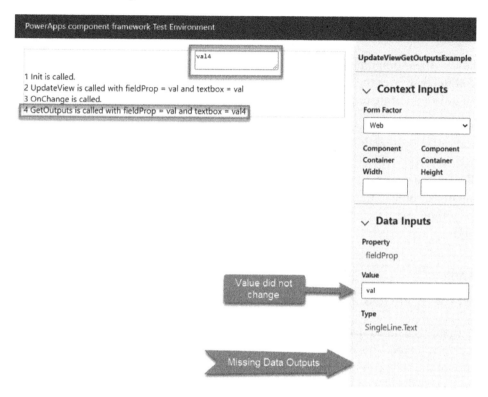

Figure 10.11 – Omitting updates to a value based on a condition

As you can see, when the value in the text box was changed, no entry was populated in **Data Outputs**, which proves that if you do not return the property in the getOuputs method, then no value is sent to the host. However, on the contrary, even if you send **undefined**, a null value is sent to the host.

By combining these scenarios, you can let your code components determine the values that need to be sent to the host.

Now that we've learned about the updateView and getOutputs methods, we will look at the caching mechanism provided by the framework.

Inspecting the caching mechanism

Caching is a technique that's used to store frequently used data in memory so that, when the same data is needed again, it can be retrieved from memory, thus saving time and improving the performance of the component. Let's look at the caching mechanism provided by the framework.

The Power Apps component framework provides a third parameter in the `init` method, called **state**, that saves the states of objects in a single session for a user. So, let's see how we can utilize the **state** to persist the data in the code component.

Saving the state in the code component is very straightforward. The framework provides a method called `context.mode.setControlState`, which takes in one parameter of the `Dictionary` type. This is provided by the framework. Before we start, we are going to follow a strategy similar to the one we used in *Chapter 5, Code, Test, and Repeat*, where we initialized some of the properties at a class level because they were only available in the `init` method. First, we need to initialize a class variable, as shown in the following code snippet:

index.ts

```
private theState : ComponentFramework.Dictionary = {};
```

This variable is defined inside the class but outside of all the methods and is of the `Dictionary` type. This is provided by the framework. It will persist the data for a single instance of the code component on the same record for a user. Now, inside the `init` method, we will add some key-value pairs and invoke the method to save the state, as follows:

index.ts

```
this.theState["sampleKey"] = "sampleValue";
context.mode.setControlState(this.theState);
```

The first line of code will add the key-value pair to the `Dictionary` type provided by the framework, while the second line of code will allow the values within the `Dictionary` type to persist.

Now that we understand how to add values and enable them to persist, let's look at an example where the text box will show a default value of `not cached` if the state does not exist; otherwise, it will show the value from the state. Before we start adding logic to persist the data, we need to declare some class variables. These are as follows:

index.ts

```
private mainDiv: HTMLDivElement;
private textbox: HTMLTextAreaElement;
private cacheButton: HTMLButtonElement;
private outputLabelDiv: HTMLDivElement
private outputLabel: HTMLLabelElement;
private counter: number;
private theNotifyOutputChanged: () => void;
private theContext: ComponentFramework.Context<IInputs>;
private theState: ComponentFramework.Dictionary = {};
private persistedTextboxValue: string;
```

These variables are defined inside the class but outside of all the methods. Let's take a look at these variables in detail:

- `mainDiv` will be our DOM element and will contain a child text box and a label.

- `textbox` is our main control and will accept inputs from users.

- `cacheButton` will display a button that will invoke the logic for setting the state of the component.

- `outputLabel` will display the status of the events getting invoked and data being cached.

- `counter` is a variable that counts the number of messages being displayed on `outputLabel`.

- `theNotifyOutputChanged` is a parameterless function variable that will be used to invoke the `getOutputs` method when a user interacts with the text box control. This was discussed in *Chapter 4, Project Overview and the Component Life Cycle.*

- `theContext` is a context object at the class level and can be accessed throughout the scope of the class.

- `theState` is like a context object at the class level and can be accessed throughout the scope of the class.

- `persistedTextboxValue` is a class-level string variable that will hold the persisted value.

Now that we've created the necessary class variables, we will move on and add logic to the init method. The following code snippet needs to be added inside the init method:

index.ts

```
this.theNotifyOutputChanged = notifyOutputChanged;
this.theContext = context;
if (state) {
    this.theState = state;
    this.persistedTextboxValue =
        this.theState["TextboxValue"];
}
// State not persisted -- set variable to default values
if (!this.persistedTextboxValue) {
    this.persistedTextboxValue = "not cached";
}
this.textbox.value = this.persistedTextboxValue;
```

Let's take a look at the code in detail:

- We assigned the notifyOutputChanged function that's provided to us by the framework in the init method to the function variable we defined at the class level. This variable is called theNotifyOutputChanged.

- Similarly, we assigned context to a class-level variable named theContext.

- If the state is not **undefined**, then we must assign state to the theState class-level variable and assign the value from state to persistedTextboxValue with the TextboxValue key.

- If persistedTextboxValue does not gets assigned, then a default value of not cached is set on it.

- Finally, we set the text box with whatever value the persistedTextboxValue variable holds.

> **Note**
> The code provided in this chapter are just snippets. Please refer to the example library for the complete code.

Inside the `init` method, while creating the UI, we have the `OnClick` method, which is bound to the button. Due to this, we need to define a custom method, as shown in the following code snippet:

index.ts

```
private OnClick(): void {
    this.theState["TextboxValue"] = this.textbox.value;
    this.theContext.mode.setControlState(this.theState);
}
```

The `OnClick` method assigns the text box value to the state with the `TextboxValue` key. This is followed by setting the state dictionary object on the context, which allows the framework to persist the value in memory. As we saw earlier, this persisted value is captured in the `init` method, which gets populated in the text box.

We need to deploy this code to a Dataverse environment using the quick push function and configure it on any single-line text field available on the form. Once this has been deployed and configured, we can open the first record and enter any text into the provided text box of the component. The following screenshot shows the logic in the `OnClick` function before and after the state has been set on the context:

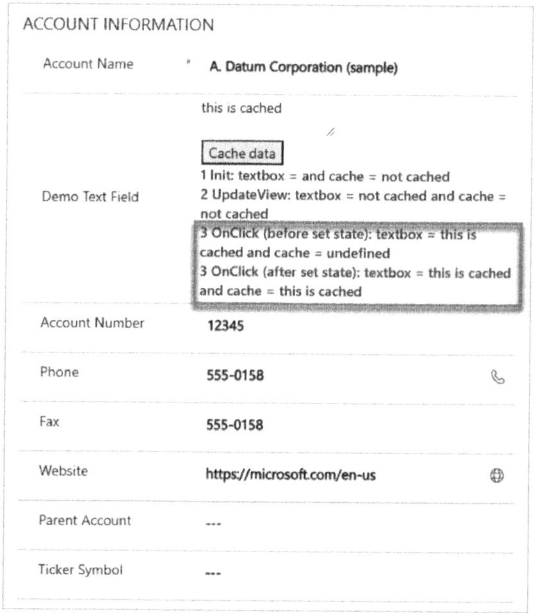

Figure 10.12 – Setting the state in the `OnClick` method

When you click the **Cache data** button, the `OnClick` function is invoked, which sets the state on the context. To test this caching functionality, enter some text into the text box provided by the code component and click **Cache data**. Now, close the record and open a second record for editing. You will see that the default value of **not cached** is shown on the second record. Let's go back to the first record. Here, we will see that the same text we had entered previously persists on this record, whereas the second record was showing the default text. The following screenshot depicts the value being persisted on the first record but shows a default value on the second record:

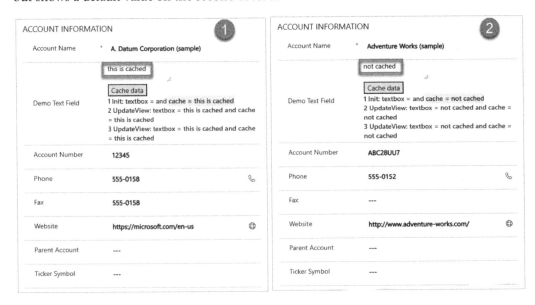

Figure 10.13 – Two records; one with the value persisted and another with the default value

As we can see, the first record, **A. Datum Corporation (sample)**, shows the persisted value, whereas the second record, **Adventure Works (sample)**, shows the default value. However, this value only persists in that session; if the user refreshes or closes their browser, the value in the state is lost.

Insights

Most modern web browsers provide a web storage mechanism. But as per the Microsoft documentation, using web storage is insecure and unsupported in the Power Apps component framework. The ability to access web storage could be blocked in the future, so be cognizant of using it in your code components.

Next, we will look at the process of working with external devices such as cameras, audio, video, and more within code components.

Working with external devices

When applications allow you to interact with external devices, it enhances the user's experience and provides meaningful data. This is exactly what the Power Apps component framework offers: the ability for us to work with external devices and capture correct data. In this section, we are going to learn how to harness the power of interacting with devices such as audio, video, images, barcodes, locations, and select files.

We will be creating a simple code component that will utilize all these external devices. This code component will contain a button for each of the device functions provided by the framework. Since we have six functions, we will be adding six buttons to the UI in the code component. Each of these buttons will have their own function on the click event.

Before you begin adding the code, you must enable the necessary features in the manifest file. As we will be utilizing all the device's features, we will only enable the features we need in the `ControlManifest.Input.xml` file, as shown in the following screenshot:

```xml
<feature-usage>
  <uses-feature name="Device.captureAudio" required="true" />
  <uses-feature name="Device.captureImage" required="true" />
  <uses-feature name="Device.captureVideo" required="true" />
  <uses-feature name="Device.getBarcodeValue" required="true" />
  <uses-feature name="Device.getCurrentPosition" required="true" />
  <uses-feature name="Device.pickFile" required="true" />
  <!-- THESE FEATURES ARE NOT USED IN THIS PCF CODE COMPONENT -->
  <!--
  <uses-feature name="Utility" required="true" />
  <uses-feature name="WebAPI" required="true" />
  -->
</feature-usage>
```

Figure 10.14 – Features enabled in the ControlManifest.Input.xml file for external devices

First, let's look at the process of capturing audio, video, and images from a device. We will add the following code for each of these functions, as shown here:

index.ts

```
private async OnCaptureAudio(): Promise<void>>{
   let aud = await this.theContext.device.captureAudio()
           .catch(err => this.displayOutput(err.message));
   if (aud) {
     this.displayOutput(aud.fileName);
   }
}
```

```
private async OnCaptureVideo(): Promise<void> {
  let vid = await this.theContext.device.captureVideo()
              .catch(err =>this.displayOutput(err.message));
  if (vid) {
    this.displayOutput(vid.fileName);
  }
}
private async OnCaptureImage(): Promise<void> {
  let img = await this.theContext.device.captureImage()
              .catch(err => this.displayOutput(err.message));
  if (img) {
    this.displayOutput(img.fileName);
  }
}
```

Each function returns a `Promise`. This is why we used `async/await` to capture the result. All three functions return a `Promise` of the `FileObject` type provided by the framework. This `FileObject` provides four properties; namely, `fileContent`, `fileName`, `fileSize`, `mimeType`. All of them are string data types.

> **Note**
> At the time of writing this book, all these device features only work on a Power Apps mobile app except for `pickFile`.

Once you have created the code component that implements the usage of external devices, deploy the code component to a Dataverse environment and configure it on a form. Now, using your mobile device, go to the Power Apps mobile app and start the app where you have added the code component. Click on any of the three buttons; for instance, if you click on the **Capture Image** button, a camera application will start to capture the image. Once you have captured the image, the code component will provide you with the image's content, as well as its filename, size, and mime type. You can use the response however you want. In this instance, the code component will show you the image's filename and render the captured image on the UI, as shown in the following screenshot:

Figure 10.15 – Preview of the image capture using an external device camera in the Power Apps mobile app

You can use the **Capture Audio** and **Capture Video** buttons as well; both will render the output. Now, let's look at the process of capturing the barcode, current location, and pick file of a device. We will add the following code for each of these functions, as shown here:

index.ts

```
private OnCaptureBarcode(): void {
   let code = await this.theContext.device.getBarcodeValue()
              .catch(err => this.displayOutput(err.message));
   if (code) {
     this.displayOutput(code);
   }
}
private OnShowCurrentLocation(): void {
    let pos = await this.theContext.device.getCurrentPosition()
              .catch(err => this.displayOutput(err.message));
   if (pos) {
     this.displayOutput(
```

```
            `Lat:${pos.coords.latitude},
            Long:${pos.coords.longitude}`);


    }
 }
private OnPickFile(): void {
    let files = await this.theContext.device.pickFile()
                .catch(err => this.displayOutput(err.message));
    if (files) {
       this.displayOutput(`File Name identified:
          ${files[0].fileName}`);
    }
 }
```

Similar to the previous three features, these features also return a Promise, but each of them has different object types. getBarcodeValue returns a string, getCurrentPosition returns a DeviceApi.Position object, as provided by the framework, and pickFile returns an array of FileObject, as provided by the framework.

Extending our earlier example, bind these three new functions to the remaining three buttons. Once you've done this, deploy the code component to your Dataverse environment. Now, clicking on each of those buttons will trigger the logic for invoking the device's feature. In this example, we will click on **Show Current Location**, which will provide the *latitude* and *longitude* of the current location, as shown in the following screenshot:

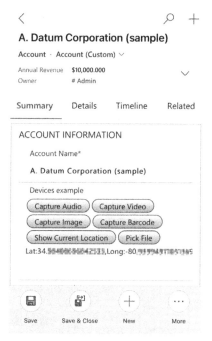

Figure 10.16 – Model-driven app showing the user's current location in the Power Apps mobile app

The `Position` object provides more properties, but this example should have helped you understand how to use them when building a code component.

Now, let's understand how to work with Dataverse's Web API methods within a code component.

Exploring the Web API

At times, you may have to interact with the Dataverse Web API inside your code component. For example, let's say you have a Primary Contact defined on an account, but you want to update that contact information on the account form itself. So, you create a code component that will show all the relevant information about that contact on the account, but also allows you to update their contact information. In order to update the primary contact, you will have to utilize the Dataverse Web API. The framework provides five functions for interacting with the data in Dataverse: `createRecord`, `updateRecord`, `deleteRecord`, `retrieveRecord`, and `retrieveMultipleRecords`.

In this section, we will look at how to use these functions by creating a simple code component. Similar to the code component we created for external devices, we will add five buttons, each of which will represent the five functions provided by the Web API. Each of these buttons will be bound to its own function on the click event.

Before you begin adding the code, you must enable the necessary features in the manifest file. Since we will be utilizing the Web API's features, we will enable them in the `ControlManifest.Input.xml` file, as shown in the following screenshot:

```
<feature-usage>
  <!-- WILL NOT BE USING DEVICE or UTILITY FEATURES -->
  <!--
  <uses-feature name="Device.captureAudio" required="true" />
  <uses-feature name="Device.captureImage" required="true" />
  <uses-feature name="Device.captureVideo" required="true" />
  <uses-feature name="Device.getBarcodeValue" required="true" />
  <uses-feature name="Device.getCurrentPosition" required="true" />
  <uses-feature name="Device.pickFile" required="true" />
  <uses-feature name="Utility" required="true" />
  -->
  <uses-feature name="WebAPI" required="true" />
</feature-usage>
```

Figure 10.17 – Features enabled in the ControlManifest.Input.xml file for the Web API

First, let's look at the process of creating a contact record, with the first name as **WebApi** and the last name as **Testing**. We will also look at the process of updating the job title to **Power** on that same contact.

> **Note**
> WebApi methods cannot be tested in test harness provided by the Power Apps component framework. You can use any deployment methods you learned in the previous chapters to deploy the code to your preferred Dataverse environment for testing.

Both these functions are shown in the following code snippet:

index.ts

```typescript
private async OnCreateButtonClicked(): Promise<void> {
  let contactData: ComponentFramework.WebApi.Entity = {};
  contactData["firstname"] = "WebApi";
  contactData["lastname"] = "Testing";
  contactData["fullname"] = "WebApi Testing";
```

```
    let resp = await this.theContext.webAPI
            .createRecord("contact", contactData)
            .catch(err => console.log(err.message));
    if (resp) {
      // Currently there is a bug
      // with EntityReference definition
      // It should be resp.id.guid as per doc
      // but response contains the record GUID at resp.id
      // Workaround is to typecast resp.id into any
      this.contactEntityId = (<any>resp.id);
      this.outputLabel.innerHTML =
        `Contact created with id = ${this.contactEntityId}.`;
    }
  }
  private OnUpdateButtonClicked(): void {
    if (this.contactEntityId) {
      let contactData: ComponentFramework.WebApi.Entity = {};
      contactData["jobtitle"] = "Power";
      this.theContext.webAPI.updateRecord(
        "contact", this.contactEntityId, contactData);
    }
    else {
      //Contact id is not defined
    }
  }
```

Once these functions have been bound to the create and update buttons, you can deploy the code component to your desired **Dataverse** environment and configure it on any field on a table. Now, open any record on the table where you configured your code component; you should see the buttons. When you click on the create button, a new contact record called **WebApi Testing** should be created. When you click on the update button, the job title on the contact should be populated with a value of **Power**.

Note

The code in this chapter are just snippets. Refer to the example library for the complete code.

Both the create and update methods require a parameter of the `Entity` type; this is provided by the framework. This object is a generic key-value pair, where `key` is the *attribute name* and `value` is the *attribute value*. In the create method, we capture the record ID that gets generated by the system when the record is created. This record ID is used in the update method to perform the update on the same record that was created in the create method. Both methods return a `Promise` of the `EntityReference` type. At the time of writing this book, there is a bug when retrieving `EntityReference` from these methods. To circumvent this issue, we must typecast the `EntityReference` response as `any`.

Now, let's look at the logic for the next two methods; that is, `retrieve` and `delete`. First, we will retrieve the full name and job title of the contact we created, and then we will delete the contact record we created. The following code snippet will help you understand this process:

index.ts

```
private async OnRetrieveButtonClicked(): Promise<void> {
  if (this.contactEntityId) {
    let con = await this.theContext.webAPI
            .retrieveRecord("contact",
            this.contactEntityId,
            "?$select=fullname,jobtitle")
            .catch(err => console.log(err.message));
    if (con) {
      this.outputLabel.innerHTML =
        `Contact info retrieved: <br/>Full Name:
        <b>${con.fullname}</b><br/>Job Title:
        <b>${con.jobtitle}</b>`;
    }
  }
  else {
    //Contact id is not defined
  }
}
pprivate async OnDeleteButtonClicked(): Promise<void> {
  if (this.contactEntityId) {
    let con = await this.theContext.webAPI
            .deleteRecord("contact", this.contactEntityId)
```

```
                .catch(err => console.log(err.message));
        if (con) {
            this.contactEntityId = undefined;
            this.outputLabel.innerHTML = `Contact was deleted.`;
        }
    }
    else {
        //Contact id is not defined
    }
}
```

In the retrieve method, you have three parameters; the first is `table` name, the second is `record id` (in this instance, the record ID is captured during the create method), and the third is `OData query`, which provides the `$select` and `$expand` options for retrieving your data. The retrieve method returns a `Promise` of the `Entity` type, which is a key-value object provided by the framework. In the delete method, to delete a record from the system, you must provide the record's table name and record ID. The response from the delete method is a `Promise` of the `EntityReference` type.

Now, let's look at the process of fetching multiple records using a query. The following code snippet shows us how to retrieve the top three contacts that have *sample* in their name:

```
pprivate async OnRetrieveMultipleButtonClicked() {
    let result = await this.theContext.webAPI
                .retrieveMultipleRecords("contact",
                "?$select=fullname
                &$filter=contains(fullname,'sample')
                &$top=3")
                .catch(err => console.log(err.message));
    if (result) {
        this.outputLabel.innerHTML =
            `Contact info where fullname contains sample.`;
        result.entities.forEach(ele => {
            this.outputLabel.innerHTML += `<br/>${ele.fullname}`;
        });
    }
}
```

The retrieve multiple method takes in two parameters; one is the name of the table that you want to retrieve the data from, while the other is an ODat a query, which supports the $select, $top, $filter, $expand, and $orderby options in the query. The retrieve method returns a Promise of the RetrieveMultipleResponse type, which contains two properties: one is the array of Entity and another is the URL that returns the next set of records. Using the array of an Entity, you can loop through your records and retrieve the data you want.

Summary

In this chapter, we learned about many of the advance features provided by the Power Apps component framework. We got a better understanding of the context and explored the updateView method. We then understood the importance of the getOutputs method and learned about its caching mechanism. After that, we learned how to work with external devices and Web APIs. Now, that you have learned all this, you can use a combination of these features to build complex code components.

In the next chapter, we will enhance the dataset code component that we built in *Chapter 5, Code, Test, and Repeat.*

Test your knowledge

1. In which of the following scenarios is the updateView method invoked? (*100 points*)

    a. First time rendering the code component on a form

    b. When the data inside the state has changed

2. Which function provides the parameter that enables us to cache the data? (*100 points*)

    a. init

    b. updateView

3. Which is the feature that works on web, phone, and tablet? (*100 points*)

    a. getBarcodeValue

    b. pickFile

4. What happens when you invoke the `updateRecord` Web API method with an undefined record ID? (*200 points*)

    a. You get an error stating *Uncaught UciError: Value should be of type: guid: Parameter Name: id*

    b. You don't receive an error, but the record isn't updated

Further reading

- Additional information on the Power Apps component framework's context can be found in Microsoft's documentation at `http://bit.ly/PCF-Context`.

- Additional information on the `updateView` method can be found in Microsoft's documentation at `http://bit.ly/PCF-UpdateView`.

- Additional information on the `getOutputs` method can be found in Microsoft's documentation at `https://bit.ly/PCFGetOutputs`.

- Additional information on setting the state provided by the framework can be found in Microsoft's documentation at `http://bit.ly/PCF-SetControlState`.

- Additional information on working with external devices can be found in Microsoft's documentation at `https://bit.ly/PCF-Device`.

- Additional information on working with the Dataverse Web API inside a code component can be found in Microsoft's documentation at `https://bit.ly/PCF-WebApi`.

- Additional information on working with retrieve records using the Web API can be found in Microsoft's documentation at `http://bit.ly/WebApi-RetrieveRecord`.

- Additional information on working with retrieve records using the Web API can be found in Microsoft's documentation at `http://bit.ly/WebApi-RetrieveMultiple`.

11
Creating Advanced Dataset Code Components

In this chapter, we would learn advanced features that can be added to a dataset code component to enhance the user experience. We will be reusing the dataset code component we had created in *Chapter 5, Code, Test, and Repeat*, and extend it with advanced features; like sorting, paging, custom filtering, opening a selected record, integrating with out-of-the-box options available with the datasets. By the end of this chapter, you have a complete dataset code component that provides all the needed features

In this chapter, we are going to cover the following main topics:

- Recap of what was built
- Sorting the data in a dataset
- Implementing pagination on a dataset
- Integrating code components with out-of-the-box options
- Understanding the technique to open a record from a dataset
- Defining properties on a dataset

Technical requirements

In order to work through this chapter, you need to install all the prerequisites mentioned in *Chapter 1, Introduction to the Power Apps Component Framework*, that will help you with the development process. Download the example library from `https://github.com/PacktPublishing/Extending-Microsoft-Power-Apps-with-Power-Apps-Component-Framework/tree/master/Chapter11`. There are different folders for each section; make sure you are using the right project for the right section by checking the folder name. You will also need to install **Visual Studio Code** and **Google Chrome**.

Recap of what was built

In *Chapter 5, Code, Test, and Repeat*, we built a simple dataset code component that only displayed the data. But we did not implement any additional features that would enable users to interact with the data. In this chapter, we will expand the same code component and add some advanced features that will provide interaction capabilities to the code component.

When building the basic dataset code component in *Chapter 5, Code Test and Repeat*, we learned the importance of identifying whether the dataset was still loading and waiting for it to complete loading before rendering the user interface. This is one of the features provided by the framework that lets you detect the status of dataset loading and helps you execute your logic at the correct time. If you do not check the dataset loading status, you might execute the logic to render the user interface multiple times.

Now, we will be enhancing the existing dataset code component by adding the following capabilities:

- Sorting
- Paging
- Interacting with the command bar
- Searching
- Opening a record from a dataset

These features are always crucial to any dataset code component.

Let's first look at the process of implementing sorting on a dataset code component.

Sorting the data in a dataset

The ability to sort the data in a column is always required on a dataset and provides a good user experience, but in some cases, based on the user interface, it may not be needed.

In our example code component, we will add a configurable property on the control manifest file that a user can provide to specify on which column they want to implement the sort while configuring the control. The following are the details of the property that will be added to the control manifest file:

ControlManifest.Input.xml

```xml
<data-set name="datasetGrid" display-name-key="Data Cards">
</data-set>
<property name="sortColName"
    display-name-key="Column Name to Sort"
    description-key="Column schema name to sort"
    of-type="SingleLine.Text"
    usage="input"
    required="true"
/>
```

As you can see, we defined a new property called `sortColName`, which will capture the column on which the `sort` command should be performed. If the code component is showing a typical grid, then the `sort` command can be performed on the click of the column header. But in our code component, we do not have a typical table, so we will add a button that will perform the sort. This button will be declared as a class variable in the code and the details will be provided in the `init` method. We also need to capture the `sortColName` property value; so, we will define a class-level string variable. The following are the details of that button in the `init` method:

index.ts

```ts
this.sortColName = context.parameters.sortColName.raw || "";
this.sortButton = document.createElement("button");
this.sortButton.innerHTML = `Sort ${this.sortColName}`;
this.sortButton.addEventListener(
    "click", this.SortColumn.bind(this));
```

Observe that the captured column name from the property value is displayed as a label on the button that will perform the sorting. Also, this button is bound to a function named SortColumn, which we will define next. This function performs the core logic to sort the data in the dataset, which is as follows:

index.ts

```
private SortColumn() {
    let dataset = this.theContext.parameters.datasetGrid;
    let columnClicked = this.sortColName;
    const oldSorting =
        (dataset.sorting || [])
            .find((sort) => sort.name === columnClicked);
    const newValue: DataSetInterfaces.SortStatus = {
        name: columnClicked,
        sortDirection: oldSorting != null ?
            (oldSorting.sortDirection === 0 ? 1 : 0) : 0
    };
    while (dataset.sorting.length > 0) {
        dataset.sorting.pop();
    }
    dataset.sorting.push(newValue);
    dataset.paging.reset();
    dataset.refresh();
}
```

In this function, first, we are identifying the current sort details. Next, using the current sort details, we change the sort direction and call this newValue. This is followed by clearing the sorting array using the dataset.sorting.pop function. Next, we add the new sorting captured in newValue and add it to the sorting array, followed by resetting the page and refreshing the dataset.

Now, you can build and deploy these changes to your Dataverse environment. Once deployed, configure the control on the form and navigate to the same form. You can see a new button named **Sort fullname** as shown in the following screenshot:

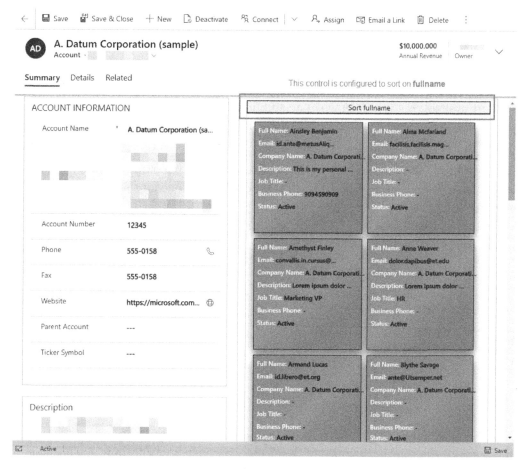

Figure 11.1 – Preview of the control with the sort button

Now, that we have learned how to perform sorting on data in a code component, let's learn how to perform pagination.

> **Note**
>
> Some of these features won't work in canvas apps as both model-driven and canvas apps interact differently with the code component.

Implementing pagination on a dataset

Every dataset code component will need to implement pagination because when you configure your code component on a sub-grid or a view of the application, it provides you with a way to configure the number of records that will be initially displayed by your control. By default, on a sub-grid, this setting is set to 10 records, and on a view, it is set to 50 records.

If you recall when we built the dataset code component in *Chapter 5*, *Code, Test, and Repeat*, we added a **Load More...** button on the dataset that shows up when additional pages are available but is hidden when no additional pages are available. At that time, we did not add any logic to this button that would implement showing the data from those additional pages.

Now, we will add an event listener on this button in the `init` method and bind it to a function that will perform pagination. The following is the code for the function that will perform the pagination:

index.ts

```
private LoadMorePages() {
  if (this.theContext
    .parameters.datasetGrid.paging.hasNextPage)
  {
    this.theContext
        .parameters.datasetGrid.paging.loadNextPage();
  }
}
```

Once you make these changes to the code component, deploy it to a Dataverse environment. After the deployment of the changes, navigate to the form where the code component is configured and click on the **Load More...** button. This will load the next page of data as shown in the following screenshot:

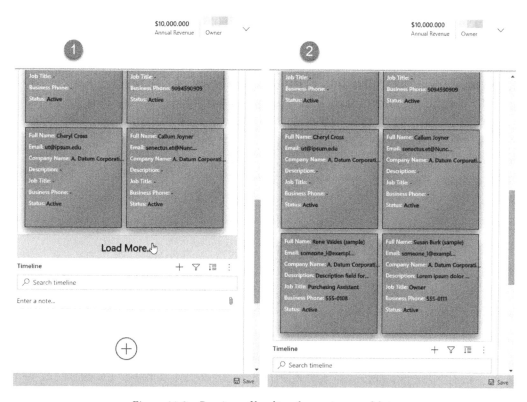

Figure 11.2 – Preview of loading the next page of data

As you can observe, when you click on the **Load More...** button, the next page of data is loaded, and the button gets hidden because there are no more pages left to load.

The framework provides four functions on the dataset parameter related to pagination, which are as follows:

- `hasNextPage`: This function returns true if there is an additional page to load, otherwise it returns false.

- `loadNextPage`: This function will load the next page.

- `hasPreviousPage`: This function returns true if there is a previous page available, otherwise it returns false.

- `loadPreviousPage`: This function will load the previous page.

The `hasNextPage` and `hasPreviousPage` functions will help you decide whether to show or hide the next and previous buttons, for example, as they are used in the `toggleLoadMoreButton` method in the dataset code component.

But pagination works differently in model-driven and canvas apps. When you invoke the `loadNextPage` method, in model-driven apps, the next page of data will be appended to the existing data, whereas in canvas apps, the next page of data will load on top of the existing data.

The following screenshot portrays the behavior of pagination in a code component on a model-driven app:

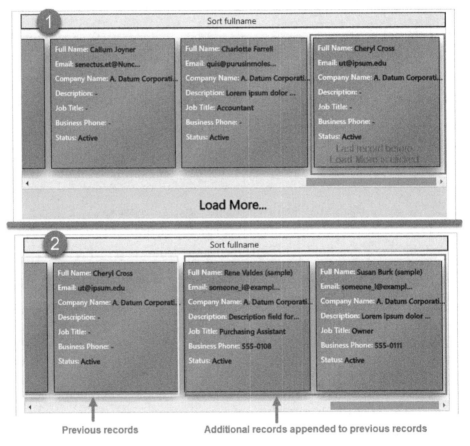

Figure 11.3 – A before and after screenshot of clicking the Load More… button in a model-driven app

As you can observe, when you scroll to the last record, you see a contact with the name **Cheryl Cross** and after you click the **Load More…** button, two additional records appear appending the existing records.

The following screenshot portrays the behavior of pagination in a code component on a canvas app:

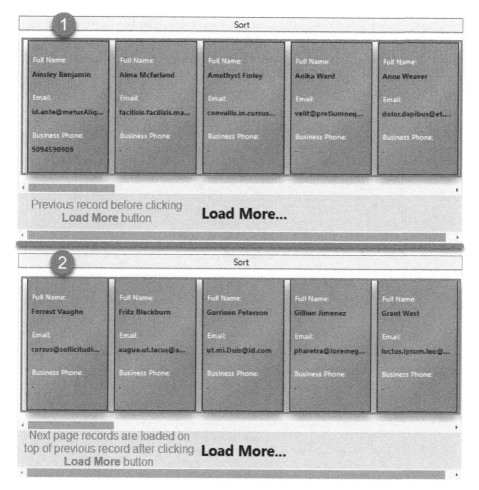

Figure 11.4 – A before and after screenshot of clicking the Load More... button in canvas app

As you can observe, with the code component in a canvas app, when the app loads, you have **Ainsley Benjamin** as the first record, but when you click the **Load More...** button, the entire set of records is replaced with records from the next page.

Another method provided by the framework is the `totalResultCount` method, which provides the total number of records available on the server for the current dataset. But this method also behaves differently in model-driven and canvas apps. In model-driven apps, it correctly provides you with the count of total records in the current dataset, whereas in canvas apps, in the `init` method, the total record count will be *-1*. When you click on the **Load More…** button, the count will increment, and this count will keep on increasing as you load the next pages. This is shown in the following screenshot:

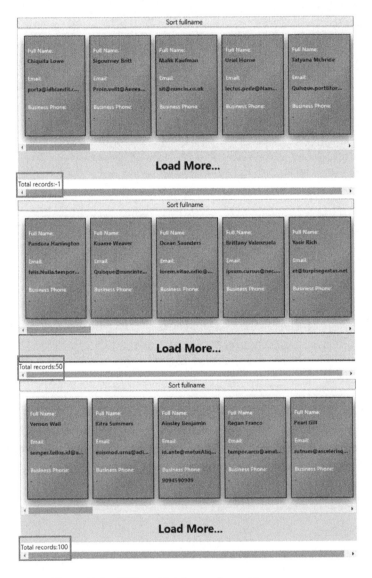

Figure 11.5 – Different total record count in canvas apps

As shown in the figure, initially, the total record count is **-1**. When the **Load More…** button is clicked, the total record count shown is **50** and when another **Load More…** button is clicked, it shows **100** even though the actual total record count is **115**. So, when building a code component that will support both model-driven and canvas apps, please be mindful of the behavior difference when it comes to the `totalResultCount` method.

Next, let's understand the process of making the dataset code component seamlessly integrate with out-of-the-box options provided by the model-driven app.

Integrating code components with out-of-the-box options

The application provides three out-of-the-box options on every view or sub-grid: namely, the command bar, the view selector, and quick search. These options not only enhance the user interface but also closely interact with the data on the view or sub-grid. The way the command bar interacts with the dataset is if you select a record from the dataset, then the list of buttons on the command bar will change. The view selector provides a different dataset query, which changes the data on the dataset. The quick find enables the user to search and filter the records within the dataset.

PCF provides an additional parameter that you can define on the `data-set` tag in the `ControlManifest.Input.xml` file. You can enable or disable which of the options you want your dataset to integrate with the options provided by the application. The following snippet sets all three options as true, which means that they are enabled to integrate:

ControlManifest.Input.xml

```
<data-set name="datasetGrid"
  display-name-key="Data Cards"
  cds-data-set-options=
    "displayCommandBar:true; // command bar option
    displayViewSelector:true; // view selector option
    displayQuickFindSearch:true; // Homepage quick find option
    displayQuickFind:true" // Sub-grid quick find option
 />
</data-set>
```

The parameter is `cds-data-set-options` and the value of this parameter is a string that contains three comma-separated key-value pairs that define the three options. The values for all three options are true or false.

> **Note**
> Since CDS was renamed to Dataverse, there is a possibility that the `cds-data-set-options` property might be renamed in the future.

Once you have added these options to the `ControlManifest.Input.xml` file, deploy it to your Dataverse environment. Now, navigate to the form where your dataset code component is configured, and you will see a command bar, view selector, and quick find search bar appear above your code component. The following screenshot shows the enabled options:

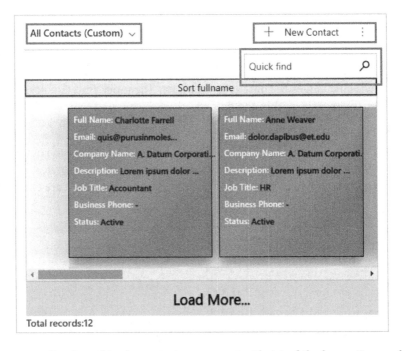

Figure 11.6 – Preview of the dataset code component with out-of-the-box options enabled

If you change the view, then the data inside your code component will also change. If you try to search for a record, the data will filter and show you only the matching records in your dataset.

> **Note**
> The view selector and quick find options should also be enabled on the sub-grid from the form customization.

The command bar will not react to any changes on the dataset. For example, if your dataset allowed the selection of records, then the expectation is that the command bar will show different buttons such as **Edit**; but we need to add additional code to indicate the command bar of the activity that happens in the dataset code component. So, let's look at how we can seamlessly integrate with the command bar.

PCF provides a function called `setSelectedRecordIds` that enables us to let the framework inform the command bar on the host that certain records were selected in the code component. Let's expand our dataset by adding record selection, and to do so, we need to add a string array class-level variable that will hold the selected record IDs and a checkbox on the card that will enable us to select those records. The following code snippet will provide the details to the checkbox in the `createCard` method:

index.ts

```
this.selectCheck = document.createElement("input");
this.selectCheck.type = "checkbox";
this.selectCheck.value =
  gridParam.records[currentRecordId].getRecordId();
this.selectCheck.addEventListener("click",
  this.RecordSelection.bind(this));
gridRecord.appendChild(this.selectCheck);
```

Observe that, on this checkbox, we have defined an event listener named `RecordSelection`, which we need to define. This method will set and unset the record selection as follows:

index.ts

```
private RecordSelection(selectedControl: any): void {
  if (selectedControl.target.checked) {
    this.selectionIds.push(selectedControl.target.value);
    this.theContext.parameters.datasetGrid
      .setSelectedRecordIds(this.selectionIds);
  }
  else {
```

```
this.selectionIds = this.selectionIds.filter((n) => {
    return n != selectedControl.target.value
});
this.theContext.parameters.datasetGrid
    .setSelectedRecordIds(this.selectionIds);
    }
}
```

Based on whether the checkbox is checked or not, we have to either add or remove the record ID from the string array, followed by setting the new value in the string array that will indicate the host of these changes using the `setSelectedRecordsIds` method. The following screenshot shows the difference when a record is selected and not selected:

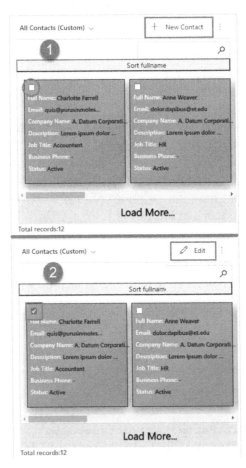

Figure 11.7 – The command bar reacts to the record selection on a sub-grid in a model-driven app

As you can see in the figure, when you *check* the first checkbox, the command bar button changes from **New** to **Edit** and when you *uncheck* the checkbox, the command bar button is reset to the original.

Now that you have learned how to integrate your code components with out-of-the-box options, let's learn about the process to open a record from your code component.

Understanding the technique to open a record from a dataset

The current out-of-the-box sub-grid allows you to open a record when you double-click on it and shows a hyperlink to the lookups, which makes it more user-friendly. But when you create code components, you have to implement these features on your own and it will vary based on the design of your code component.

Let's expand our code component that will show a hyperlink on the primary field and lookups, which when clicked will open those records. We will update the createCardItems method to check whether the datatype of the column is a lookup or primary field, then add a class that will display this record differently than all other records. The following is the updated code snippet on the createCardItems method:

index.ts

```
if (columnItems.dataType.startsWith('Lookup.') ||
  columnItems.isPrimary) {
    content.classList.add("gridText", "gridTextLookup");
    content.addEventListener("click",
      this.NavigateToRecord.bind(this));
    if (columnItems.dataType.startsWith('Lookup.')) {
      let lookupER = gridParam.records[currentRecordId]
        .getValue(columnItems.name) as
          ComponentFramework.EntityReference;
      content.id = lookupER.id.guid;
      content.setAttribute(
        lookupEntityName, lookupER.etn ?? "");
    }
    if (columnItems.isPrimary) {
      content.id = gridParam
        .records[currentRecordId].getRecordId();
      // Unsupported
```

```
            content.setAttribute
              (lookupEntityName, (<any>gridParam
                .records[currentRecordId].getNamedReference()
              ).entityName ?? "");
      }
  }
```

In this method, we are determining whether the datatype is a lookup or primary and adding the gridTextLookup class to the span tag. Next, we determine whether the datatype is a lookup, then we fetch the ID and entity name from the dataset and assign it on the span tag so we can retrieve these details when it is clicked. Similarly, we retrieve the ID and entity name and assign it to the span tag. The reason for two different if statements is that the retrieval of the ID and entity name process is different for those two types as highlighted in the code. Also, as highlighted, we add an event listener on the click event that will invoke the NavigateToRecord method. This method is shown as follows:

index.ts

```
private NavigateToRecord(selectedControl: any): void {
  this.theContext.navigation.openForm({
    entityName: selectedControl.target
                    .getAttribute(lookupEntityName),
    entityId: selectedControl.target.id
  });
}
```

In this method, we call the openForm method provided by the framework that enables us to open a specific record when supplied with the proper entity name and ID. Because we saved the entity name and ID on the span tag, we retrieve them from the control's target and pass those values to the openForm method.

Next, let's add some styling to the new class we added, so that the lookups and primary field will look different. The following is the `gridTextLookup` class we define in the stylesheet:

MyDataCard.css

```css
.PowerMeUp\.MyDataCard .gridTextLookup {
    text-decoration: underline;
    color: mediumvioletred !important;
    cursor: pointer;
}
```

Now, you need to build and deploy the code component to a Dataverse environment. Once deployed, open the form or a view where the code component is configured, and you will observe that the primary field and lookup are now highlighted in red with an underline. The following screenshot shows how the code component will look once the changes are applied:

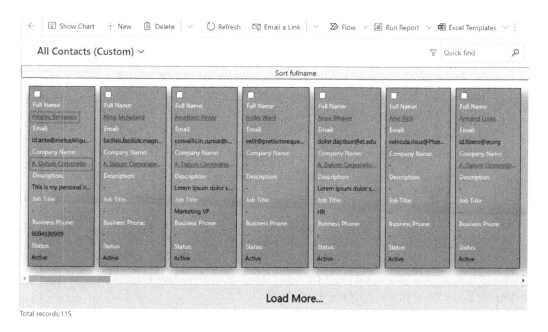

Figure 11.8 – Styling on the lookup and primary field

If you click on the highlighted fields, then you will navigate to that record. If no value exists on the lookup, then there is no style applied and clicking on such fields will have no effect.

Next, let's learn how to make sure certain data points are always available to us when building a dataset code component even if that data point is not part of the view.

Defining properties on a dataset

The `dataset` tag in the `ControlManifest.Input.xml` file allows you to define properties on a dataset. These properties are like the properties defined in a field-type code component, but instead, the tag is named `property-set`. When a property is defined on a dataset, the framework includes that property as a column in the dataset, making sure it is available at runtime even when it is not part of the view.

In our example dataset, we will add a `property-set` to capture a mobile phone number and any record that does not have a mobile phone number will be highlighted in a different color. First, we need to add the `property-set` in the `ControlManifest.Input.xml` file, which is shown in the following snippet:

ControlManifest.Input.xml

```xml
<data-set name="datasetGrid"
  display-name-key="Data Cards"
  cds-data-set-options=
    "displayCommandBar:true;displayViewSelector:true;
    displayQuickFindSearch:true;displayQuickFind:true">
      <property-set name="mobilePhone"
        display-name-key="Mobile Phone"
        description-key="Mobile Phone"
        of-type="SingleLine.Phone"
        usage="bound" required="true" />
</data-set>
```

As we have added a new property, we need to rebuild the PCF project so that the `ManifestTypes.d.ts` file will be regenerated with the new property definition. Once the build is successful, we need to add a new CSS class that will highlight the card. The following is the code snippet for the new class:

MyDataCard.css

```css
.PowerMeUp\.MyDataCard .gridItemHighlight {
  margin: 5px;
  width: 200px;
```

```
    color: white;
    border: solid thin black;
    padding: 5px;
    text-align: left;
    float: left;
    background-color: #1f2cdb;
    background-image:
      linear-gradient
        (141deg, #9fb8ad 0%, #1f2cdb 51%, #2c48e8 75%);
    box-shadow: 0 10px 16px 0 rgba(0,0,0,0.2),
      0 6px 20px 0 rgba(0,0,0,0.19) !important;
}
```

This class is a copy of the `gridItem` class but with a different `background-color` and `background-image` as highlighted in the code.

Next, we need to check whether the mobile phone number exists on a record and accordingly assign the appropriate CSS class name. This code needs to be added in the `createCard` function, as shown in the following code snippet:

index.ts

```
private createCard(columnsOnView: DataSetInterfaces.Column[],
    gridParam: DataSet,
    currentRecordId: string): HTMLDivElement {
    let mobilePhone = gridParam.records[currentRecordId]
      .getFormattedValue("mobilePhone");
    let isMobilePhoneExists =
      mobilePhone != null && mobilePhone !=
      "" ? true : false;
    let gridRecord: HTMLDivElement =
      document.createElement("div");
    gridRecord.className =
      isMobilePhoneExists ? "gridItem" :
      "gridItemHighlight";
}
```

The `createCard` function has three parameters: `columnsOnView`, `gridParam`, and `currentRecordId`. Assume that we have not configured the `mobilePhone` field on the view where this dataset is going to be configured. Hence, `columnsOnView` will not have the `mobilePhone` column data as it is not part of the view, but you can still access the data using `gridParam` because it is part of the dataset records; you just need to hardcode the value that you defined in the manifest file even though the actual schema name could be different. The reason for using the `property-set` name is to make it generic as you have defined the `property-set` name, which won't change, and that `property-set` can be bound to any field.

Once all the changes are implemented, you can deploy the code component and configure the view again as the new property needs to be bound to a **Mobile Phone** column or any column you want. The following is a screenshot of a view on the **Contact** entity when the code component is configured on a mobile phone number:

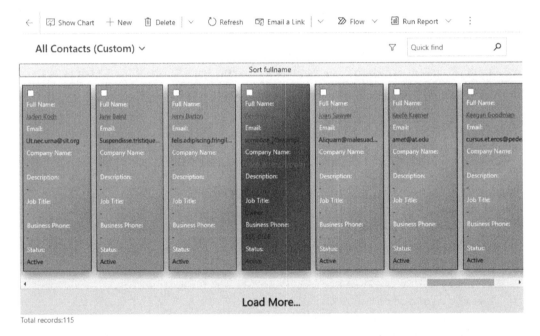

Figure 11.9 – Data card highlighted when no mobile phone exists on a record

As you can see from the screenshot, even though **Mobile Phone** is not displayed on the card, one of the records is highlighted as that record does not have a mobile phone number populated.

Summary

In this chapter, we learned how to sort data and implement pagination on a dataset. We also learned the best way to integrate with the out-of-the-box options provided by the application and understood the technique to add styling based on a condition. Finally, we learned how to open a record from a code component. These advanced features will help you build complex code components that can provide a rich and integrated user experience for the host application.

In the next chapter, we will learn how to enrich your development experience, implementing a testing framework and building a code component using React plus Fluent UI.

Test your knowledge

1. Which of the following functions is provided by the framework? (*100 points*)

    a. `context.parameters.dataset.sorting.sortAscending`

    b. `context.parameters.dataset.paging.loadNextPage`

2. Which of the following will show the quick find search box on the home page? (*100 points*)

    a. `displayQuickFindSearch`

    b. `displayQuickFind`

3. What happens when the `id` parameter in the `openForm` method is an empty string? (*200 points*)

    a. An error with the following message is returned by the function: **The requested record was not found or you do not have sufficient permissions to view it**.

    b. A new form for the specified entity is opened by the application.

Further reading

- Additional details on sort status can be found on Microsoft Docs at `http://bit.ly/PCF-SortStatus`.

- More details on implementing sorting in code components were discussed on a forum thread that can be found at `http://bit.ly/ForumThread-Sorting-PCF`.

- Additional details on pagination can be found on Microsoft Docs at `http://bit.ly/PCF-Paging`.

- Details on dataset properties can be found on Microsoft Docs at `http://bit.ly/PCF-DataSetElement`.

- Additional details on navigation besides opening a form can be found on Microsoft Docs at `http://bit.ly/PCF-Navigation`.

12

Enriching Your Dev Experience

In the previous chapters, we learned about the process of creating a complex dataset and looked into more advanced features provided by the framework. In this chapter, we will learn about features that are not provided by the framework but are part of modern web development. We will learn how to use Prettier and Lint, setting up a testing framework, using React and Fluent UI to build a code component. By the end of the chapter, you should be able to set up your PCF project with these features, which will enhance your development experience.

In this chapter, we are going to cover the following main topics:

- Using Lint and Prettier
- Setting up a testing framework
- Using React and Fluent UI to build code components

Technical requirements

In order to work through this chapter, you need to install all the prerequisites that will help you with the development process mentioned in *Chapter 1, Introduction to the Power Apps Component Framework*. Download the example library from https://github. com/PacktPublishing/Extending-Microsoft-Power-Apps-with-Power-Apps-Component-Framework/tree/master/Chapter12. There are different folders for each section; so, make sure you are using the right project for the right section by checking the folder name. You will also need to install **Visual Studio Code**, **PCF Builder**, and **Google Chrome**.

Using Lint and Prettier

When you write code, if it is not readable or each developer uses their own coding styles, then the code review might be affected, which can lead to the creation of bugs and issues. This is where Lint and Prettier come in handy.

Understanding the process of linting your code

Linting is an automated process to check your code for programming and styling errors. This process is accomplished by using lint tools, also called **linters**. When we are dealing with **TypeScript**, there are two linters available to us: one is called **ESLint** and the other is **TSLint**. As **TSLint** is now deprecated, we will only be working with **ESLint**.

First, we will initialize a new PCF project. Once the project is initialized, install all the required **ESLint** packages using the following command in the VS Code integrated terminal as shown in the screenshot:

```
npm install eslint @typescript-eslint/parser @typescript-eslint/eslint-plugin --save-dev
```

Figure 12.1 – Command to install ESLint packages

We are using the `--save-dev` attribute because these packages are not needed for the execution of the application but instead are only needed for improving the development process. The following are the descriptions for each of the packages we just installed:

- `eslint`: This is the core **ESLint** package that provides the core linting features.

- `@typescript-eslint/parser`: This package allows you to lint TypeScript code.

- `@typescript-eslint/eslint-plugin`: This package contains several **ESLint** rules specific to TypeScript code.

Next, we need to add a configuration file named `.eslintrc.json` for **ESLint** in the root directory of our PCF project and the following will be the contents of that file:

.eslintrc.json

```json
{
    "parser": "@typescript-eslint/parser",
    "env": {
        "browser": true,
        "commonjs": true,
        "es6": true
    },
    "extends": [
        "plugin:@typescript-eslint/recommended"
    ],
    "parserOptions": {
        "project": "./tsconfig.json"
    },
    "plugins": [
        "@typescript-eslint"
    ]
}
```

When working with **React,** you will have to enable a few more options in the **ESLint** configuration file. These options are shown in the following snippet:

.eslintrc.json

```json
{
    ...
    "settings": {
        "react": {
            "pragma": "React",
            "version": "detect"
        }
    },
    "extends": [
        "plugin:@typescript-eslint/recommended",
```

```
        "plugin:react/recommended",
    ],
    ...
}
```

As you can see from the highlights, when working with React we had to add a `settings` section and an extra option under the `extends` section.

Next, let's look at the process to invoke the linting process. There are two ways to execute the linter: one is using the ESLint **command-line interface** (**CLI**), and another is using the ESLint VS Code extension. We will first learn how to use the **ESLint CLI**.

To start with the ESLint CLI, we need to globally install the core CLI package using the following command, which needs to be executed only once:

```
npm install -g eslint
```

After the CLI package is installed, you can run the command `eslint ./**/*.ts --fix` in the VS Code integrated terminal, which will showcase all the issues in the current code files. Alternatively, you can add this command in the `package.json` file under script.

Now let's see how we can use a VS Code extension to help us use **ESLint**. First, we need to install the extension from the following URL: `http://bit.ly/VSCodeExt-ESLint`. Next, using your command palette, type `ESLint` in the command palette bar and click on **Manage Library Execution**, which will show a prompt; click **Allow** to enable the linting for this specific project or **Allow Everywhere** to enable it globally. This will start showing all the errors and warnings on the *TypeScript* code files, which means your **ESLint** extension is configured.

Next, let's configure the Prettier extension, which, in conjunction with a linter, will help you define rules for your development.

Integrating Prettier with a linter

Prettier is a code formatter extension that parses and formats your code with its own rules. This helps with the consistent styling of code throughout your project team.

In the same PCF project, we will first install Prettier using the following command:

```
npm install prettier --save-dev --save-exact
```

As you can see, we have used the --save-dev attribute as previously mentioned, but in addition to that, we also used the --save-exact attribute because even a slightly different version of **Prettier** can result in different formatting. Using the --save-exact attribute makes sure that all the team members are using the same version of Prettier.

Now, we need to install a couple of packages that will help us integrate Prettier with ESLint. The command shown in the following screenshot is to install those packages:

```
npm install eslint-config-prettier eslint-plugin-prettier --save-dev
```

Figure 12.2 – Command to integrate the Prettier plugin

Let's look at the description for each of the packages we just installed:

- prettier: This is the core Prettier package that provides the rules for formatting.
- eslint-config-prettier: This package helps in disabling the rules provided by ESLint that conflict with Prettier.
- eslint-plugin-prettier: This package runs Prettier as an ESLint rule.

Next, we need to add a configuration file named .prettierrc.json for **Prettier** in the root directory of your PCF project and the following will be the contents of that file:

.prettierrc.json

```
{
    "semi": true,
    "trailingComma": "all",
    "singleQuote": false,
    "printWidth": 120,
    "tabWidth": 2,
    "endOfLine":"auto"
}
```

As we have added prettier on the PCF project, we need to work on integrating Prettier with ESLint. This is done by editing the ESLint configuration file. The following snippet showcases the new edits you will have to make in the ESLint configuration file:

.eslintrc.json

```json
{
    ...
    "extends": [
        ...
        "plugin:prettier/recommended",
        "prettier",
        "prettier/@typescript-eslint"
    ],
    ...
    "plugins": [
        "@typescript-eslint",
        "prettier"
    ],
    "rules": {
        "prettier/prettier": "error"
    }
}
```

The highlighted edits will enable the linting process to prettify your code using rules from Prettier. We have also added a rule in the `rules` section that will highlight any formatting issues identified by Prettier as an error. If you are working with a React application, then add `prettier/react` in the `extends` section of the ESLint configuration file.

Let's now see how these work in conjunction with each other.

Working with ESLint and Prettier

Once both these extensions are integrated with each other, we can add some code to our PCF code component. If you have installed the ESLint VS Code extension, you will see the errors and warnings instantaneously. The following screenshot shows us one such error when using the ESLint VS Code extension:

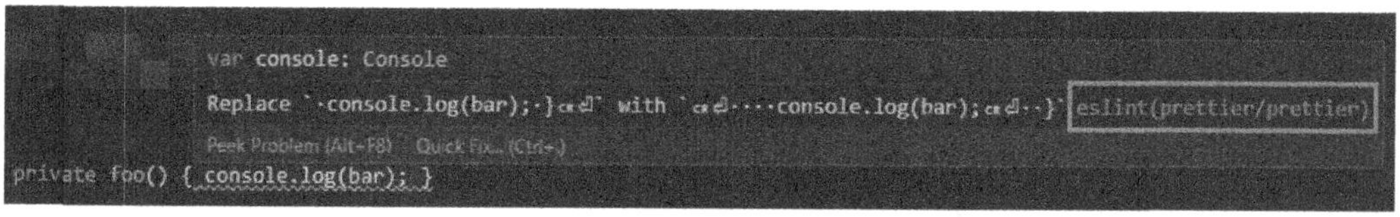

Figure 12.3 – ESLint and Prettier in action

As you can see from the screenshot, the ESLint VS Code extension is showing a formatting issue identified by Prettier as an error in the code.

Let's now add a Prettier VS Code extension that will help us format the documents. To install the Prettier VS Code extension, navigate to the following URL: `http://bit.ly/VSCodeExt-Prettier`. Once you have installed the extension, when you format the code using the default keyboard shortcut *Shift + Alt + F*, you might be asked by VS Code to select your formatter. You can choose Prettier as your default formatter and this setting will be saved globally. The following is a screenshot of the prompt you will see when you format a document:

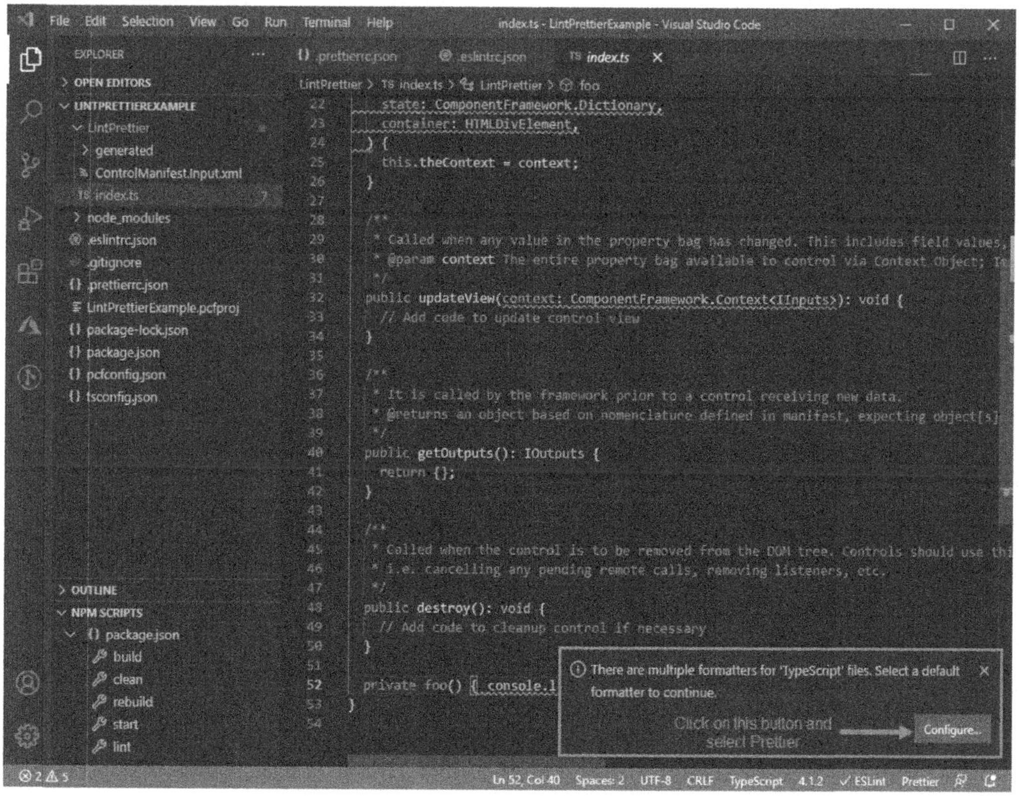

Figure 12.4 – Selecting a default formatter globally

On this prompt, click on the **Configure** button and select **Prettier – Code formatter** for `TypeScript` files. As soon as you do that, the code will be formatted as per the formatting rules defined by Prettier and you can save your files.

You can also enable the setting to format the document every time you save the file. This can be done by going to **File > Preference > Settings** from the menu bar and searching for `format on save` in the search box. This will present you with multiple settings options. Look for **Editor: Format On Save** and check the provided checkbox to enable the formatting of a document on saving. This is shown in the following screenshot:

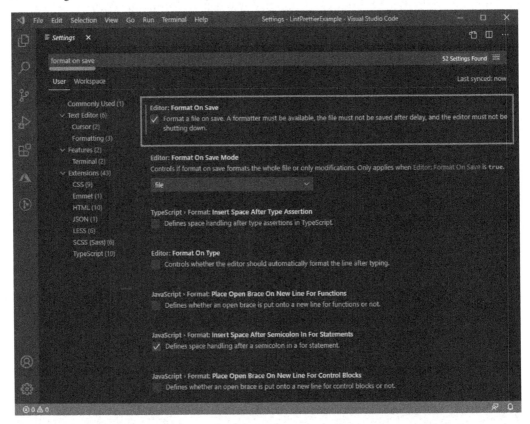

Figure 12.5 – Setting for enabling the formatting of a document on saving

Once enabled, whenever you save an unformatted document, VS Code will invoke the default formatter. In this case, it will invoke Prettier and format the document before saving.

Next, let's learn how to set up a testing framework on our PCF project.

Setting up a testing framework

We will be using **Jest** as our testing framework tool. It was initially developed for JavaScript, hence the name **Jest**. But today it works with various projects using TypeScript, React, Node.js, Angular, and so on.

First, we need to install Jest in our project using the following command:

```
npm install jest @types/jest ts-jest --save-dev
```

Similar to the previous section, we use the `--save-dev` attribute as this activity will only be performed during the development phase and has no effect on running the application.

Now, let's add a folder named `tests` and create a configuration file named `jest.config.js` in the root directory of your PCF project for Jest to run its test cases. The following is the sample configuration file for Jest:

---

jest.config.js

```
module.exports = {
  verbose: true,
  rootDir: ".",
  testMatch: ["<rootDir>/tests/*.(spec|test).(j|t)s"],
  transform: {
    "^.+\\.(ts|tsx)$": "ts-jest",
  },
};
```

The attribute values defined in the Jest config file are described as follows:

- `verbose`: This determines whether the output produced by Jest during testing should contain in-depth details of the execution or should be just an overview of the outcome of test execution.

- `rootDir`: This specifies the root directory based on the placement of your Jest config file. In our instance, the Jest config file is in the root directory; it has **.** as the value.

- testMatch: By default, test files are located next to the code files in a folder named __tests__. But you can change that setting by using the testMatch attribute. It contains an expression that helps Jest to search for test files. In our instance, the test files can be found in the tests folder in the root directory where the name of the file can be anything followed by a . and either spec or test with the extension js or ts. For example, these are valid filenames: index.test.js, index.test.ts, index.spec.js, and index.spec.ts.

- transform: This attribute in the config specifies that Jest uses ts-jest for ts or tsx files.

Using our code component from the example library, let's create a test file named index.spec.ts under the tests folder in the root directory. Before you start creating your test files, you must ensure that the project contains testable code. If you write code with low coupling and a clear distinction between logic and presentation, then you can test the individual functions independently. With that in mind, the code in this PCF project where we are creating a *Character Counter* control from the example library is slightly different than the *Character Counter* control we created in *Chapter 5, Code, Test, and Repeat*. The following is an example of a test file:

index.spec.ts

```
import { MyCharacterCounter } from "../MyCharCount/index";
describe("CharacterCounter", () => {
  let instance: MyCharacterCounter;
  beforeEach(() => {
    instance = new MyCharacterCounter();
  });
  it("should get positive number", () => {
    expect(instance).toBeInstanceOf(MyCharacterCounter);
    const chars = instance.GetCharacterCount(100, 90);
    expect(chars).toEqual(10);
  });
  it("should get negative number", () => {
    expect(instance).toBeInstanceOf(MyCharacterCounter);
    const chars = instance.GetCharacterCount(100, 110);
    expect(chars).toEqual(-10);
  });
});
```

In this file, we are testing the `GetCharacterCount` function in the `MyCharacterCounter` class, which takes in two parameters of type number and returns the number of characters left from the maximum character limit, which is a numerical value. As you can see, this test file has two test cases: one is to test whether the output is a positive number and the second is to test whether the output is a negative number. Once you have added the code in the test file, you can invoke Jest to run the test cases by using the following command in the VS Code terminal:

```
npx jest
```

This will run all the test files and all the test cases within those test files. The following is a screenshot of the execution after running the `npx jest` command:

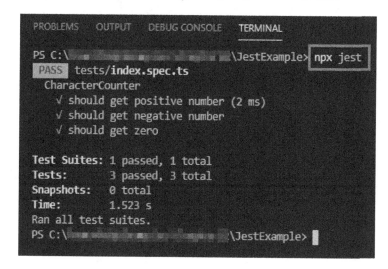

Figure 12.6 – Preview of the test case execution by Jest

Alternatively, you can also add `"test"` : `"jest"` under `scripts` section in the `package.json` file, which will initiate the execution of Jest from `npm scripts`. If you have added this to your `package.json` file, then you can also execute test cases by using the `npm run test` command. If you want to run a specific test file, then you can execute the same command followed by the filename; for example, if you wanted to run tests from the `index.spec.ts` file, then the command will be `npm run test index`.

If you want to get test coverage, then you can append the `--coverage` attribute to the `jest` command. This will produce a table that will show the percentage of the coverage and identify the line numbers of uncovered test cases. The following screenshot shows the coverage of the example code component we built in this section:

```
PS C:\                            \2.JestExample> npx jest --coverage
 PASS   tests/index.spec.ts
  CharacterCounter
    √ should get positive number (2 ms)
    √ should get negative number (1 ms)
    √ should get zero

----------|---------|----------|---------|---------|-------------------
File      | % Stmts | % Branch | % Funcs | % Lines | Uncovered Line #s
----------|---------|----------|---------|---------|-------------------
All files |      30 |        0 |   42.86 |   27.59 |
 index.ts |      30 |        0 |   42.86 |   27.59 | 33-55,63-70,78
----------|---------|----------|---------|---------|-------------------
Test Suites: 1 passed, 1 total
Tests:       3 passed, 3 total
Snapshots:   0 total
Time:        3.318 s
Ran all test suites.
PS C:\                            \2.JestExample>
```

Figure 12.7 – Preview of the test case execution by Jest using coverage

Execution of coverage also creates a folder named `coverage` in your project directory that contains a detailed report for the test coverage in your project.

Now, let's look at how to utilize React and Fluent UI to build code components.

Using React and Fluent UI to build code components

React is an open source JavaScript library that helps you build user interface libraries and components. **Fluent UI**, on the other hand, is a cross-platform design system created by Microsoft that provides you with a framework to create user interfaces that include accessibility, internationalization, and performance.

Most of the code components on PCF Gallery are created using React because it provides a rich user interface. In this section, we will be building a simple user persona with an adjustable size that can be controlled by a slider. This code component will use both React and Fluent UI.

First, we need to initialize a PCF project. In order to do this, we will use PCF Builder for VS Code. Here are the steps to create the project:

1. Start your command palette using the keyboard shortcut *Ctrl + Shift + P*.

2. Search for `PCF Builder`, and select **Initialize Component (Simple)**.

3. Enter `PowerMeUp` as a namespace.

4. Enter `ResizablePersona` as the name of the control.

5. Select `Field` as the type of the code component.

6. Select **React + Fluent UI**, which will install the required libraries for React and Fluent UI on this project.

This will initialize a new project that will contain React and Fluent UI libraries.

Let's add a new extension file named `Persona.tsx` inside the `ResizablePersona` folder. In this file, import the required React and Fluent UI component libraries. The following is the code that needs to be added:

Persona.tsx

```
import * as React from "react";
import { IPersonaSharedProps,
  Persona,
  PersonaSize,
  PersonaPresence,
} from "@fluentui/react/lib/Persona";
import { Slider } from "@fluentui/react/lib/Slider";
import { Stack } from "@fluentui/react/lib/Stack";
import { TestImages } from "@uifabric/example-data";
```

As we are creating this as an example, we are using some example data that is made available from the @ui-fabric library. Currently, you will see an error on this import; so, let's resolve that error by installing that library as well. This is shown in the following command:

```
npm install @uifabric/example-data
```

Once this package is installed, the error should disappear. Next, let's create the class that will contain the user interface. The following is the code for the class that you can add below the import statements:

Persona.tsx

```tsx
export const CustomPersona: React.FunctionComponent = () => {
  return (
    <Stack tokens={{ childrenGap: 10 }}>
      <Slider
        label="Control the size of Persona"
        max={5}
        onChange={sliderOnChange}
      />
      <Persona
        {...examplePersona}
        size={personaSizeValue}
        presence={PersonaPresence.online}
      />
    </Stack>
  );
};
```

As you can observe, we defined two main controls, – a slider and a persona, both of which are provided by the Fluent UI library. At this point, you will have a couple of errors. Let's rectify those. We need to define some constant variables inside the function component. First, let's define examplePersona as follows:

Persona.tsx

```tsx
const examplePersona: IPersonaSharedProps = {
  imageUrl: TestImages.personaFemale,
```

```
    imageInitials: "AL",
    text: "Annie Lindqvist",
    secondaryText: "Software Engineer",
    tertiaryText: "In a meeting",
    optionalText: "Available at 4:00pm",
};
```

Next, we need to define the `state` variable to hold slider and persona size values. This is accomplished with the following code:

Persona.tsx

```
const [sliderValue, setSliderValue] = React.useState(0);
const [personaSizeValue, setPersonaSizeValue] =
    React.useState(
        PersonaSize.size32
    );
```

In this code, we set the slider value default to *0* and the persona size value default to `size32`. Now, we need to define the `sliderOnChange` method to complete the user interface for this component. This is as follows:

Persona.tsx

```
const sliderOnChange = (value: number) => {
  setSliderValue(value);
  switch (value) {
    case 0:
      setPersonaSizeValue(PersonaSize.size32);
      break;
    case 1:
      setPersonaSizeValue(PersonaSize.size48);
      break;
    case 2:
      setPersonaSizeValue(PersonaSize.size56);
      break;
    case 3:
      setPersonaSizeValue(PersonaSize.size72);
```

```
        break;
      case 4:
        setPersonaSizeValue(PersonaSize.size100);
        break;
      case 5:
        setPersonaSizeValue(PersonaSize.size120);
        break;
      default:
        break;
    }
  };
```

We are using the `switch` statement because `PersonaSize` is an enum but the slider value is an integer. So, in this method, we define which slider value corresponds to which persona size.

Once your component is ready, we need to add it to the index file provided by Power Apps Component Framework. In your `index.ts` file, you need to import the React library along with the component extension file we just created. The following are the `import` statements that need to be added:

index.ts

```
import * as React from "react";
import * as ReactDOM from "react-dom";
import { CustomPersona } from "./Persona";
```

`CustomPersona` is the name of the function component defined in the `Persona.tsx` file. Next, in the `init` method, we need to render the component we created in the extension file using the following code:

index.ts

```
ReactDOM.render(
  React.createElement(CustomPersona),
  container
);
```

The `render` method of `ReactDOM` will render the user interface built in the `CustomPersona` function component on the container element provided by the framework.

Now, you can build and test your component. The following is a screenshot of the code component we built:

Figure 12.8 – Preview of the code component built using React and Fluent UI

Once you initiate a test harness, you can use the slider to increase or decrease the value, which will increase or decrease the size of the persona. When the size of the persona changes, you can observe that the secondary and tertiary text also changes based on the size. Thus, using React and Fluent UI makes it easier to create user interfaces in code components.

Summary

In this chapter, we learned about the process of linting code and integrating Prettier with a linter to format code that provides consistency throughout a project team. We also learned about the process of setting up a test framework using Jest and executing test cases. Lastly, we built a code component using React and Fluent UI. These settings will help you develop better code components by enriching your development experience.

Test your knowledge

1. The `--save-exact` attribute saves the package dependency as one of the dev dependencies. Is this statement correct? (*100 points*)

   a. True

   b. False

2. On which attribute do we define an expression to search for test files in the configuration file for Jest? (*100 points*)

   a. `matchTests`

   b. `testMatch`

3. Which **ESLint** package is required when using `plugin:react/recommended` in the ESLint configuration file? (*200 points*)

   a. `eslint-plugin-react`

   b. `eslint-react`

Further reading

- Additional details on setting up Lint and Prettier can be found at `http://bit.ly/ScottDurow-Linting`.

- Additional information on using ESLint and Prettier can be found at `https://www.robertcooper.me/using-eslint-and-prettier-in-a-typescript-project`.

- To get started with the Jest testing framework, you can find more details at `https://jestjs.io/docs/en/getting-started`.

- A tutorial on getting started with React can be found at `https://reactjs.org/tutorial/tutorial.html`.

- An overview of Fluent UI by Microsoft can be found at `https://developer.microsoft.com/en-us/fluentui`.

Answers to Knowledge Tests

Chapter 1

1. **Correct Answer**: a

   a. Yes, we still need both HTML web resources and code components built using PCF. We discussed this in the section *How are code components different from HTML web resources?*.

   b. This is incorrect as we discussed the reason why we need both HTML web resources and code components in the section *How are code components different from HTML web resources?*.

2. **Correct Answer**: b

   a. This answer is incorrect because, as discussed in the section *Getting to know the licensing requirements*, whenever an app consumes a code component that uses an external service, the user will need a premium Power Apps license to access that app.

   b. This is the correct answer; as discussed in the section *Getting to know the licensing requirements*, whenever an app consumes a code component that uses an external service, the user will need a premium Power Apps license to access that app.

3. **Correct Answer**: b

   a. You can use any integrated development environment and not necessarily Visual Studio Code and hence this is the incorrect answer.

   b. Power Apps CLI is the most crucial tool you will need on your machine as this is the tool that enables you to interact with Power Apps Component Framework and hence is the correct answer.

Chapter 2

1. **Correct Answer**: b

   a. There are no `pcf` commands. Power Apps CLI provides `pac` commands.

   b. Power Apps CLI is a command-line interface that not only provides access to PCF but also provides support for other project types and hence the commands it offers are `pac` commands.

2. **Correct Answer**: a

   a. Because it is a project file that supports PCF, the extension for such a file is `.pcfproj`.

   b. There is no such file with the extension `.pcf` created.

3. **Correct Answer**: b

   a. The PCF `Initialization` command does not allow spaces in `namespace` and `name` and hence this option is the incorrect answer.

   b. The command properly follows all the guidelines when initializing a PCF project, such as no spaces in `namespace` or `name` attribute and the correct option is selected for template attribute. All Power Apps CLI commands have aliases that can be utilized using a single dash (`-`) and for a full name, you need to use a double dash (`--`).

Chapter 3

1. **Correct Answer**: a

   a. PCF Builder is available on XrmToolBox, which provides a graphical user interface, and on Visual Studio Code it provides a guided experience.

   b. PCF Builder is not available on Visual Studio 2019 and Azure DevOps.

2. **Correct Answer**: a

   a. When you have a code component to submit on PCF Gallery, you can use the following direct link: `https://pcf.gallery/submit`.

   b. This is an invalid link. If you want to submit a code component on PCF Gallery, then you need to use `https://pcf.gallery/submit` as the link.

3. **Correct Answer**: b

   a. The attribute for skipping a solution is of type Boolean, which accepts `true` or `false` as valid values.

   b. This command correctly passes the `true` value to skip the creation of a Dataverse solution project.

Chapter 4

1. **Correct Answer**: b

   a. The Power Apps CLI command provides a basic folder structure.

   b. PCF Generator provides the recommended folder structure with all the references added in the `ControlManifest` file.

2. **Correct Answer**: b

   a. None of these functions except `destroy` are provided by Power Apps Component Framework.

   b. Power Apps Component Framework provides these four default functions with each of those playing an important role in the component's life cycle.

3. **Correct Answer**: a

   a. A code component initialized with the dataset template can also contain the `property` tag in the `ControlManifest` file along with the `data-set` tag. It can also contain multiple `data-set` tags.

   b. The `data-set` tag and `property` tag can co-exist on a `ControlManifest` file for dataset control, but not vice versa.

Chapter 5

1. **Correct Answer**: b

   a. The command `npm start` will just initiate the testing but will not watch the files for changes.

   b. The command `npm start watch` indicates to the local web server to watch for any file changes. If any file is changed, then it will rebuild the project and reload the browser with new changes.

2. **Correct Answer**: a

    a. The template with the option `dataset` is used to initialize the PCF project for views and sub-grids. The word `dataset` is used because we are creating a code component for multiple rows of data.

    b. There are only two options available when creating a PCF project; one is `field`, and another is `dataset`. The option `field` is used to initialize a PCF project for a single field or an attribute, whereas the option `dataset` is used to initialize a PCF project for a view or a sub-grid.

3. **Correct Answer**: a

    a. The default file that the test harness accepts is the `.cvs` file.

    b. No matter how you format your `.xlsx` file, it will not be parsed by the test harness. The only file that has worked so far is the `.cvs` file.

4. **Correct Answer**: b

    a. A single PCF project cannot contain multiple code components and it can only build one code component at a time.

    b. Currently, SCSS files aren't supported by the PCF project.

Chapter 6

1. **Correct Answer**: b

    a. There is no such expression called `(?control)`.

    b. The regular expression with `(?insx)` ensures that case-insensitivity and a few other options are turned on. For more information on this, read the official reference guide from **Telerik** at `http://bit.ly/AutoResponder-Regex`.

2. **Correct Answer**: a

    a. When in edit mode for canvas apps, the `bundle.js` file is loaded from this location and that is the reason you must configure the rule in **AutoResponder** to replace this with the location of `bundle.js` from the local directory.

    b. This is an invalid choice because the `bundle.js` file is referenced with `Resources0Controls0` in the path in canvas apps.

3.   **Correct Answer**: a

   a. After the hard reload, do not forget to add a debug pointer in the index file so you can start debugging in DevTools. Also, when you make any changes to the code, you need to rebuild the PCF project so that the `bundle.js` file is recreated, which gets picked up by AutoResponder.

   b. When you perform a hard reload, the cache is already cleared so you do not need to clear it again. Start watch will initiate testing local but because the code component is already deployed to a model-driven app, you would want to rebuild the PCF project instead.

Chapter 7

1.   **Correct Answer**: a

   a. The command `pac org who` provides you with all the details of the currently active profile.

   b. This command provides you with a list of all the profiles created on a system and shows you the currently active profile but does not provide complete details of the active profile.

2.   **Correct Answer**: b

   a. A publisher prefix can contain a number.

   b. The length of a publisher prefix cannot be more than five characters.

3.   **Correct Answer**: b

   a. This statement is incorrect as you can reuse the publisher prefix for the deployment of multiple code components.

   b. This statement is correct as the tool will append new code components to an existing solution if the prefix matches the one that was deployed earlier.

Chapter 8

1.   **Correct Answer**: b

   a. This command needs to be executed when building the solution project for the first time as it will restore all the project dependencies and then build the project.

b. The `rebuild` switch notifies the `msbuild` command to clean the output directory before starting the build process, making sure you always have the latest build output.

2. **Correct Answer**: a

a. Just as a solution is a container for multiple components, similarly, a Dataverse solution project is a container for multiple project references, especially PCF projects. Hence, when you build a solution project, the output solution file will contain multiple code components.

b. A single PCF project can only be used to create one code component.

3. **Correct Answer**: b

a. A solution that is packaged using the production version has the minified version of the code component, making it difficult to understand and debug the code.

b. As was learned in *Chapter 7 Authentication Profiles*, when using the `pac pcf push` command, the name of the solution file will be a constant `PowerAppsTool_` appended with the prefix you provided in the command.

Chapter 9

1. **Correct Answer**: b

a. A view is a dataset so we can configure code components for type dataset on views.

b. Charts are a different type of component in Dataverse and, currently, code components cannot be configured on charts.

2. **Correct Answer**: a

a. You can have multiple code components of any type inside a gallery component.

b. This is an incorrect answer because we learned in the sub-section *Add a code component in a gallery component* that we can configure field and dataset type code components inside a gallery.

3. **Correct Answer**: a

a. Yes, a canvas app component can contain code components like any other component. And yes, a gallery component that is on a canvas app component can contain code components.

b. A canvas app component treats code components like regular components, hence it can contain code components.

Chapter 10

1. **Correct Answer**: a

    a. As was learned in the section *Exploring the updateView method*, during the first-time load, the updateView method is invoked after the init method.

    b. Any changes to the value in the state would not invoke the updateView method. Learn more about when the updateView method is invoked in the section *Exploring the updateView method* of this chapter.

2. **Correct Answer**: a

    a. The init method provides four parameters: the third parameter, named state, which is of type ComponentFramework.Dictionary, is the one that allows us to cache the data.

    b. The updateView method only has one parameter and that is the context of the component framework.

3. **Correct Answer**: b

    a. The method getBarcodeValue, as of the writing of this book, only works on the Power Apps mobile app.

    b. The method pickFile will work on all devices and will allow you to pick a file from your device.

4. **Correct Answer**: b

    a. The updateRecord method does not throw an error if record ID is sent as undefined.

    b. As of the writing of this book, the updateRecord method did not throw any error messages if record ID was sent as undefined.

Chapter 11

1. **Correct Answer**: b

    a. The framework provides SortStatus, which gives you the current sorting details on the column but does not provide a SortAscending method.

    b. The loadNextPage method helps in paging through additional data.

2. **Correct Answer**: b

    a. Initially, the documentation had an incorrect entry with the option `displayQuickFindSearch`, which is now fixed.

    b. The option `displayQuickFind` is used to display the search box for a dataset code component on both the home page and sub-grid.

3. **Correct Answer**: b

    a. When the `id` parameter is empty, that indicates a new record needs to be created. Hence, the application shows a **create form** for that specific table. If the *table name* is misspelled, then you will get an error but not when `id` is empty.

    b. This is correct – a new form will be shown for that specific table.

Chapter 12

1. **Correct Answer**: b

    a. The attribute `--save-dev` is used to indicate to **npm** to install the package as a `dev` dependency.

    b. This is correct as `--save-exact` means to save the exact version of the package getting installed. This ensures every machine the project is loaded on always has the same version of that package.

2. **Correct Answer**: b

    a. An attribute with this name does not exist.

    b. Yes, this is correct. The attribute `testMatch` contains expression that helps Jest identify the location of test case files in the project.

3. **Correct Answer**: a

    a. Yes, this is correct. Whenever using *React* in the PCF project, install the `eslint-plugin-react` package and modify the ESLint configuration file to include settings for linting React code.

    b. Such a package does not exist. We need to use `eslint-plugin-react` as the package when extending the lint for *React* files.

`Packt.com`

Subscribe to our online digital library for full access to over 7,000 books and videos, as well as industry leading tools to help you plan your personal development and advance your career. For more information, please visit our website.

Why subscribe?

- Spend less time learning and more time coding with practical eBooks and Videos from over 4,000 industry professionals

- Improve your learning with Skill Plans built especially for you

- Get a free eBook or video every month

- Fully searchable for easy access to vital information

- Copy and paste, print, and bookmark content

Did you know that Packt offers eBook versions of every book published, with PDF and ePub files available? You can upgrade to the eBook version at `packt.com` and as a print book customer, you are entitled to a discount on the eBook copy. Get in touch with us at `customercare@packtpub.com` for more details.

At `www.packt.com`, you can also read a collection of free technical articles, sign up for a range of free newsletters, and receive exclusive discounts and offers on Packt books and eBooks.

Other Books You May Enjoy

If you enjoyed this book, you may be interested in these other books by Packt:

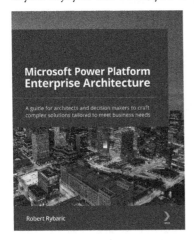

Microsoft Power Platform Enterprise Architecture

Robert Rybaric

ISBN 978-1-80020-457-7

- Understand various Dynamics 365 CRM, ERP, and AI modules for creating Power Platform solutions

- Enhance Power Platform with Microsoft 365 and Azure

- Find out which regions, staging environments, and user licensing groups need to be employed when creating enterprise solutions

- Implement sophisticated security by using various authentication and authorization techniques

- Extend Power Apps, Power BI, and Power Automate to create custom applications

- Integrate your solution with various in-house Microsoft components or third-party systems using integration patterns

Fundamentals of CRM with Dynamics 365 and Power Platform

Nicolae Tarla

ISBN: 978-1-78995-024-3

- Get to grips with Power Platform for building and enhancing Dynamics 365 apps
- Integrate Dynamics 365 CRM with Microsoft 365, Azure, and other platforms
- Discover how you can customize existing entities and create new ones
- Explore various security features and grant users access to CRM data and functions
- Find out which CRM attributes are used to automate operations with programming
- Use internal and external social data to help users to make informed decisions

Packt is searching for authors like you

If you're interested in becoming an author for Packt, please visit `authors.packtpub.com` and apply today. We have worked with thousands of developers and tech professionals, just like you, to help them share their insight with the global tech community. You can make a general application, apply for a specific hot topic that we are recruiting an author for, or submit your own idea.

Leave a review - let other readers know what you think

Please share your thoughts on this book with others by leaving a review on the site that you bought it from. If you purchased the book from Amazon, please leave us an honest review on this book's Amazon page. This is vital so that other potential readers can see and use your unbiased opinion to make purchasing decisions, we can understand what our customers think about our products, and our authors can see your feedback on the title that they have worked with Packt to create. It will only take a few minutes of your time, but is valuable to other potential customers, our authors, and Packt. Thank you!

Index

Symbols

.NET Framework 10, 11

A

Application Life Cycle
    Management (ALM) 154
authentication profiles
  about 138
  changing, with Power Apps
    CLI 141, 142
  creating 138
  creating, with PCF Builder 139, 140
  creating, with Power Apps CLI 138, 139
  deleting, with Power Apps CLI 142, 143
  managing 141
  managing, with PCF Builder 144-147
  selected profile details, retrieving 143
  used, for deploying 147
AutoResponder
  used, for debugging 129-135

B

bound properties 214
breakpoints
  used, for debugging 125-127

C

caching mechanism
  inspecting 222, 224-226
canvas app
  code component, adding 192-194
  debugging in 132
code component
  adding, to canvas app 192-194
  adding, to gallery component 199-201
  building, for sub-grid 105
  building, for view 105
  building, with Fluent UI 272-277
  building, with React 272-277
  deploying, with PCF Builder 150, 151
  development cycle, for building 174, 175
  elements, inspecting 122, 123

integrating with
    out-of-the-box options 249-253
versus HTML web resources 7, 8
code linting process 262-264
Common Data Service (CDS) 4
component life cycle
  about 80
  data changes, by app 80-84
  data changes, by user 80
  page, loading 80
console logs
  inspecting, to evaluate scripts 123-125
context 206, 208
ControlManifest file
  about 67-69
  devices 76
  supported data types 75, 76
  supported features 76
  using, for dataset type code
      components 74
  using, for field type code
      component 70-73
  utility 77
  Web API 77, 78
Custom Control Framework (CCF) 5

D

dataset
  control manifest file, updating for 106
  pagination, implementing on 244-249
  PCF project, initializing for 105
  properties, defining 256-258
  technique, for opening record
      from 253-256
dataset code component
  adding, to specific view of table 181-183
  adding, to sub grid 186-189

adding, to table 184, 185
configuring, in model-driven app 181
configuring, on dashboard 189-192
logic, adding 106-114
styling, adding 114, 115
testing 115, 116
dataset type code components
  configuring, on screen 197-199
  ControlManifest file, using for 74
Dataverse 4, 26
Dataverse solution project
  about 16
  building 161
  code component, adding 155-161
  creating, with Power Apps CLI 66
  default build process 162
  initializing 155-161
  multiple code components,
      adding 166-168
  output, obtaining 161
  overview 154, 155
  package types, generating 162
  production version, creating 163, 164
  ZIP file, exploring with Power Apps
      CLI commands 172, 173
debugging
  breakpoints, using 127
  in canvas apps 132
  in model-driven apps 127
  with AutoResponder 129-135
  with breakpoints 125, 126
  with DevTools 132, 133
  with test harness 121
development machine
  preparing 9
development machine, prerequisite
  .NET Framework 10, 11
  Node.js 9

npm 9
Power Apps CLI 12
TypeScript 10
Visual Studio Code 11
DevTools
  used, for debugging 132, 133

E

ESLint
  about 262
  working with 266, 268
ESLint CLI 264
example library
  downloading 12
existing Dataverse solution project
  code components, adding with
    PCF Builder 170-172
  code components, deploying 168
  solution clone command, using 168, 169
external devices
  working with 227-231

F

Fiddler Classic
  configuring 128
  download link 127
  installing 128
field
  code components, building 90
  control manifest file, updating 91-93
  null value, setting 217, 218
  PCF project, initializing 90
  updates, omitting to 220, 221

field, based on condition
  values, setting 218, 219
field code component
  enriching, by using preview
    image 103, 104
  logic, adding to 94-97
  observed issues, fixing 99-101
  styling, adding 101, 103
  testing 97, 98
field type code component
  adding, to model-driven app 178-181
  configuring, on screen 194-197
  ControlManifest file, using for 70-73
Fluent UI
  used, for building code
    components 272-277

G

getOutputs method
  importance 214-217

H

HTML web resources
  versus code components 7, 8

I

index.ts file
  about 78
  destroy method 79
  getOutputs method 79
  init function 78
  updateView method 79

J

Jest
  testing framework, setting
      up with 269-272

L

Lint
  using 262
linters
  about 262
  Prettier, integrating with 264-266
linting process 262
low-code-no-code platform 6

M

Microsoft Power Apps CLI 5
model-driven apps
  dataset code component,
      configuring 181
  debugging 127
  field type code component,
      adding 178-181

N

Node.js
  about 9
  URL 9
Node Package Manager (npm)
  about 9, 17, 18
  commands 17
  reference link 17

P

pagination
  implementing, on dataset 244-249
PCF Builder
  about 26, 138
  graphical user interface version 26
  guided experience version 32
  installing, from VS Code 33
  installing, from XrmToolBox library 28
  used, for creating authentication
      profiles 139, 140
  used, for creating PCF Builder
      for XrmToolBox 30-32
  used, for creating PCF Builder
      for VS Code 35
  used, for deploying code
      components 150, 151
  used, for initializing PCF Builder
      for XrmToolBox 29
  used, for managing authentication
      profiles 144-146
PCF Builder, for VS Code
  advantages 33
PCF Builder, for XrmToolBox
  about 161
  advantages 27
PCF Gallery
  about 55, 56
  code component, submitting 57
  code component, using from 56, 57
PCF Generator
  about 41
  advantages 46
  command-line arguments, using 45

installing 42
integrating, in PCF Builder 46-55
used, for creating PCF Generator 47-51
used, for initializing PCF projects 66
used, for installing PCF Generator 42
versus Power Apps CLI 45
PCF project
  components 60
  creating, with PCF Generator 47-50
  files and folder structure 63
  initializing, with Command Prompt 42
  initializing, with PCF Generator 42, 66
  initializing, with Power Apps CLI 63, 64
  initializing, with VS Code 43
  recommended folder structure 65
  types 60
PCF project components
  about 60
  implementing 62
  manifest file 61, 62
  resource files 62
Power Apps CLI
  about 16, 138
  download link 12
  used, for changing profiles 141
  used, for creating authentication
    profiles 138, 139
  used, for creating Dataverse
    solution projects 66
  used, for creating Power Apps
    component framework
    (PCF) project 20-22
  used, for deleting authentication
    profiles 142, 143
  used, for deploying 148-150
  used, for initializing PCF projects 63, 64

Power Apps component framework (PCF)
  advantages 8
  code components, versus HTML
    web resources 7, 8
  licensing requirements 8
  overview 4, 5
  target audiences 6
Power Apps component
    framework (PCF) project
  creating, with Power Apps CLI 20-22
  initializing 19, 20
Prettier
  integrating, with linter 264, 266
  using 262
  working with 266-268
preview image 103

R

React
  used, for building code
    components 272-277
  working with 263

S

state 222

T

test harness
  overview 120, 121
  used, for debugging 121
testing framework
  setting up, with Jest 269-272
TSLint 262
TypeScript 10, 262

U

updateView method
  exploring 208
  working 208-214

V

Visual Studio Code (VS Code)
  about 11
  download link 11
  PCF Builder project, creating with
    PCF Builder extension 35, 37-41
  PCF Builder project, initializing
    with PCF Builder extension 34
Visual Studio Marketplace
  tool, rating 34

W

Web API
  exploring 231-236
Web API methods 232
web resources 4

X

Xrm context 4
XrmToolBox
  about 26
  PCF Builder, installing from 28
  PCF Builder project, creating
    with PCF Builder 30-32
  PCF Builder project, initializing
    with PCF Builder 29
  tool, rating 29

Y

Yeoman 41